THE ROUGH GUIDE

Website Directory

Andrew Clare, Peter Buckley
and Duncan Clark

www.roughguides.com

Credits

The Rough Guide Website Directory

Text, Layout & Design:
Andrew Clare, Peter Buckley & Duncan Clark
First edition created by: Angus J. Kennedy
Proofreading: Stewart J Wild
Production: Aimee Hampson

Rough Guides Reference

Series editor: Mark Ellingham
Editors: Peter Buckley, Duncan Clark,
Tracy Hopkins, Sean Mahoney, Matthew Milton,
Joe Staines, Ruth Tidbull
Director: Andrew Lockett

Publishing Information

This sixth edition published September 2006 by
Rough Guides Ltd, 80 Strand, London WC2R 0RL
345 Hudson St, 4th Floor, New York 10014, USA
Email: mail@roughguides.com

Distributed by the Penguin Group:

Penguin Books Ltd, 80 Strand, London WC2R 0RL
Penguin Putnam, Inc., 375 Hudson Street, NY 10014, USA
Penguin Group (Australia), 250 Camberwell Road, Camberwell, Victoria 3124, Australia
Penguin Books Canada Ltd, 10 Alcorn Avenue, Toronto, Ontario, Canada M4P 2Y3
Penguin Group (New Zealand), 67 Apollo Drive, Mairangi Bay, Auckland 1310, New Zealand

Printed in Italy by LegoPrint S.p.A

Typeset in Minion and Myriad to an original design by Duncan Clark & Peter Buckley

A catalogue record for this book is available from the British Library

ISBN 13: 978-1-84353-729-8
ISBN 10: 1-84353-729-X

1 3 5 7 9 8 6 4 2

Contents

contents

contents

Read this first

You already know how to use the Internet and you know how to use Google to find what you want. Basically you know what you're doing, so why on earth do you need this book? Well, although you can find a lot of stuff using search engines, you also have to spend a lot of time trawling through all the rubbish to find the useful sites. Think of this book as a shortcut – a general purpose links page. Or, even better, just use it to dip into every now and then to find something you didn't even know you were looking for.

How else would you discover, for example, that you can have the carbon extracted from your deceased body and transformed into a diamond for your loved ones (www.lifegem.com), or that you can buy camping toilet roll impregnated with seeds (www.enviro-roll.com), medicinal leeches (www.biop-harm-leeches.com) or even coffee beans vomited up by weasels (www.cybercandy.co.uk)?

Today, thanks to the Internet, you can buy pretty much any item or service imaginable. Wherever you see the ☺ symbol it means there's the possibility of money changing hands. We've kept the shopping elements of this book as UK-oriented as possible, but there are a top foreign sites thrown in. When comparing prices on local and overseas sites, be mindful of shipping costs and import taxes. Also consider voltage ratings of foreign electrical equipment and whether or not the item you're purchasing is likely to need any kind of repair should it develop a fault.

Of course, it's not all about buying stuff. We also point you at the best information portals for everything from art to zoology, plus hundreds of sites that are simply interesting or entertaining. What this book *doesn't* cover is how to actually use the Internet, or the ins and outs of trading safely online. For that kind of information – and for tips on everything from broadband to blogging – pick up a copy of this book's sister volume, *The Rough Guide to the Internet*.

Alright then, go fill yer boots!

Amusements

Looking for a chuckle or perhaps to extend your lunchbreak into the late afternoon? Click through the following directories to enter a whole new dimension of time-wasting:

Open Directory dmoz.org/Recreation/Humor
Yahoo! dir.yahoo.com/Entertainment/Humor

If you have a high-bandwidth connection or are blessed with abnormal patience, you might like to investigate the world of online animation. Offerings range from clones of old-school arcade games to feature-length Flash cartoons. Peruse the galleries and links from:

Animation dmoz.org/Arts/Animation
b3ta www.b3ta.com
Flasharcade www.flasharcade.com
Newgrounds www.newgrounds.com
Shockwave www.shockwave.com.

Boing Boing
www.boingboing.net
Cultural blog and directory, there's always something worth taking a look at here.

Comedy Central
www.comedycentral.com
Download full *South Park* episodes, listen to comedy radio and see what's screening across the network. More of a station promo than a source of laughs.

Complaint Letter Generator
www.pakin.org/complaint
Punch in a name for an instant dressing-down.

Exorcist Bunnies
www.angryalien.com/0204/exorcistbunnies.html
It's short, it's sharp, it's scary and it's got bunnies in it – what more do you want?

Eyezmaze
www.eyezmaze.com
An inventive little site offering beautiful mind-bending abstract games. Growcube is the current favourite here.

The Flash Mind Reader
www.flashpsychic.com
Be amazed. Be slightly amazed.

The Frown
www.thefrown.com
Bitter and twisted cartoons.

amusements

Gary Duschl's Gumwrapper Chain
www.gumwrapper.com
If only you had so much ambition.

Graffiti The Web
www.yeahbutisitart.com/graffiti
Vandalise websites for fun.

Guimp
www.guimp.com
The world's smallest fully featured website?

Gumshoe Online
www.gumshoe-online.com
Fancy yourself as a bit of a cybersleuth? Interrogate suspects and solve puzzles to reveal the truth.

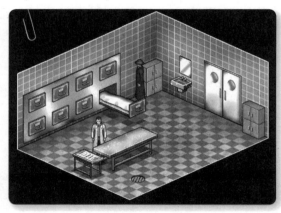

Half Bakery
www.halfbakery.com
Questionable concepts.

Horrorfind
www.horrorfind.com
A helpful hand into the darkness.

Hot or Not?
www.hotornot.com
Post a picture of yourself or someone else, and passing chumps will rate your attractiveness on a scale of one to ten. So popular it's spawned a plethora of similar sites where you can rate everything from goths to architecture:
www.archibot.com/ratings
www.ratemyface.com
www.cutelittlekittens.com/
www.gothornot.com
www.amigeekornot.com

I Love Bacon
www.ilovebacon.com
Most of the gags that arrive in your inbox courtesy of your caring friends will wind up in these, or similar, archives sooner or later. Usually before you see them. Don't go near the galleries if you're a bit sensitive.
www.collegehumor.com

In the 70s
www.inthe70s.com
Re-enter the landscape that wallpapered your childhood memories; and if you are a little younger than that, try one of these:
www.inthe80s.com
www.inthe90s.com

Japanese Engrish
www.engrish.com
Copywriters wanted, English not a priority.

Jay Is Games
jayisgames.com
Reviews and links to a comprehensive selection of quality flash games and puzzles.

Joke Index
www.jokeindex.com
So many jokes it's not funny. And there's loads more to be found here, here, here, here and here:

www.humordatabase.com
www.humournet.com

Kelman To The Rescue

www.abc.net.au/gameon/kelman/kelmangame.htm
Stunning flash game based loosely on the arcade classic "Defender".

La Pate A Son

www.lecielestbleu.com/media/pateasoncontent.htm
Beautiful and compelling musical toy. Replace parts of a machine from a conveyer belt and send little multi-coloured nuggets bouncing between different sound-making devices.

Mansion Impossible

3form.net/mansion_impossible/
Buy and sell property in this fast moving game.

The Official Rock-Paper-Scissors Strategy Guide

www.worldrps.com
Master such techniques as Speed Play, Rusty and Lowball, then make like Gary Kasparov and play the computer.

The Onion

www.theonion.com
Unquestionably the finest news satire on or off the Net. See also:
www.private-eye.co.uk
www.satirewire.com

Online Etch-A-Sketch

babygrand.com/games
It doesn't quite have the tactile wonder of the original game, but it's a whole lot of fun.

Pet Fish

www.petfish.com
Turn your monitor into a virtual fish tank.

Pop Cap

www.popcap.com
Loads of games to play online or download.

The Post-Modernism Generator

www.elsewhere.org/cgi-bin/postmodern
Sprinkle your next essay with "postsemanticist dialectical theory" and fool your teacher.

The Prank Institute

www.prank.org
Mischief for every occasion. Or for a history of hoaxes, visit:
www.museumofhoaxes.com

Rather Good

www.rathergood.com
See what all the fuss is about. This is one Flash site not to be missed. Kittens as you've never seen them before playing "Independent Woman" as you've never heard it before. And more!

amusements

Real Ultimate Power
www.realultimatepower.net
The official Ninja site.

Rec.humor.funny
www.netfunny.com/rhf
Archives of the rec.humor.funny newsgroup, updated daily.

The Simpsons Zombie Shootout
www.thesimpsons.com/zombie
As you might imagine, *The Simpsons'* website is a great place to kill some time ... and some zombies.

Sissyfight
www.sissyfight.com
Scratch, tease and diss your way to playground supremacy.

Snowballing
www.3form.net/snowbawling/
Ever wanted to throw something at Jamie Oliver or Craig David? Now's your chance.

Star Wars Asciimation
www.asciimation.co.nz
The *Star Wars* saga rendered in vivid ASCII text – George Lucas would be spinning in his grave if he were dead.

Stick Figure Death Theater
www.sfdt.com
Stickcity citizens meet their sticky ends.

Stumble Upon
www.stumbleupon.com
A hybrid on-line community/search tool where you can browse recommendations from other surfers and rate the pages you visit.

The Surrealist Compliment Generator
www.madsci.org/cgi-bin/cgiwrap/~lynn/jardin/SCG
"In caressing your follicles I am only vaguely reminded of the bitter harvest", and other bons mots.

Things People Said
www.rinkworks.com/said/
"Coming home, I drove into the wrong house and collided with a tree I don't have."

Vectorpark
www.vectorpark.com
Interact with the exhibits in the park or play the balancing game.

Web Economy Bullshit Generator
www.dack.com/web/bullshit.html
Learn how to "leverage leading-edge mindshare" and "incubate compelling interfaces".

Xiaoxiao
www.xiaoxiaomovie.com
The Jackie Chan and Bruce Lee of the stick-figure world battle to the death. Head straight for "No. 3".

Zefrank
www.zefrank.com
Weblog of frequently updated amusing links.

Antiques & collectables

These days many dealers have set up shop on eBay, so it can be a useful starting point, especially if you're already familiar with the interface. If you're thinking of selling your own items it's also a good place to get a feel for the market. In addition there's a huge variety of dealers and information sites all over the internet which can be a valuable resource for even the most obscure collector. Whether you're after snuff boxes, corkscrews or something larger, take a look around these sites:

Bonhams www.bonhams.com
Christie's www.christies.com
eBay www.ebay.co.uk
I Collector www.icollector.com
Sotheby's Collectibles www.sothebys.com

Antiques

Antique Hot Spots
www.antiquehotspots.com
No-nonsense and very comprehensive set of links to online antique dealerships. See also:
www.antiques.co.uk
www.atg-online.com

Antiques on the Web
www.bbc.co.uk/antiques
The BBC's superb antiques site includes buying advice from *Antiques Roadshow* experts, feature articles, hints on scoring big at car boot sales, exhibition listings and the latest finds from the *Roadshow*.

Antiques UK
www.antiques-uk.co.uk
Similarly to most antique portals it offers links to dealers and salvage warehouses, but it has an excellent want ads feature.

Cartophilic Society of Great Britain
www.csgb.co.uk
Homepage of the organization devoted to card collecting. See also:
www.londoncigcard.co.uk
www.cardmine.co.uk

Christer Schultz Antiques
www.schultz-antiques.com
Easy-to-use catalogue specialising in high-quality English and northern European antiques, ranging from Georgian secretaires to Victorian chandeliers.

Collectics
collectics.com/education.html
A variety of helpful essays on collectable antiques covering Clarice Cliff to Lalique.

antiques & collectables

Auctions

You know how auctions work: the sale goes to the highest bidder, as long as it's above the reserve price. Or, in the case of a Dutch auction, the price keeps dropping until a buyer accepts. Well, it's similar online. You simply set your maximum and the auction site will raise your bid incrementally until that ceiling is reached. If you're the highest bidder when the auction ends, the deal is struck.

Once the deal's been settled, it's up to the buyer and seller to arrange delivery and payment, though both can be arranged through trusted third parties. There are millions of goods for sale in hundreds of categories across thousands of online auctions. These days most people turn to eBay, the grand-daddy of all auction sites, to satisfy their needs:

eBay www.ebay.co.uk

Here are a few more specialist auction sites, mixed in with a handful that you may find useful as you navigate the auction universe:

Auction Seller's Resource
www.auction-sellers-resource.com
Free advice, tips, and resources for eBay sellers.

Heritage
coins.heritagegalleries.com
Specialists in numismatic auctions, also has a handy guide for evaluating a coin's value.

I Collector
www.icollector.com
Home to over 650 auction houses, this American site aims to be a high-end eBay with an emphasis on art and antiques. One for the serious collector.

National Fraud Information Center
www.fraud.org
If you're worried about getting swindled by an online auctioneer, this excel-

lent American site has all the information you need to protect yourself.

Sotheby's
www.sothebys.com
You won't find that signed Kylie picture disc here, but if you've got money to burn, sites don't come any classier than this online home of the august auction house. For similar service, try Bonham's or Christie's:
www.bonhams.com
www.christies.com

Vendio
www.vendio.com
Tools and services for the serious online auction seller. Also see:
www.lotwatch.co.uk/tools
www.SpoonFeeder.com

Disturbing Auctions
www.disturbingauctions.com
Looking for a golfing dead frog or attacking puppet? Look no further.

Collector Café
www.collectorcafe.com
A collecting community portal with channels for just about everything from advertising memorabilia to writing instruments. For a UK-based portal, try:
www.antiquesbulletin.com
www.antiquesworld.co.uk
www.worldcollectorsnet.com

The Design Gallery
www.designgallery.co.uk
An online catalogue of restored late-19th and early-20th-century furniture from the Arts and Crafts and Art Deco movements. It's also worth paying a visit to www.artfurniture.co.uk

The Howard Gallery
www.thehowardgallery.article7.co.uk
This well-stocked dealer is a specialist in 17th- and 18th-century furniture, but also has a limited range of clocks and porcelain.

Invaluable
www.invaluable.com
If you can't get to the *Antiques Roadshow* or you're a serious collector, the online branch of *Invaluable* magazine provides an appraisal service. If you've had an item stolen, it also has a tracer service to improve your odds of recovering it. These don't come cheap, but you can try them for free.

In the trade

Whether you are a dealer yourself, or a punter looking for some insider information, it's worth keeping half an eye on a few of the trade websites. **Antiques Trade Gazette** is probably the best – it features articles, auction calendars and a page where you can report stolen items – but there are loads to choose from:

Antiques Trade Gazette www.atg-online.com
British Antique Dealers' Association www.bada.org
WebStall www.webstall.net

LAPADA
www.lapada2.co.uk/index.html
The homepage of the Association of Art and Antique Dealers features a directory of members, fair and auction listings and advice on buying, selling, taking care and providing security for antiques.

Lassco
www.lassco.co.uk
An architectural antiques salvage company that offers a glorious selection of fixtures and fittings saved from old buildings. Apart from the more traditional baths, radiators and recycled flooring, you may also find treasures such as old telephone kiosks and huge brass doors from closed bank branches.

Richard Gardner Antiques
www.richardgardnerantiques.co.uk
This classy operation displays an enormous selection of truly lovely pieces of quality furniture and decorative items.

Watchnet
www.watchnet.com
Online hub for the vintage wrist-watch collecting community.

Coins & stamps

Coin Dealers Directory
www.numis.co.uk
Comprehensive regional database of coin dealers across the UK.

Coint Talk Forum
www.cointalk.org
Swap tips with the numismatic community.

Harlan J Berk
www.harlanjberk.com
Probably the most professional site for numismatists on the Web. The range of coins available covers a huge period of history and spans the globe.

Royal Mail
www.royalmail.com
Worth checking the Stamps & Collecting section in their portal for their latest gift sets, and yearbooks.

Royal Mint
www.royalmint.com
A clean, well-structured site with an impressive, well-presented stock of commemorative coins and gifts.

Sandafayre
www.sandafayre.com
Auctions and information from the world's largest mail bid company..

Memorabilia, toys & comics

Action Figure Collectors
www.actionfigurecollectors.com
Looking for that elusive Lando Calrissian toy? Try here first.

Advertising Icon Museum
www.advertisingiconmuseum.com
A delightful gallery spanning a century of American consumer product mascots from the Jolly Green Giant to Tony The Tiger.

Collecting Airfix Kits
www.djairfix.freeserve.co.uk
Everything you wanted to know about plastic modelling but were afraid to ask.

Comics International
www.comics-international.com
This gateway features a near-definitive directory of UK stockists, an excellent links page, comics reviews and unusually informative FAQs. Also see:
comicbooks.about.com

Feeling Retro
www.feelingretro.com
Charming site where you can add memories associated with various products to an ever growing list. For table-top arcade cabinets, Audrey Hepburn coasters, and Only Fools And Horses board games, visit:
www.letsgoretro.co.uk

Kitsch
www.kitsch.co.uk
UK site for collectors of retro-chic featuring *Dukes of Hazzard* items, Presleyana, lava lamps, James Bond paraphernalia, etc.

Labelcollector.com
www.labelcollector.com
Salute the golden era of fruit crates and jars.

Memorabilia Mania
www.memorabiliamania.co.uk
For anything with a signature on it.

Old Bear
www.oldbear.co.uk
Don't throw away that beat-up, moth-eaten old teddy bear – it might be worth a few sovereigns. This site will tell you if you can start a trust fund with your Gund or if you're stuck for life with your Steiff.

Tracks
www.tracks.co.uk
Whether it's a Yellow Submarine Kaleidoscope or Hard Day's Night mug you're after, this is the place to go for all your contemprorary Beatles regalia. Or if you'd prefer to spend $14,495 on a signed copy of the Sgt Pepper album visit:
www.rarebeatles.com

TV Toys
www.tvtoys.com
One of the best sites to explore the ever-expanding world of TV memorabilia with knowledgeable articles about collecting certain shows and links to eBay auctions and collectables for sale.

Wolfgang's Vault
www.wolfgangsvault.com
This US site hosts a cornucopia of rock memorabilia from Allman Brothers ticket stubs to Frank Zappa posters.

World War II Collectibles
www.wwii-collectibles.com
Beneath the visual clutter lies a treasure trove of stamps, coins, posters, propaganda material and military ephemera.

Architecture

Archibot
www.archibot.com
If you're interested in contemporary architecture and design, this is the best portal on the Web with daily updates on news and links. It also has busy forums and an excellent metasearch engine.

Architecture.com
www.architecture.com
The Royal Institute of British Architects site allows you full access to their database of article abstracts; has a find-an-architect function if you're redesigning your garden shed; and has an exhaustive array of links.

Architecture Mag
www.architecturemag.com
One of the top online architecture magazines. The others include:
www.arplus.com
www.ArchitectureWeek.com
www.metropolismag.com

Arcspace
www.arcspace.com
Excellent Danish site devoted to contemporary architecture, with copiously illustrated exhibits, feature articles and portfolios.

Building Conservation
www.buildingconservation.com
Preserve your palace.

Design for Homes
www.designforhomes.org
UK Knowledge centre for housing design, has interesting articles on subjects like perceptions of privacy and density in housing, and details about the housing design awards winners. See also:
www.buildingforlife.org

Glass, Steel and Stone
www.glasssteelandstone.com
A fun site, with browsable galleries (including ones devoted to haunted and odd architecture), forums and news stories that are updated daily.

Great Buildings Online
www.greatbuildings.com
An exemplary resource. If you download free Design Lite software you can get three-dimensional models of Stonehenge, Chartres Cathedral, Falling Water and other masterpieces by Alvar Aalto, Le Corbusier and Ludwig Mies van der Rohe. Of course, there are also flat photographs and information on the architects of over a thousand great buildings.

Icon Town
www.icon-town.net
Design an icon-sized building pixel by pixel, pick a plot of land and submit it to the town council.

Art

If you're an artist, you can post photos of your work online: it's cheap gallery space and your disciples can visit at any time without even leaving home. You may find it's worth taking up supplementary residence at one of the on-line communities such as myspace (www.myspace.com) in order to take advantage of its networking potential.

If you're looking for online exhibitions turn to the Museums and Galleries section (p.159). The following section is devoted to portals, art education sites, artist resources, and art buying.

A.A. Art
www.1art.com
For budding Constables, this excellent arts education site offers free online painting lessons, video workshops and forums on technique.

Arts councils

For information on everything from National Lottery funding and government grants (they'll only spend it on guns if you don't use it) to online exhibition spaces, this is the place to check. You'll also find click-throughs to even more regional Arts Council websites.

England www.artscouncil.org.uk
Northern Ireland www.artscouncil-ni.org
Wales www.acw-ccc.org.uk
Scotland www.sac.org.uk

Art Capital Group
www.artcapitalgroup.com
Borrow posh pictures to hang in your snooker room.

Art Crimes
www.graffiti.org
The first and still the best graffiti site on the Web. Art Crimes features an amazing array of burners, interviews with the best-known writers, a good FAQ page and an untouchable set of graf links.

Artindustri
www.artindustri.com
Comprehensive portal for the art community, this site has a regular magazine alongside portfolio space, links to resources, advice, and an extensive reference section.

ArtLex
www.artlex.com
This visual arts dictionary is a truly superb resource for students, experts and bluffers alike. Containing extensively cross-referenced definitions of over three thousand terms and examples, this is one of the most useful art sites on the Web.

Art Net
www.artnet.com
With its frighteningly comprehensive artists' index, excellent exhibition listings and articles both breezy and dense, the homepage of Art Net magazine probably serves as the best art portal out there.

The Association of Illustrators
www.theaoi.com
Invaluable resource for illustrators offering advice, seminars, news, on-line portfolios and articles.

British Arts
www.britisharts.co.uk
Friendly portal which offers British artists the usual trappings (news, advice, etc) and has a decent amount of articles and links covering gallery space, printing, fraud protection, education, funding, and a whole lot more.

Creativity Portal
www.creativity-portal.com
Articles and ideas to help you increase your creativity and inspiration.

Grove Dictionary of Art Online
www.groveart.com
Freeload for a day on the definitive work of art reference.

World Wide Arts Resources
www.wwar.com
Its URL may lead you to believe that this is a site for military enthusiasts, but this list bank is probably the most comprehensive art search engine, with links to just about everything from art supplies and atelier services to gallery spaces and arts education courses. Also worth a gander is:
www.artcyclopedia.com

Buying art

It's not all overpriced sunflowers and piles of bricks, today it's easier than ever to buy original work by up-and-coming young British artists with prices varying between the cost of a new hi-fi and a secondhand car. For those of you with deeper pockets and an eye for the classics, try Christie's and Sotheby's
www.christies.com
www.sothebys.com

 Art Connection
www.art-connection.com
Check out and buy work by emerging artists selected by knowledgeable folks from the Big Apple.

 Art for Sale
www.artforsale.co.uk
London-based Art for Sale serves as a useful introduction to new artists and media. You can browse through an A to Z catalogue featuring such names as Patrick Caulfield, Tracey Emin and Paul Maze, or simply select a medium and price range to view a selected section. Prices start from £150 up to around £9,000.

 Art Is A Tart
www.art-is-a-tart.com
Limited edition paintings by contemporary artists, bronze resin sculptures and greetings cards are all on sale at a site which never quite lives up to the chutzpah in its title.

art

Posters & prints

There are countless stores on-line where you can buy art prints and posters, handy for plastering over the cracks in you bedroom wall. Many offer special deals and discounts, here's a handful to get on with:

www.allaboutart.com
www.allposters.com
www.artland.co.uk
www.artrepublic.com
www.easyart.com
www.postershop.co.uk
www.worldgallery.co.uk

 **Contemporary Posters**
www.contemporaryposters.com
Like the (Russian) Fine Arts Gallery, this site's name is missing a key word – 'Polish'. That caveat aside, the site offers a breathtaking selection of vintage Polish circus posters.

 **Rare Posters**
www.rareposters.net
A stonking collection of exhibition and museum posters, with more Roy Lichtensteins than even the Lichtenstein family might want.

Visoni Poster Art
www.visoni.com
Good, if small, stock of classic posters, mostly from the tourism industry.

Brit Art
www.britart.com
Although held fast in the modern vein, the huge selection still manages to encompass a wider range of styles from the abstract to figurative and landscapes. With prices ranging from hundreds to thousands, it may be worth taking advantage of the facility to make an offer on a work, rather than just paying up for it or passing it by. See also:
www.britisharts.co.uk/gallery.htm

 D'Art
dart.fine-art.com
A giant online art marketplace with more than five thousand participating sites and tens of thousands of works.

Eyestorm
www.eyestorm.com
Flashy site which offers contemporary art and art photography from A (Marina Abramovic) to W (James Welling). The breadth of artists on display is impressive, but the work on show may not always be their finest.

New British Artists
www.newbritishartists.co.uk
Reasonably priced selection of work from British artists you may not have heard of, complete with potted biographies of each prodigy.

Asian interest

British Born Chinese
www.britishbornchinese.org.uk
Articles, humour, links, a newsletter and more for the British Chinese population.

Click Walla
www.clickwalla.com
Probably the most wide-ranging site serving Britain's Asian community, Click Walla comprises sections devoted to music, film, news, students, weddings, food, listings, beauty and fashion, health and Asian businesses. Other UK portals worth checking out include:
www.redhotcurry.com
www.ukasian.co.uk
www.asiancommunity.net

Criss Cross
www.crisscross.com/jp/
What's really happening in Japan.

India Abroad
www.indiaabroad.com
The focus here is largely on the US and Canada, but this huge site has extensive news coverage, a broad array of channels, immigration advice, in-depth interviews and shopping facilities.

Lankaweb
www.lankaweb.com
A virtual community for Sri Lankans across the world.

Sada Punjab
www.sadapunjab.com
Devoted to keeping Punjabi culture alive. The site's features include a literature archive of folktales, ghazals and poems; a Punjabi jukebox; an archive of Sikh religious texts; language tutorials; and a magazine. See also Punjab Online and Punjabi Network:
www.punjabonline.com
www.punjabi.net

South Asia Network
www.southasia.net
This portal features the South Asia search engine and serves as a useful gateway to information on Bangladesh, Bhutan, India, the Maldives, Nepal, Pakistan and Sri Lanka.

Tehelka
www.tehelka.com
A very influential Internet newsletter from India, which has had a role in exposing corruption in politics and breaking cricket's match-fixing scandal.

Babies & parenting

Aware Parenting Institute
www.awareparenting.com
A garish site, but an excellent resource for those interested in child-centred parenting.

Babies "R" Us
www.babiesrus.co.uk
The baby Toys "R" Us offers nappies and gadgets as well as more heavy-duty items like prams and high chairs.

BabyCentre
www.babycentre.co.uk
Probably the most complete baby site on the Web, with advice on everything from conceiving to lullaby lyrics to sleep routines to coping with your kid bursting into tears on a plane.

BabyNamer
www.babynamer.com
Why not give your babe a cutesy name like Adolph? It apparently means "noble hero". More suggestions to scar it for life at:
www.babynames.com
www.baby-names-meanings.com

Baby Supplies
www.baby-supplies.co.uk
Award-winning site with some good specials and clearance items.

Babyworld
www.babyworld.co.uk
The homepage of *Babyworld* magazine offers all the usual chat rooms, shopping facilities and pregnancy diaries, plus one of the most detailed health sections around.

Boots
www.boots.com
Functional rather than flashy. The baby section is broken down into crystal clear categories ranging from Pregnancy and Birth to Nappies and Toilet Training.

Dooce
www.dooce.com
Heather B. Armstrong's insightful blog about motherhood. For more 'momoirs' visit dotmoms:
www.roughdraft.typepad.com/dotmoms

Diaper Goop
www.innopharm.com
Here's a top product for those parents whose babies tend to get nappy rash.

Fathers Direct
www.fathersdirect.com
UK resource for fathers, with in-depth articles, news, training, and information for working parents.

Ferti Magazine
www.fertimagazine.com
On-line journal with the latest in fertility news.

 Genius Babies
www.geniusbabies.com
All sorts of products designed to hothouse your little prodigy. The Embryonics section includes a range of goods to 'encourage' a brainy foetus, like the Mozart Womb Songs CD. And what concerned parent could be without a Baby Shakespeare video?

 Green Baby
www.greenbabyco.com
Environmental concerns lie close to the heart of this site but it's not all reusable nappies and organic babygros. You can also pick up a cutting-edge three-wheeled stroller along with your Olive Oil Soap Flakes.

Homebirth
www.homebirth.org.uk
Advice for parents choosing to give birth at home, including birth stories and pain relief options as well as recommended books, videos and articles. Also try:
www.birthchoiceuk.com

Kids Health
kidshealth.org
Thoughtfully divided into three separate sections for parents, kids, and teens with health answers and advice appropriate to each.

 Mischief Kids
www.mischiefkids.co.uk
What parent could be without a Donna Karan romper suit for their bambino? This site has a warm, personally written approach which helps take the sting out of the designer prices. See also:
www.peppermint.co.uk

 Mothercare
www.mothercare.com
The Mothercare site offers a comprehensive range of products and a useful comparison facility to help you make your mind up. The own-brand stuff offers a good budget option.

Mothers Who Think
www.salon.com/mwt
As with just about everything else on Salon, this section is funny, informative, engaging and well written, and a perfect antidote to all the sites and publications that treat mums as scarcely more intelligent than their babies.

Mums Network
www.mumsnet.com
A no-nonsense guide to parenting with the emphasis on practical, realistic advice and extensive product reviews. See also:
www.theparentclub.com

National Childbirth Trust
www.nctpregnancyandbabycare.com
The NCT's official site is a good place to find out

Maternity

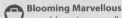
Active Birth Centre
www.activebirthcentre.com
Giving birth needn't be all about misery and enemas. This straightforward site gives advice (on why massaging your wriggler is a good thing, for example) and sells everything from bras to birth balls (for optimal foetal positioning).

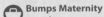
Blooming Marvellous
www.bloomingmarvellous.co.uk
This site has a great selection of fashionable maternity and lovely baby clothes. It's also good for presents for new parents or pregnant friends.

Bumps Maternity
www.bumpsmaternity.com
Bumps specialises in maternity clothes for pregnant women not satisfied with sack dresses. Sizing guides are on hand and prices are good, generally within the same range as pre-pregnancy clothes.

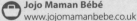
Formes
www.formes.com
Maternity fashion with bags of French chic: everything from jeans to jackets, pedal pushers to pullovers.

Jojo Maman Bébé
www.jojomamanbebe.co.uk
The maternity section offers some useful business clothes and pretty nursing tops to help with discreet breastfeeding. You'll find lots of attractive kids' clothes too, plus useful gadgets and basic equipment.

about antenatal classes, breast-feeding counsellors, mothers' groups and the NCT's own books on pregnancy and childbirth.

Net Doctor
www.netdoctor.co.uk/children
Certainly among the best UK health sites, Net Doctor's specialist pages are filled with largely jargon-free information for mother and child. See also: www.drgreene.com

Parents.com
www.parents.com
The homepage of the American magazine *Parents* doesn't skimp on online content, and because of its ties to a respected publication, the advice and information is authoritative.

SheilaKitzinger.com
www.sheilakitzinger.com
Sheila Kitzinger is one of the gurus of childbirth. There's a wealth of information here on breast-feeding, water births, home births and other related issues.

Sunday Best
www.sundaybest.co.uk
The christening outfits have names like The Fauntleroy, The Country Squire and The Bronte, which gives you a clue what to expect – lots of velvet and lace, and more frills than you could shake a rattle at.

Teeny Tots
www.teeny-tots.com
Items for playtime, bedtime, bathtime and all-terrain stroller time, with prices to suit every pocket.

The Total Baby Shop
www.thetotalbabyshop.com
A comprehensive selection of products with the occasional bargain thrown in for good measure.

UK Parents
www.ukparents.co.uk
An informative, unpatronizing parenting e-zine, covering pretty much everything from pre-conception to sending the young 'uns off to school.

Vertbaudet
www.vertbaudet.co.uk
Baby clothing ranges from newborn essentials through chic christening outfits to down-to-earth play wear. Prices are good for the quality and styling, and the baby basics are seriously good value.

Betting & gambling

It's tempting to say that online betting is for those who like that extra added element of risk, but if you stick to well-known bookmakers who've invested heavily in their security systems and avoid the casinos (which are often pretty dodgy and sometimes require you to buy a CD-ROM or install software) you should be fine. To find a bookie, try **Bookies Index** (www.bookiesindex.com) or go straight to one of the big names:

BlueSQ www.bluesq.com
Coral Eurobet www.eurobet.co.uk
Ladbrokes www.ladbrokes.com and www.bet.co.uk
Littlewoods www.betdirect.net
Paddy Power www.paddypower.com
Sporting Index www.sportingindex.com
Tote www.totalbet.com
Victor Chandler www.victorchandler.com
William Hill www.williamhill.co.uk

National Lottery
www.national-lottery.co.uk
It could be you…but it probably won't be.

Oddschecker
www.oddschecker.co.uk
Useful site that allows you to view the odds that all the bookies are offering, linking directly to their sites so you can place a bet.

The Racing Post
www.racingpost.co.uk
The online home of the venerable tip sheet.

Settle-a-Bet
www.settle-a-bet.co.uk
How to beat the odds.

24 Dogs
www.24dogs.com
Comprehensive, Wembley-owned greyhound resource and betting service. Also see The Dogs: www.thedogs.co.uk

UK Betting Guide
www.uknetguide.co.uk/Sports/Betting
Pretty comprehensive portal that will give you hundreds of ways of parting with your cash online.

Win 2 Win
www.win2win.co.uk
One of the very few free horseracing tipster services on the Web, it also has a section devoted to different betting systems.

World of Gambling
www.gamble.co.uk
News, reviews and advice on everything from baccarat to slot machines.

Bikes

Bicycle Net
www.bicyclenet.co.uk
Here you'll find a glossary for beginners and tips on what model you need according to your inside leg measurement. Their stock ranges from kids' bikes to BMX to folding bikes.

Bikes 2U Direct
www.bikes2udirect.com
Competitively priced bikes for all ages, with handy guides for choosing the right type and size of cycle.

Bike for All
www.bikeforall.net
A joint initiative of the Bicycle Association and the Department for Transport provides links to practical information, such as where to get training, what bike to buy and everything else you need to know about the ins & outs of getting on yer bike. See also: www.bike2work.info

Cycle Centre Online
www.cyclestore.co.uk
A long list of topics and brand names from bottom brackets to Vredestein bikes. There's also a good range of bikes to choose from.

CycleXpress
www.cyclexpress.co.uk
The range of bikes is limited, but there are plenty of categories and accessories here. The major plus point is the upgrade advice service, which helps you improve your bike bit by bit.

Cycling and Mountain Biking
cycling.timeoutdoors.com
Advice from a team of experts with useful information about events, clubs, training, cycling holidays, and more.

Halfords
www.halfords.com
Wide selection of bikes, accessories and spares from one of the main high-street traders. They also offer a comprehensive cycle maintenance plan.

Ultimate Bikes
www.ultimatebikes.com
The logo of a crumpled bike may not look promising – actually it's one of those recumbent jobs in which they specialise – but this site promises access to eight thousand components for all kinds of bikes, with discounts of up to twenty percent.

Black interest

All Africa
allafrica.com
This portal offers some of the most comprehensive African news coverage on the web. See also:
www.africaguide.com
www.africahomepage.org

Afrocentric Forum
www.afrocentricforum.com
Bustling bulletin board for all things nubian. Has a separate recipe forum too.

Big Culture
www.bigculture.com
This directory should be your first port of call for anything relating to Jamaican culture.

Black Search
www.blacksearch.co.uk
Search engine and directory for "Black Orientated" sites, with links to over nine thousand sites covering a range of catergories from arts to dating to history.

Black Britain
www.blackbritain.co.uk
Part of Colourful Network – which also includes blackenterprise.co.uk – this site is an extensive gateway to black British culture with a friendly, inclusive feel. Regular columns on Africa and Europe, the Americas, and the Caribbean. Also try Black Net:
www.blacknet.co.uk

Black Information Link
www.blink.org.uk
The 1990 Trust's bulletin board for the UK's black community serves two functions: it provides news, events listings and links; and it serves as a forum for political advocacy.

Black Presence
www.blackpresence.co.uk
A forum and resource for researchers and other people interested in the history of black culture in Britain. Also includes news, features on music and articles on contemporary figures such as Chris Ofili.

Windrush
www.bbc.co.uk/history/community/multicultural/windrush
The BBC's celebration of fifty years of Afro-Caribbean culture in Britain, with a heavy slant towards education: timelines, achievements, first-person remembrances, poetry and a literature guide.

Blogs

Blogs, or weblogs, are essentially diaries – logs of a person's thoughts, what they did, what's interesting them, and news. They still represent an important development in the Web's democratization of culture: due to their immediacy and their liberation of the means of production, blogs are being hyped as the new publishing revolution. Following are some blogging resources and some of the best blogs on the Web. See also RSS Newsfeeds (p.176).

Apparently Nothing
www.apparentlynothing.com
Regular photographic postings and commentary. See also:
snowsuit.net
www.day26.com
www.chromasia.com

Belle de Jour
belledejour-uk.blogspot.com
"The diary of a London call girl"; but is it fact or fiction?

Blogdial
irdial.com/blogdial/
An intelligent free-thinking collective blog from the respected Irdial record label, encompassing innovations in music production, security, politics and anything else that takes their interest.

Blogger.com
www.blogger.com
Links, news and everything you need to create your own blog.

BlogSearchEngine
blogsearchengine.com
In case you hadn't guessed, this is a blog search engine. It also boasts loads of articles and blog news features.

Call Centre Confidential

callcentrediary.blogspot.com

The gripping diary of a call-centre team leader.

Coolfer

www.coolfer.com

The definitive Big Apple blog, covering "for the most part" music and the music industry, and, of course, NYC.

The Daily Report

www.zeldman.com/coming.html

Web guru Jeffrey Zeldman dishes up tech advice and links, and the wickedly funny "If the great movies had been websites".

The Diary of Samuel Pepys

www.pepysdiary.com

Every day brings an entry from the renowned 17th-century diarist. If you've missed his exploits to date, there's a "story so far" page.

DAYPOP

www.daypop.com

"Search 59,000 news sites, weblogs and RSS feeds for current events and breaking news."

Eatonweb Portal

portal.eatonweb.com

A huge list of blogs you can browse by category.

Going Underground

london-underground.blogspot.com

Adventures below the streets of London.

KICK-AAS

kickaas.typepad.com

"Kick All Agricultural Subsidies" is a brilliant blog devoted to third-world issues.

La Coquette

www.lacoquette.blogs.com

Don't hate her because she lives in Paris.

Librarian.net

www.librarian.net

A model blog, with a crucial insight into the subterranean world of the librarian.

The Londonist

www.londonist.com

Award-winning blog covering all sorts of stuff, from news and reviews to cinema and culture. The site is well laid-out and funny.

Ma.gnolia

ma.gnolia.com

Not strictly a blog but an interesting social bookmarking tool, this allows you to share your bookmarks and site recommendations with a growing community. It's also worth paying a visit to stumble upon: www.stumbleupon.com

MetaFilter

www.metafilter.com

Long-standing community weblog.

Mocoloco

www.mocoloco.com

Modern contemporary design news and views. For art visit: www.mocoloco.com/art

nyclondon

www.nyclondon.com/blog

Stunning photoblog.

blogs

Overheard in New York
www.overheardinnewyork.com
"Teen girl #1: You shouldn't chew gum; it makes you stupider.
Teen girl #2: Oh yeah?
Teen girl #1: Yeah, I heard that somewhere.
Teen girl #2: Well, I heard somewhere that you're an idiot. No, wait, that was right here."

Overheard in the Office
www.overheardintheoffice.com
"Boss: We had so many ideas outside of the box we needed a box to keep them in."

Photo Blogs
www.photoblogs.org
A resource designed to help people find all kinds of photoblogs. Their database currently holds listings for 16,868 photoblogs in 106 countries and 52 languages.

Pop Culture Junk Mail
www.popculturejunkmail.com
Your guide to the flotsam of post-industrial society.

PostSecret
postsecret.blogspot.com
PostSecret is an ongoing community art project where people mail in their secrets anonymously on one side of a homemade postcard.

PubSub
www.pubsub.com
Subscribe to this service, enter a few keywords and PubSub will let you know when there are new blog posts that match your interests.

Shiny Shiny
shinyshiny.tv
What the world has been waiting for – a girls' guide to gadgets.

Talking Points Memo
www.talkingpointsmemo.com
All the dirt from the Washington DC Beltway.

The Best Page in the Universe
maddox.xmission.com
Beneath the onion layers of misanthropy and delusions of grandeur you'll find a soulless husk.

Vagabonding
www.vagabonding.com
Great travel blog by Mike Pugh.

World Changing
www.worldchanging.com
Interesting site based on the premise that the tools, models and ideas for building a better future lie unconnected all around us and which aims to bring some of those elements together to promote change.

Boats

Admiralty Easytide
easytide.ukho.gov.uk
Provides tidal data and forecasts for over six thousand ports worldwide together with a host of other useful information.

Apollo Duck
www.apolloduck.co.uk
Looking to buy or sell a boat? With free photo ads, email updates and hundreds of boats for sale around the UK this should be your first port of call. See also:
www.yachtsnet.co.uk

Berth Search
www.berthsearch.com
This handy site allows you to search specific areas for available berths. Its international selection is quite weak but has comprehensive listings for the UK.

Boating Advice
www.boatingadvice.com
Does exactly what it says on the tin.

Canal Junction
canaljunction.com
Fancy taking in the world at four miles per hour? Maybe you need a narrow boat holiday. This site has canal guides and maps, links to boat hire sites and all the tips and advice you'll need to get started. For nation-wide bookings check Black Prince or Drifters:
www.black-prince.com
www.drifters.co.uk

Global Crew Network
www.globalcrewnetwork.com
Agency for worldwide yachting jobs.

Granny Buttons
www.grannybuttons.com
A charming blog all about canal boating.

Living On Boats
www.livingonboats.co.uk
Helpful site aimed at providing information and contacts to anyone thinking of living on a houseboat.

The Main Sail
www.themainsail.com
Sailing portal with forums, advice, news, buyer's guides, competitions, and gear reviews. See also Yachting and Boating World:
www.ybw.com

 Marinestore Chandlers
www.marinestore.co.uk
There's enough kit here to build a boat from scratch. Galley equipment and deck fittings line up next to items like plastic glasses in case Hurricane Charlie upsets your gin and tonic. See also:
www.pcsboatbits.co.uk
www.force4.co.uk

Books & literature

If a squillion Web pages aren't enough to satisfy your lust for the written word, maybe you should use one to order a book. You'll be spoilt for choice, with hundreds of shops offering millions of titles for delivery worldwide. That includes many Web-only superstores such as **Amazon** as well as most of the major high-street chains (many of which operate their sites "in partnership" with **Amazon** or another online retailer). These superstores typically lay on all the trimmings: user ratings, reviews, recommendations, sample chapters, author interviews, bestseller lists, press clippings, publishing news, secure ordering and gift-wrapping. They also generally offer serious reductions, though these are usually offset by shipping costs. The UK big boys are:

Amazon www.amazon.co.uk
Blackwell's www.blackwells.com
BOL www.uk.bol.com
Bookzone www.bookzone.co.uk
Country Books www.countrybookshop.co.uk
Tesco www.tesco.com/books
Waterstone's www.waterstones.co.uk
WHSmith www.bookshop.co.uk

You can search across many stores simultaneously for availability and the best price by going to:

AddAll www.addall.com
BookBrain www.bookbrain.co.uk
Kelkoo www.kelkoo.co.uk

Can't find what you're looking for online? Why not try searching by specialism in the **BookSellers.org** directories for UK listings…

BookSellers www.booksellers.org.uk

Alternatively, browse the following selection of the best book and literature sites…

Advanced Book Exchange
www.abebooks.com
Describes itself as the world's largest network of independent booksellers, with an Amazon-like interface. A good place to start if you want old, out-of-print books, even if they're in paperback.

Audiobook Collection
www.audiobookcollection.com
Thousands of audiobook titles for sale. A further selection can be found at Listen2Books and the American site, Talking Book World:
www.listen2books.co.uk
www.talkingbooks.com

Audioville
www.audioville.co.uk
This friendly site sells downloadable talking books, magazines, and other content in MP3 format. If you

can't find what you're looking for here try Audible.com or for completeley free stuff visit Audio Books For Free:

www.audible.com

www.audiobooksforfree.com

Banned Books Online

onlinebooks.library.upenn.edu/banned-books.html

Extracts from books that riled the righteous.

Bartleby

www.bartleby.com

Online versions of such classic reference texts as *Gray's Anatomy*, Strunk & White's *The Elements of Style*, the King James Bible and works of fiction and verse by H.G. Wells, Emily Dickinson and many others.

Bibliomania

www.bibliomania.com

Houses the digital versions of some eight hundred classic literary works. However, Bibliomania also features study aids as well as digital versions of reference books, plus a shopping facility if you'd prefer the real thing.

Book-A-Minute

www.rinkworks.com/bookaminute

Knock over the classics in a lunch hour.

Book Crossing

www.bookcrossing.com

Print out a unique ID label, stick it on your finished-with book and then leave it on a train or park bench. If someone finds it and likes it, they'll follow the instructions on the label, go to the site, leave a message and review and then "release" it again. Some

books have now changed hands more than twenty times.

Book Ninja

www.bookninja.com

One of the top literary sites in the world and a nexus for literary news and opinion.

The Bookseller

www.thebookseller.com

UK book trade news, bestseller lists and more. For US publishing news, complete with author road schedules and content from *Publisher's Weekly* and *Library Journal*, see:

www.bookwire.com

Bookslut

bookslut.com

Review, news, features and interviews all available on this excellent site.

Book Wrap Central

www.bookwrapcentral.com

Watch video interviews of authors talking about their work.

The British Library

www.bl.uk

The British Library's site is more use to academics and researchers than to most ordinary Joes, but bookworms will delight in the ability to search the entire catalogue online as well as view select exhibits from the library's collection. There are also some beautifully

books & literature

presented, fully interactive versions of classic texts, complete with turning pages and a magnifying glass: www.bl.uk/onlinegallery/ttp/ttpbooks.html

Carol Hurst's Children's Literature Site
www.carolhurst.com
Don't let the austere style put you off, this site has extensive reviews of books for kids, as well as ideas on how to incorporate them into the curriculum.

 ### Chthonios Books
www.esotericism.co.uk
This stocks new and antique esoterica from neoplatonism and gnosticism to alchemy, mysticism and paganism. More can be found over at Watkins: www.watkinsbooks.com

Classic Novels – In Five Minutes a Day
www.classic-novels.com
Get masterworks such as *Oliver Twist* or *Huckleberry Finn* emailed to you in free bite-sized instalments.

Complete Review
www.complete-review.com
This well-organized, easy-to-search compendium of book reviews includes editor's picks and bestseller lists by year. You can read the site's own reviews or click to read reviews published elsewhere.

The Electronic Labyrinth
eserver.org/elab
An exploration of the implications that the hyperlink has for the future of literature.

The Electronic Text Center
etext.lib.virginia.edu
The University of Virginia's digital archive project is similar to the others but it includes more foreign language texts than any of the competition, so if you're after esoterica like Mescalero Apache texts or just Voltaire's *Candide* in the original French (and why wouldn't you be?), this is the place to look.

E Server
www.eserver.org
Over thirty thousand online works, including classic novels, academic articles, journals, recipes and plays.

The Internet Public Library
www.ipl.org
Browse online books, magazines, journals and newspapers.

Jubilee Books
www.jubileebooks.co.uk
Divided into ages and then again into school terms, there are books for literacy, mathematics, PE or the arts. Information about each book – including how and why it was selected – is included. A brilliant resource.

January Magazine
www.januarymagazine.com
Dissecting books and authors.

Journal Storage
www.jstor.org
Organization devoted to digitally archiving scholarly journals.

JournalismNet
www.journalismnet.com
Tips and tools for tapping into the big cheat sheet. More facts for hacks at:
www.facsnet.org
www.usus.org

Literary Marketplace
www.literarymarketplace.com
Find publishers and literary agents to pester with your manuscript.

London Review of Books
www.lrb.co.uk
Everything you'd expect from the paper version of this literary institution, including a good – if not complete – archive of articles from writers such as Christopher Hitchens, Iain Sinclair, Edward Said and Marjorie Garber. See also *The New York Review of Books*:
www.nybooks.com

 ## Love Reading
www.lovereading.co.uk
Useful new book site which allows you to download first chapters of books, read exclusive reviews and get tailored recommendations based on your reading tastes.

 ## Maps Worldwide
www.mapsworldwide.co.uk
A must for armchair travellers.

MysteryNet
www.mysterynet.com
Hmm, now what could this be?

New York Public Library
www.nypl.org
Contains links to a plethora of resources from magazines, journals and databases online to archives &

manuscripts, and the audio and ebooks you can download.

Online Book Pages
onlinebooks.library.upenn.edu
Searches and links to around twenty thousand free online books.

 ## Ottakar's
www.ottakars.co.uk
This independent bookstore has access to a comprehensive stock of titles. There are also links to Outland, Ottakar's own sci-fi and fantasy site, a daily quiz, and its own columnist, Yossarian. Good discounts too.

Perseus Digital Library
www.perseus.tufts.edu
Hundreds of translated Greek and Roman classics.

Poetry.com
www.poetry.com
Your complete poetry resource, featuring literally millions of poets, plus advice on rhyming and technique, online poetry slams, the hundred greatest poems

E-books

As if the Internet hadn't already sparked enough publishing, along comes the electronic book or eBook. At the moment, most eBooks are simply regular books converted into a special eBook format – or plain old Acrobat.pdf format – so you can read them either on a computer, a pocket PC, a palmtop or a dedicated eBook device.

Once you have the necessary software:

Adobe www.adobe.com/products/ebookreader
Microsoft www.microsoft.com/reader

You can choose titles from a specialist eBookshop:

eBooks www.ebooks.com
GemStar www.gemstar-ebook.com
PeanutPress www.PeanutPress.com
Mobipocket www.mobipocket.com

Or from someone offering free eBooks:

Blackmask www.blackmask.com
Xdrive www.xdrive.com

Or from the eBook departments of the major book retailers:

Amazon www.amazon.co.uk/ebooks
Barnes and Noble ebooks.barnesandnoble.com

For news, reviews and info on eBook hardware and software, visit:

Planet eBook www.planetebook.com
Ebook Reviews www.ebook-reviews.net

Or to try and get your own eBook published, go to:

Authors Online www.authorsonline.co.uk
Online Originals www.onlineoriginals.com
Mushroom eBooks www.mushroom-ebooks.com

 Ebooks.com
www.ebooks.com
This American site has 50,000 titles to choose from. Should keep you going for a while…

 E-Book Mall
www.ebookmall.com
A well organised and comprehensively stocked (over 125,000 titles!) store.

 FictionWise
www.fictionwise.com
Aiming to provide the most comprehensive selection of fiction on the Internet, this site offers high-quality reading and some top authors. It's strong on short stories and science fiction (Isaac Asimov for less than 50¢), but it also republishes out-of-print works and non-fiction.

and love poems. If you're good enough, they'll even publish yours.

Poetry Society

www.poetrysociety.org.uk
A halfway house for budding poets and their victims. Give it a go – you won't be the worst in the class. Also rhyme your way to:
www.poets.org

 Politicos
www.politicos.co.uk
With anything from the latest political blockbuster to memorabilia, this site has almost everything the political buff could desire.

PowerPoint Hamlet

www.myrtle.co.uk/art/hamlet
The Bard's greatest work as a PowerPoint presentation. And if you fancy reading the Sonnets on your iPod, or the plays as PDFs, visit:
www.westering.com/ipod
www.hn.psu.edu/faculty/jmanis/shake.htm

Project Gutenberg

www.gutenberg.net
Copyrights don't live for ever; they eventually expire. In the US, that's seventy-five years after first publication. In Europe, it's some seventy years after the author's death. With this in mind, Project Gutenberg

is gradually bringing thousands of old texts online, along with some more recent donations.

Random Access Memory

randomaccessmemory.org

A truly wonderful concept: this vast repository of memories (of anything at all) is the embodiment of what the Web is meant to be all about. Simple, compelling, about real people and real lives, with no corporate intrusion.

Religious and Sacred Texts

davidwiley.com/religion.html

Links to online versions of the holy books of many of the world's major religions – everything from the Bhagavad Ghita to the Zand-i Vohuman Yasht.

Science Fiction Reader

www.sfreader.com

Extensive reviews of science fiction, speculative fiction and fantasy novels. See also:
www.sffworld.com

Shakespeare

www.opensourceshakespeare.com

There's loads of Will's work to be found online. Also see:
absoluteshakespeare.com
shakespeare.palomar.edu

Simon Finch

www.simonfinch.com

For rare books, especially early printed books. For first editions, biographies, and more visit:
www.deiltak.com

The Slot: A Spot For Copy Editors

www.theslot.com

Soothing words of outrage for grammar pedants.

Soccer Books

www.soccer-books.co.uk

Particularly valuable for its extensive stock of foot-ball books and videos, including a huge portfolio of coaching videos.

Text files

www.textfiles.com

Chunks of the junk that orbited the pre-Web Internet. For a slightly more modern slant, see:
www.etext.org

Vatican Library

bav.vatican.va/en/v_home_bav/home_bav.shtml

A beautiful website heaving with beautiful religious book type stuff.

Village Voice Literary Supplement

www.villagevoice.com/vls

The online version of *The Village Voice*'s literary supplement is the complete printed version for non-New York residents and includes writing from major new voices and insightful reviews.

Web Del Sol

webdelsol.com

A portal for small literary reviews and journals, hosting such prestigious American names as *Kenyon Review*, *Mudlark*, *Sulfur* and *Prairie Schooner*.

Word Counter

www.wordcounter.com

Paste in your composition to rank your most over-used words.

The Word Detective

www.word-detective.com

Words never escape him. See also:
www.quinion.com/words

Word Exchange

www.collins.co.uk/wordexchange

This innovative site from Collins encourages you to submit and discuss articles about words as well as submit new words or new meanings of existing words to their database. Your neologisms could

Business

These homepages of prominent business magazines offer much of the same content as their paper versions, but often at a cost:

Advertising Age www.adage.com
Adweek www.adweek.com
Barrons www.barrons.com
Fast Company www.fastcompany.com
Financial Times www.ft.com
Forbes www.forbes.com
Wall Street Journal www.wsj.com

See also News, Newspapers and Magazines (p.173) and Money and Banking (p.154). Or browse a few of these worthy sites:

AccountingWeb
www.accountingweb.co.uk
Safe playpen for British beancounters.

Adbusters
www.adbusters.org
Headquarters of the world's culture jammers, dedicated to declaring independence from the ever-encroaching corporate state. More culture jamming to be found at ®TMArk:
www.rtmark.com

Ad Critic
www.adcritic.com
Make a cuppa while you wait for this year's best US TV ads. For the best of the past twenty, see:
www.usatvads.com

Ad Forum
www.adforum.com
Gateway to thousands of agencies, their ads and the humble creatives behind them. Also visit:
www.sourcetv.com

Annual Report Gallery
www.reportgallery.com
View the annual reports of over two thousand publicly traded companies for free.

Bizymoms
www.bizymoms.com
Crafty ways to cash up without missing the afternoon soaps.

Disgruntled customer sites

The Web may be the most important business tool ever invented, but it just may be the most important consumer tool ever invented as well. This is what happens when companies don't follow the "customer is always right" rule, or just get too big for their boots.

BT Open Woe www.btopenwoe.co.uk
Ford Really Sucks www.fordreallysucks.com
Fuck Microsoft www.fuckmicrosoft.com
Fuck McDonalds www.fuckmcdonalds.co.uk
I Hate Dell www.ihatedell.net
Paypal Sucks www.paypalsucks.com

And if you want to tell the corporate scum how you feel, first take a moment to search **Google** for "complaint letter of the year" for a little inspiration.

Business.com
www.business.com
Attempting to become the Yahoo! of business sites.

Business Advice Online
www.businessadviceonline.org.uk
Information and advice on taxes, regulations, e-commerce and consultations from the Small Business Service.

Business Ethics
www.business-ethics.com
Apparently it's not an oxymoron.

BVCA
www.bvca.co.uk
Homepage of the British Venture Capital Association, offering basic advice for businesses seeking funding.

City Wire
www.citywire.co.uk
Probably the best place to come for UK financial news. City Wire also contains research reports on what the directors are up to.

Clickz
www.clickz.com
The Web as seen by the marketing biz.

Cluetrain Manifesto
www.cluetrain.org
Modern-day translation of "the customer is always right". Read it or perish.

Complaints.com
www.complaints.com
A database of personal, first-hand, consumer experiences with products and services.

Confederation of British Industry
www.cbi.org.uk/home.html
Tomorrow's public policy today.

Customers Suck!
www.customerssuck.com/board
Grumbling dispatches from the retail front.

Delphion Intellectual Property Network
www.delphion.com
Sift through a few decades of international patents plus a gallery of obscurities. Ask the right questions and you might stumble across tomorrow's technology long before the media. For UK patents see: www.patent.gov.uk

DTI
www.dti.gov.uk
The homepage of the Department for Trade and Industry offers policy news and resources that affect every UK business.

Entrepreneur.com
www.entrepreneur.com
"Get rich now, ask us how."

Flame Broiled
www.geocities.com/capitolhill/lobby/2645
The disgruntled ex-Burger King employee homepage. If only every company had one.

The Foundation Center
fdncenter.org
Companies who might happily spare you a fiver.

Garage.com
www.garage.com
Matchmaking agency for entrepreneurs and investors founded by Apple's Guy Kawasaki.

Guerrilla Marketing
www.gmarketing.com
Get ahead by metaphorically butchering your competitors' families and poisoning your customers' water supply.

Inc
www.inc.com
Online presence of American mag for entrepreneurs and small businesses; includes advice and services such as assistance with creating marketing plans, health insurance quotes and financing.

International Trademark Association
inta.org
Protect your brand identity.

Internal Memos
www.internalmemos.com
Leaked.

Interparcel
www.interparcel.com
Compare prices for ANC, Parcelforce, Parceline and DHL deliveries and book at discount through this courier broker.

Jot Spot
www.jot.com/gallery
Some useful business services and applications offered here, including 'Project Manager' which allows users to share to-do lists, comments, and files from a common remote source.

Mondaq
www.mondaq.com
Regulatory information and financial commentary on over eighty world economies.

Patent Café
www.patentcafe.com
Protect your crackpot schemes and see them through to fruition.

Setting up shop online

Check out the services offered by these sites:

FreeMerchant www.freemerchant.com
BigStep www.bigstep.com
BizFinity www.bizfinity.com
JumboStore www.jumbostore.com
Click and Build www.clickandbuild.com
Yahoo! store.yahoo.com

Or to set up an online shop for next to nothing try one of the big names, such as **eBay** or **Amazon**; alternatively turn to **Cafepress** and its growing network of over two million people:

Cafepress www.cafepress.co.uk

Once things take off you'll need to worry about accepting credit card payments; there are now several recognized online payment methods which are worth investigating; read the FAQs of these sites:

Worldpay www.worldpay.co.uk
PayPal www.paypal.co.uk
Nochex www.nochex.co.uk

Payloadz

www.payloadz.com
Sell downloads of all kinds via PayPal.

Planet Feedback

www.planetfeedback.com
Let US companies know what you think of their service.

Sporting Affair

www.sportingaffair.co.uk
Entertaining at Sporting and Cultural events has apparently become a very effective marketing tool. Sporting Affair provides an innovative approach to the corporate hospitality market with the promise of the best facilities at all events.

The Prince's Trust

www.princes-trust.org.uk
Learn new skills thanks to Charlie.

Quick Formations

www.quickformations.com
If you're starting a new limited company this site offers a range of packages to make it happen.

Silver Lining

www.silverlining.uk.net
Offers a selection of web-based assesment and learning tools to help your staff train themselves.

Super Marketing: Ads from the Comic Books

www.steveconley.com/supermarketing.htm
Everything from Sea Monkeys to Silly Putty. The ads that kept you lying awake at night wishing you had more money.

The Wonderful Wankometer

www.cynicalbastards.com/wankometer
Measure corporate hyperbole. Couple with:
www.dack.com/web/bullshit.html

Cars & motorbikes

Before you're sharked into signing for a new or used vehicle, go online and check out a few road tests and price guides. You can complete the entire exercise while you're there, but it mightn't hurt to drive one first. Start here:

Autobytel www.autobytel.com
Autolocate www.autolocate.co.uk
Autotrader www.autotrader.co.uk
BBC Top Gear www.topgear.beeb.com
Car Shop www.carshop.co.uk
DealerNet www.dealernet.com
Exchange & Mart www.exchangeandmart.co.uk
4 Car www.4car.co.uk
Kelly Blue Book www.kbb.com
Oneswoop www.oneswoop.com
What Car? www.whatcar.com

Aftermarket Motorcycle Parts
www.oem-uk.com
Organised by manufacturer, select your bike model from top names, then scroll through an adequate list of accessories including footpegs, oil caps and end weights.

Art Cars In Cyberspace
www.artcars.com
Fluffy dice just not doing it for you? Try something more adventurous.

Automobile Association
www.theaa.com
Not merely an online rest stop trying to hawk you memberships, the AA's site has useful free features such as a cheap petrol finder and route planner. See also the RAC or International Breakdown:
www.rac.co.uk
www.internationalbreakdown.com

Autotrader
www.autotrader.co.uk
Select a category and make your search as advanced as you like, bearing in mind how far you're willing to travel. After making your selection you are automatically linked to insurance and finance sites.

Bike Trader

www.biketrader.co.uk

Part of the Autotrader group, this site offers the same services as its parent site: good search tool, advice on buying and selling motor bikes, and links to insurance and finance companies.

Breath Testing

www.copsonline.com/breath_test.htm

Slurring your swearwords, wobbling all over the road, mounting gutters and knocking kids off bikes? Pull over and blow into this site.

Car Net

www.carnet.co.uk

Massive automotive portal, including advice and information on collecting, research facilities, trivia, forums, links, classifieds, want ads, rallying news and more.

Car Shop

www.carshop.co.uk

Simple name for a simple system. The Buy & Go section is especially straightforward. Search for the make and model of the car you wish to buy, view

specs and images of the cars on offer, choose one and put down your deposit on your credit card. Easy as one, two, three.

Chater's

www.chaters.co.uk

For all the repair manuals and vids you could want. They also stock rare and out-of print automotive literature.

Circuit Driver

www.circuitdriver.com

This e-zine for speed junkies includes racing information (with online booking facilities), car reviews, etc.

Classic Car Directory

www.classic-car-directory.com

Good resource for classic car enthusiasts, with price guides, dealer directories, events listings, classifieds and links.

Exchange & Mart

www.exchangeandmart.co.uk

You may not be able buy online but the Mart is still at the pinnacle of used car directories. Make your search as simple or complex as you choose. A price guide ensures you're not being ripped off, and there are insurance quotes and car reviews.

Find A Part

www.find-a-part.com

Find A Part does exactly that, though you'll need to know the ins and outs of your car for them to be able to help – and for engine parts you'd better know everything there is to know about your gearbox. If you can cope with this, click away and wait for them to return with help.

The Highway Code

www.highwaycode.gov.uk

Fail your driving theory test online first.

Making our roads safer

Motoring online isn't just about wide-wheels and horse-power:
www.brake.org.uk
www.safespeed.org.uk/s.p.e.e.d.html
www.speedlimit.org.uk
www.thinkroadsafety.gov.uk

Lowrider.com
www.lowrider.com
Online community for Vatos Locos and other con-noisseurs of barely-street-legal motor vehicles with the lowest clearance known to man.

MOT
www.ukmot.com
Let Malcolm the mechanic help you make your car roadworthy.

Motorcycle News
www.motorcyclenews.com
Everything on two wheels ... plus the obligatory bikini babes. Also see BikersWeb and, for a more measured approach, the Motorcycle Action Group:
www.bikersweb.co.uk
www.mag-uk.org

 ### One Swoop
www.oneswoop.com
This brilliant site offers discounted vehicles and express shopping. Search by your chosen make, model or price range and you'll find a long list of options.

Parkers Online
www.parkers.co.uk
Car price and specs database going back twenty years. For new models, try:
www.new-car-net.co.uk

Planet Campers
www.planetcampers.com
The online home of all things VW-camper-related – loads of ads, links for buying and selling and useful books. Also see:
www.vwcampers.co.uk

 ### Rainbow
www.rainbow.co.uk
BMW-mad site with bikes for hire, used bikes, spare parts, leathers, boots and helmets.

Speedtraps
www.ukspeedtraps.co.uk
A great resource for drivers who want to know, umm, where traffic flashpoints might occur.

Street Trucks Magazine
www.streettrucksmag.com
Custom trucking bible for fans of bags, grilles, rims, souped-up air intake manifolds and other such things.

 ### What Car?
www.whatcar.co.uk
Like Exchange & Mart site, the What Car? site includes a good price guide for used cars. There's also a sophisticated search engine, and you get the chance to sell your old car for less than a fiver.

Woman Motorist
www.womanmotorist.com
The demographic group that motor vehicle insurers prefer. For the best deals, try:
www.diamond.co.uk

 ### World Parts
www.world-parts.com
If you're seeking a hubcap or an entire engine, tell this site the car's make and model and the country in which you live, and it will tell you who stocks your part.

Gossip & celebrities

Every celebrity has at least one obsessive fan site in their honour, but finding them can sometimes be tricky. If they're not listed in **Yahoo!**, try:

Celebhoo www.celebhoo.com
CelebSites www.celebsites.com
Celebrity Site Of The Day www.csotd.com
Webring www.webring.org

Search engines tend to find porn scuttlers who've loaded their HTML meta tags with celebrity names – easy bait, when you consider that most fans would be more than happy to catch a glimpse of their idol in various states of undress:

Celebrity Nudity Database www.cndb.com

If they succeed in catching your attention, at least have the sense not to pull out your credit card. Adding -**naughty** -**naked** -**nude** to your search term, or enabling an adult filter such as **Google**'s SafeSearch (under Preferences), might help weed them out.

ABC News Entertainment
abcnews.go.com:80/sections/entertainment
Rumours and legit showbiz news from one of America's big three TV networks.

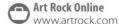 **Art Rock Online**
www.artrock.com
Online utopia for rock and pop fans, selling posters, T-shirts and other items from a huge range of musicians and bands.

Arundel Autograph Gallery
www.autographs.co.uk
This site offers signed photos and letters from public figures, including movie stars, sportsmen and politicians. Everyone from Caprice to Winston Churchill.

Beat Box Betty
www.beatboxbetty.com
Gossip and industry news "with a twist of blonde".

Celebrity Baby Blog
celebritybabies.typepad.com
This blog is overflowing with snaps of celebrity tots, all the gossip surrounding them and, most importantly, what they are wearing this season.

Cinescape
www.cinescape.com
The latest insider industry news. Not as good as *The Hollywood Reporter*, but you don't have to subscribe.

Drudge Report
www.drudgereport.com
Rumours from inside the Washington Beltway with a distinctly right-wing slant, from the online columnist who almost brought down a president.

gossip & celebrities

E! Online
www.eonline.com
The latest from the States courtesy of the homepage of the American cable TV channel.

Famous Birthdays
www.famousbirthdays.com
See who shares your birthday. And then see again at: us.imdb.com/OnThisDay

Fanzine
www.fanzine.co.uk
The official addresses of the stars. For more direct access, try Chip's Celebrity Home E-mails, and if that doesn't land you with a restraining order, reach out to more stars at Celebrity Addresses and Celebrity Email:
www.addresses.site2go.com
www.writetoaceleb.com
www.celebrityemail.com

Filth2Go
www.filth2go.com
Outrageous, scandalous, rude gay gossip zine.

Find a Grave
www.findagrave.com
See where celebrities are buried.

Gawker Stalker
www.gawker.com/stalker
Celebrity sightings plotted on a google map.

Go Fug Yourself
gofugyourself.typepad.com
Fashion disasters of the rich and famous.

Hello!
www.hellomagazine.co.uk
All the jet trash and desperate celebs you expect from the glossy, only with lower production values. For an American version of the same, try:
people.aol.com

New York Post
www.nypostonline.com/gossip/gossip.htm
The latest dish from the columnists of the Big Apple's most notorious tabloid.

Popbitch
www.popbitch.com
Scurrilous, rude, fun and yes, downright bitchy, this is without question the best British pop gossip site. Their weekly mailing lists have brought down careers and halt work all over the capital every Thursday.

Pop Justice
www.popjustice.com
Fabulously bitchy site taking aim at the teen pop hordes.

Recollections
www.recollections.co.uk
Lots of autographed concert programmes and ticket stubs, along with a variety of memorabilia, much of it at very good prices.

The Smoking Gun
www.thesmokinggun.com
Tom Cruise's petition for divorce, Linda Fiorentino's nudity rider and other documents of celebrity misbehaviour.

Starstore
www.starstore.com
More than thirteen thousand items of movie and TV memorabilia, searchable by name, show or even catchphrase.

TeenHollywood.com
www.teenhollywood.com
All the latest dirt and news on Tinseltown's pretty young things.

Classifieds

Online classifieds need no explanation. They're like the paper version, but easier to search and possibly more up to date. In fact, most papers are moving their classifieds to the Net, though you might have to pay to see the latest listings. Here's a small selection:

Ad Trader www.adtrader.co.uk
Exchange & Mart www.exchangeandmart.co.uk
Excite Classifieds classifieds.excite.com
Friday-Ad www.friday-ad.co.uk
Gumtree www.gumtree.com
London Classifieds www.londonclassified.com
Loot www.loot.com
Net Trader www.nettrader.co.uk
Photo Ads www.photoads.co.uk
Preloved www.preloved.co.uk
Reel Exchange www.reelexchange.co.uk
Sell It Net www.sellitnet.com

Aquarist Classified
www.aquarist-classifieds.co.uk
For all things fishy.

Craigslist
www.craigslist.org
Local community classifieds and forums; find jobs, housing, goods & services, social activities, a girlfriend or boyfriend, advice, community information, and just about anything else -- all for free, and in a relatively non-commercial environment.

Flatmate World
uk.easyroommate.com
If you're looking for a place to live or have a spare room this is a good place to browse. Also worth a visit:
www.clickflatshare.co.uk
www.spareroom.co.uk

Freecycle
www.freecycle.org
Want to get rid of something fast? Want something for nothing? Join your local Freecycle network, you'll be surprised what you can find, or what other people are looking for.

Music 3 Ads
www.music3ads.com
Advertise anything musical here. For pro live equipment take a look at concert trade.
www.concerttrade.com

Star Now
www.starnow.co.uk
If your bass player just left or you're looking for a reality TV show to cast you into the limelight, or both, then this is the place for you. See also:
www.formingbands.co.uk

Comics

Anime Fringe
www.animefringe.com
Well presented on-line anime magazine. For more news from Japan visit:
www.animenewsnetwork.com
www.otakunews.com/uk/
www.mangalife.com

Children's Illustrators
www.childrensillustrators.com
On-line portfolios of nearly three hundred children's illustrators

Comic Art Collective
www.comicartcollective.com
Buy original work direct from your favourite comic book artists.

Comic Book Resources
www.comicbookresources.com
A great place to start when looking for comic and cartoon sites and shops. If you're really serious about your comics, check out Sequential Tart, a webzine about the industry, and these others:
www.sequentialtart.com
www.crimeboss.com
www.comicsreporter.com

Comic Foundry
comicfoundry.com
Useful Site for Comic artists and writers to network, collaborate and hone their skills. For a comprehensive list of resources for the aspiring cartoonist visit:
www.block.plus.com/Information/resources.htm

The Comic Guru
www.thecomicguru.co.uk
Online store dealing mostly in Marvel and DC stuff, with a host of statuettes and manga DVDs to boot.

Comics International
www.comics-international.com
A useful gateway site offering a virtually definitive directory of UK stockists, rated hyperlinks to great comic sites, reviews of hundreds of comics and an FAQ on comic trivia which, among other interesting things, tells you which sets of Marvel Comics are almost worthless.

The Comics Journal
www.tcj.com
Archived interviews, reviews and essays from the publication that tackles comics from an "arts first" perspective. Worth visiting for its bustling discussion board alone.

Down The Tubes
www.downthetubes.net
British Comic news and writing guides.

Drawn
www.drawn.ca
A multi-authored blog devoted to illustration, art, cartooning and drawing. An invaluable site for anyone interested in comic book art.

Fantagraphics
www.fantagraphics.com
Currently in the process of re-issuing (among other things) the complete Peanuts collection, alongside more contemporary works by Jamie Hernandez, Daniel Clowes, and many others.

Forbidden Planet
www.forbiddenplanet.co.uk
Forbidden Planet is well known for its comprehensive stock of graphic novels and comics; you can also buy DVDs, games, vinyl toys, and more.

International Catalogue of Superheroes
www.internationalhero.co.uk
More spandex than you could shake a stick at.

London Cartoon Gallery
www.cartoongallery.co.uk
Online gallery showcasing political, editorial, strip and gag cartoonists from the broadsheets, the tabloids and satirical magazines.

Mega City Comics
www.megacitycomics.co.uk
This online store has a decent selection of books and

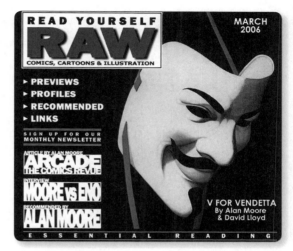

comics, with back issues and collector editions, posters and gifts. It's also worth looking at Book Palace: www.bookpalace.com

Read Yourself Raw
www.readyourselfraw.com
Excellent site with artist profiles (from Peter Bagge to Jim Woodring), a recommended list, previews & reviews, and a links list that'll keep you clicking for the rest of the year. For more, visit:
www.indyworld.com/indy/
www.paulgravett.com
www.ninthart.com

Vinyl Pulse
www.vinylpulse.com
Want the dirt on James Jarvis or Pete Fowler? Daily news from the designer toy industry can be found here. If you're shopping follow the links or visit:
www.bugvinyl.com
www.designertoystore.co.uk
www.intoyswetrust.com

Computing & tech news

Every decent PC brand has a site where you can download the latest drivers, get support and find out what's new. It won't be hard to find. Usually it's the company name or initials between a www and a com.

So you'll find **Dell** at www.dell.com, **Compaq** at www.compaq.com, **Gateway** at www.gateway.com, and so forth. Most of the big names also have international branches, which will be linked from the main site. Consult **Yahoo!** if that fails. If you're in the market for new computer bits, check out the best price across online vendors:

Kelkoo www.kelkoo.co.uk
Price Runner www.pricerunner.co.uk
Shopping.com uk.shopping.com

Popular package software vendors include:

www.amazon.co.uk
www.ebuyer.com
www.saversoftware.co.uk
www.softwareoutlet.com
www.softwareparadise.co.uk

It's worth browsing a few of the online mags for reviews before you buy; try:

Custom PC www.custompc.co.uk
Maxpc www.maxpc.co.uk

PCWorld www.pcworld.com
Personal Computer World www.pcw.co.uk

Here are a few more of our favourite tech sites:

Apple Store
www.apple.com
You can grab all your Mac and iPod products right here.

Avast
www.avast.com
Possibly the best antivirus software you can get, and for home users it's free!

Bastard Operator from Hell
bofh.ntk.net
If you work in a big office, you know this man. Or is the grass greener on the other side of the fence? Find out here:
www.techtales.com

Bios Magazine
www.biosmagazine.co.uk
Keep up to date with the latest tech news & reviews. See also:
www.hexus.net

Blue Frog
www.bluesecurity.com/blue-frog
Neat little app that integrates into your mail client to automatically report spam and put pressure on

offending companies by posting complaints on their websites.

Bright Minds
www.brightminds.co.uk

A great site where you can stock up with software for the little ones.

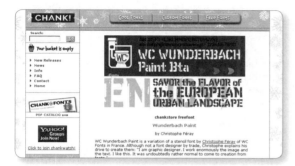

Chankstore FreeFont Archive
www.chank.com/freefonts.php

Download a wacky Chank Diesel display font free each week. If there's still space in your font sack, arrive hat in hand at:
www.1001freefonts.com
www.dafont.com
www.fontface.com
www.fontfreak.com
www.pizzadude.dk/fonts.php

Clip Art
webclipart.about.com

Bottomless cesspit of the soulless dross used to inject life into documents. Also click through to:
classroomclipart.com

Computer Manuals
www.compman.co.uk

Hefty discounts on the latest software guidebooks.

CNET
www.cnet.com

Daily technology news and features plus reviews, shopping, games and downloads, along with schedules, transcripts and related stories from CNET's broadcasting network.

Custom PC
www.custompc.co.uk

If you're thinking of building your own computer this site will give you a few pointers about what to put inside it. With in-depth news, features and benchmark tests it's a good place to start.

DABS
www.dabs.com

Dabs sells Macs as well as PCs, and at prices very competitive with Mac Warehouse. All the big PC brands are there, plus software, peripherals, components and audio-visual gear. See also:
www.novatech.co.uk

Desktop Publishing
desktoppublishing.com

Get off the ground in print. For more visit:
desktoppub.about.com

Download.com
www.download.com

Grab trial and free versions of the latest software, music, video and games from this friendly portal which has regular articles and features covering everything from making a better mix CD to removing spyware.

Easter egg archive
www.eeggs.com

A racing game in Excel, a basketball game in Windows 95 and a raygun-wielding alien in Quark Xpress? They're in there all right, but you'll never find them on your own. Here's how to unlock secrets in scores of programs.

PC help

The best place to find an answer to your computer problems is usually on Usenet. Chances are it's already been answered, so before you rush in and post, search the archives through Google Groups.

Google Groups groups.google.com

That's not to say you won't find an answer on the Web. You probably will, so follow up with a Web search. You'll find a choice of engines at the very bottom of the results page. If you click on **Google**, for example, it will perform the same search in the Web database. Apart from Usenet, there are several very active computing forums on the Web, such as:

Computing.net www.computing.net
Tek-Tips www.tek-tips.com

And there are hundreds of troubleshooting and Windows news sites, such as:

ActiveWin www.activewin.com
Annoyances.org www.annoyances.org
Virtual Dr virtualdr.com
WinosCentral www.winoscentral.com

Don't forget to keep your hardware installation drivers up to date. You'll find the latest files for download direct from the manufacturer's website, or at driver guides such as these:

DriverForum www.driverforum.com
Driver Guide www.driverguide.com
Drivers HQ www.drivershq.com

Electronic Privacy Information Center

www.epic.org
Since 1994, EPIC has been in the vanguard of the campaign to protect privacy over the Internet. For a withering attack on the UK's Regulation of Investigatory Powers Act and coverage of free speech issues on the Net, go to:
www.fipr.org
www.eff.org

Forward Garden

www.forwardgarden.com
The resting place of every piece of junk email you've ever received.

Ghost Sites: The Museum of Failure

www.disobey.com/ghostsites
A chronicle of the rise and fall of the cyber empire.

Gibson Research Corporation

grc.com
If you're at all interested in computer security or are a raving paranoiac, you owe it to yourself to check out this site. Also visit here to find out about Rootkit threats:
www.rootkit.com

The GNU Project

www.gnu.org
The homepage of Richard Stallman's efforts to create a free operating system. You might know it better as Linux, named after Linus Torvald's kernel. For more on GNU/Linux, try:
www.linux.org

Guide to Flaming

www.advicemeant.com/flame
Learn how to win friends and influence people in newsgroups, forums and chat rooms.

Hackers' Homepage

www.hackershomepage.com
Everything you shouldn't do to your computer or someone else's. Just make sure you run every anti-virus utility you've got after stopping by. More at:
www.attrition.org
www.cultdeadcow.com
www.2600.com

InfoAnarchy
www.infoanarchy.org
Turn to this site for all the latest news and views from the battle to keep information free.

Insight
uk.insight.com
Stronger on components and peripherals than on complete desktop PC systems. The main attraction here is what Insight calls its Inventory Blowout – a bargain basement where you could pick up anything from a still-boxed notebook to a slightly scuffed motherboard for a fraction of the original cost.

Internet Speed Test
www.zensupport.co.uk/speedtest
Wallow in the grim truth about the speed of your connection. More tests to be found at:
www.dslreports.com/stest
www.beelinebandwidthtest.com

ISP Review
www.ispreview.co.uk
Compare your Internet Service Provider with the rest and get the latest broadband news. Also try:
www.broadband-help.com/home.asp

IT Reviews
www.itreviews.co.uk
Independent, jargon-free reviews of hardware, software, games, etc. For more reviews, try these:
compreviews.about.com/compute/compreview
www.technologyowl.com

Laptops Direct

www.laptopsdirect.co.uk
Offers a good range of laptops and spares from brands like Acer, Fujitsu, IBM, Sony and Toshiba at competitive prices. It's also worth scouting around these other sites to compare prices:
www.shoplaptop.co.uk
www.mynewcheap.co.uk/products/laptops/

Computer viruses

Unless you're 100 percent certain that a download or attachment is safe, even if it's been sent by your best friend, DON'T OPEN IT! Instead, save it to your Desktop or a quarantine folder and examine it carefully before proceeding. That should include running it past an up-to-date antivirus scanner such as Avast (www.avast.com). You'll find everything you need to know about viruses at:

About antivirus.about.com
Faqs.org www.faqs.org/faqs/computer-virus
Grisoft www.grisoft.com
Symantec www.symantec.com/avcenter

Life Hacker
www.lifehacker.com
Lifehacker recommends downloads, web sites and shortcuts that can save time and improve your computing experience.

Mac Warehouse
www.macwarehouse.co.uk
Good site for Mac-compatible peripherals. Everything comes with a spec sheet and prices are competitive.

Microsoft
www.microsoft.com
If you're running any Microsoft product (and the chance of that seems to be approaching one hundred percent), drop by this disorganized scrapheap regularly for upgrades, news, support and patches. That includes the latest free tweaks to Windows, Office and all that falls under the Internet Explorer regime.

Modem Help
www.modemhelp.org
Solve your dial-up dramas for modems of all persuasions including cable, ISDN and DSL. And be sure to check your modem maker's page for driver and firmware upgrades.

Apple online

Apple www.apple.com

The company's own site is the essential drop-in to update your Mac, pick up QuickTime and be hard-sold the latest hardware. To top up with news, software, and brand affirmations, see:

MacAddict www.macaddict.com
Apple Insider www.appleinsider.com
Tidbits www.tidbits.com
Mac In Touch www.macintouch.com
MacNN www.macnn.com
MacSlash www.macslash.com

And if you want to know what Apple is going to come out with next, angle your one-button mouse at:

Mac Rumors www.macrumors.com

For the latest applications, hints and news on OS X Tiger, seek out:

Mac OS X Apps www.macosxapps.com
Mac OS X Hints www.macosxhints.com

If you're still desperately clinging on to your old Quadra or Performa, try:

Low End Mac www.lowendmac.com

And to diagnose your ailing Mac:

MacFixit www.macfixit.com

And if iPods are what float your boat, take a trip to one of these sites:

Apple/iPod www.apple.com/ipod
iLounge www.ilounge.com

Alternatively, pick up a copy of *The Rough Guide to iPods, iTunes & Music Online*. And while you're at it, we also recommend *The Rough Guide to Macs & OS X*.

The Museum of Counter Art
www.counterart.com
"THE showcase for over five hundred sets of counter digit artwork."

Newslinx
www.newslinx.com
Have the top Net technology stories, aggregated from around fifty sources, delivered to your mailbox daily.

Old Computers
www.old-computers.com
Relive the days when your Sinclair ZX81 or Commodore Vic 20 could barely play solitaire. More at HCM:
www.homecomputer.de

 ### Overclockers UK
www.overclockers.co.uk
Supplies high-spec computer parts carefully selected for performance. If you're serious about building a PC check here first. It's also worth visiting Scan and Misco:
www.scan.co.uk
www.misco.co.uk

Palmgear
www.palmgear.com
Know your Palm like the back of your hand. For the PocketPC, see:
www.pocketmatrix.com

PC Mechanic

www.pcmech.com/byopc

How to build or upgrade your own computer. Also see:

arstechnica.com/tweak/hardware.html

PC Tweaking

www.anandtech.com

How to overclock your processor into the next millennium, tweak your bios and upgrade your storage capacity to attract members of the opposite sex. Loads more at:

www.arstechnica.com

www.sharkyextreme.com

www.tweaktown.com

PCWebopedia

www.pcwebopedia.com

Superb illustrated encyclopedia of computer technology.

PC World

www.pcworld.co.uk

This is the non-techie end of the online buying spectrum. There's no bewildering depth or range, just well-known names and a brief selection of everything. The PC World of Computing section provides reviews, hints and tips, and a handy jargon buster.

Quiet PC

www.quietpc.com

Put a little peace and quiet back into your life. Quiet PC collects together fanless PSUs, giant CPU heatsinks, water cooling systems, acoustic treatments and everything else you could need short of earplugs. For

Online storage

Whether you want to back-up some files safely onto a remote server or transfer large amounts of data between two computers, consider signing up for some online storage. Some webspace may have come free with your Internet access account (ask your ISP). If it did, all you'll need is an FTP client to upload and download files to the space. Such as:

CuteFTP www.cuteftp.com

If it didn't, you could find some free space from:

Yahoo Briefcase briefcase.yahoo.com
Save File www.savefile.com
Stream Load www.streamload.com
Your File Link www.yourfilelink.com
You Send It www.yousendit.com

Alternatively, if you don't mind paying, sign up for a virtual disk drive service, such as:

XDrive www.xdrive.com
.Mac www.mac.com

silent fans visit:

www.dorothybradbury.co.uk

Red Light Runner

www.redlightrunner.com

Apple collectibles, from towels and sandals with the Apple logo to mugs, pens and even a 'Steve Jobs for President' sticker. Also sells those classy 'Think different' posters, featuring Miles Davis, Callas, Lucy & Desi and Martha Graham.

The Register

www.theregister.co.uk

Punchy tech news that spins to its own tune.

Slashdot.org

slashdot.org

News for those who've entirely given up on the human race.

Tech Dirt

www.techdirt.com

Keeping tabs on the dark underbelly of the Internet economy.

Tom's Hardware Guide

www.tomshardware.com

One of the most important sites on the Net, at least for the hardware industry. Tom and his reporters are credited with the delayed release of Pentium's 1GHz Pentium III processor because the site gave it a thumbs down. This is the best source for bug reports and benchmark tests. Try also:

www.tech-pc.co.uk

www.trustedreviews.com

Tucows

www.tucows.com

An excellent resource for the lastest shareware downloads, with reviews and user ratings.

WebReference

www.webreference.com

If you don't know your HTML from your XML or DHTML, try this reference and tutorials site. For more tips and tricks, try Webmonkey:

webmonkey.wired.com/webmonkey

Widget Software

www.widget.co.uk

Selling all the latest handheld systems, EPOC devices, Palm OS, Windows CE and a selection of mobiles. Psion, Compaq, Hewlett Packard and Handspring dominate each section with high-street prices throughout.

Wired News

www.wired.com

The Net's best source of breaking technology news plus archives of *Wired* magazine. For more, try Geek. com:

www.geek.com

Woody's Office Portal

www.wopr.com

Beat some sense out of Microsoft Office. For Outlook, see:

www.slipstick.com/outlook

Yahoo! Computing

www.yahoo.com/Computers

The grandpappy of all computing directories.

ZDNet

www.zdnet.com

Computing info powerhouse from Ziff Davis, publisher of *PC Magazine*, *MacUser*, *Computer Gaming World* and scores of other IT titles. Each magazine donates content such as news, product reviews and lab test results; plus there's a ton of prime Net-exclusive technochow. The best place to start researching anything even vaguely computer-related.

Crazes

With each new craze lasting about as long as a goldfish's memory span, the Internet is a wonderful tool to find the best, the worst and the weirdest.

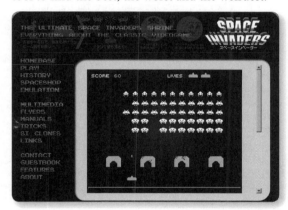

Space Invaders
www.spaceinvaders.de
The beautiful game has its own e-shrine where you can download stuff, play online or buy the T-shirt.

Tablesports
www.garlando.co.uk
Table football has raised its game with these Italian designs. Choose from elegant art deco to pub-quality coin-operated tables. For classier kicks visit Eleven Forty, and to really immerse yourself visit the British

Foosball Association:
www.elevenforty.com
www.britfoos.com

The History Of the Slinky Toy
inventors.about.com/od/sstartinventions/a/slinky.htm
"What walks down stairs, alone or in pairs, And makes a slinkity sound? A spring, a spring, a marvelous thing, Everyone knows it's Slinky…" See also:
www.poof-slinky.com

Let's Go Retro
www.letsgoretro.com
Craze memorabilia loosely grouped by era, everything from Fuzzy Felts to the Crazy Frog.

Perplex City
www.perplexcity.com
Complex puzzle-oriented game.

Rubiks
www.rubiks.com
Play the cube online.

Scoubidou Guide
www.scoubiguide.co.uk
All the instructions you need to get knotted.

Sudoku Online
www.sudoku.org.uk
Your gateway to the grids. For daily puzzles visit:
www.dailysudoku.co.uk
www.sudokufun.com

Department stores

Traditional high-street names have taken to the Net the way porcupines make love: very carefully indeed. Many still only have store locators or information on a limited selection of products with no ordering facility. Below are a handful that offer a more complete online shopping experience.

Argos
www.argos.co.uk

Offers the same range of goods as can be found in their high-street stores, with regular special offers and discounts. Also worth checking their separate spares site for cables, vacuum cleaner bags, and other less glamorous items:
www.argosspares.co.uk

Debenhams
www.debenhams.com

You'll find fashion, gifts, flowers and wedding items: search for a gift in your price range or check out fashion by brands. Top names include Jasper Conran, Pearce II Fionda, Boxfresh and Warehouse.

Fortnum & Mason
www.fortnumandmason.com

A classy site hawking a delectable range of food & wines from its Piccadilly store.

Harrods
www.harrods.com

Everything from pants to pool tables available here.

Heal's
www.heals.co.uk

A well thought-out site offering a healthy selection from their home accessories and gifts range, including stylish kitchen and tableware, modern lighting and storage, luxurious cushions and throws, office & garden furniture and more. Also has a wedding list facility.

John Lewis
www.johnlewis.com

The John Lewis site is a classy number with good descriptions of the items on offer. Everything from electrical to fashion to furniture.

LX Direct
www.lxdirect.com

Offers a wide range of goods including men and women's fashion, electrical goods, toys and gift ideas.

Marks & Spencer
www.marks-and-spencer.co.uk

Recently revamped M&S no longer sells food online, sticking to clothes and housewares.

Selfridges
www.selfridges.com

They don't sell fridges online, or anything else for that matter, but their site is beautifully designed and packed with next season's fashion tips.

Education

This chapter is perhaps a bit of a misnomer as the entire Internet is potentially the greatest single educational resource that's ever been invented: the latter-day equivalent of the library at Alexandria. Here you'll find educational resources (for students, teachers and parents), general homework sites, information on distance learning and admissions guides. For other study tools, try the Reference chapter or other subject headings (Art, Politics, History, etc).

About Education
education.about.com
They may be geared towards the US, but, as usual, About's education pages are an excellent source of information and news. Having trouble with times tables or conjugating Latin verbs? Try About Homework:
homework.about.com

Ask an Expert
www.cln.org/int_expert.html
Links to hundreds of experts who will happily answer your homework question or offer you careers advice. There are also teaching experts awaiting questions from harried pedagogues.

BBC Shop
www.bbcshop.com
The Education section sells books, videos and CD-ROMs. The range is heavily influenced by what's on the national curriculum and you'll find decent, well-produced stuff.

Brilliant Publications
www.brilliantpublications.co.uk
Brilliant has an attractive selection of posters and books, broken down by age group and the area you want to improve (literacy or maths, for example). You can even download sample pages.

Click Teaching
www.clickteaching.com
Site written by and for Primary school teachers.

Dorling Kindersley
www.dk.com/uk
DK's range of books and software are on sale here. Categories include arts and crafts, languages, DIY and science.

EduFind
www.edufind.com
Massive language education resource site, with a TEFL slant.

Evil House of Cheat
www.cheathouse.com
Thousands of college essays, term papers and reports. But beware, teachers can check for traces of plagiarism:
www.turnitin.com

Good Schools Guide
www.goodschoolsguide.co.uk
A listing of all the public information available on UK schools – from head teachers and pupil numbers through to exam results. In order to gain full access to more in-depth information you need to buy the actual book, which then allows you weekly updates and school reviews written by parents for parents.

Green Board Game Company
www.greenboardgames.com
This range of educational board games and toys is aimed at primary school ages and up, including *Antworks,* a space-age ant-farm devised by NASA to study ants in zero-gravity.

Guide to Grammar and Style
andromeda.rutgers.edu/~jlynch/Writing
Handy online guide to English language usage. It won't replace Strunk & White or *The Chicago Manual of Style*, but if you're in a pinch, could be worth a try.

International Centre for Distance Learning
www-icdl.open.ac.uk
The Open University's distance learning resource centre contains a huge database on courses and organizations as well as abstracts of journal articles and research papers pertaining to distance education.

Internet Public Library
www.ipl.org
Browse the catalogue of some sixteen thousand online texts, utilize the original resources and ask homework questions – all without a horn-rimmed librarian telling you to turn down your Discman.

ISIS
www.isc.co.uk
The homepage of the Independent Schools Information Service allows parents and teachers to search their database for information on prospective schools and employers.

Learning Alive
www.learningalive.co.uk
Offers a wide range of educational services to teachers, pupils and parents. Some services require a subscription, and others are free, such as the useful Pathways feature which provides thousands of curriculum-relevant links browsable by subject.

Linguaphone
www.linguaphone.co.uk
A staggering selection of language courses on offer from quick starter packs to more advanced studies.

Maths Net
www.mathsnet.net
For help with numbers.

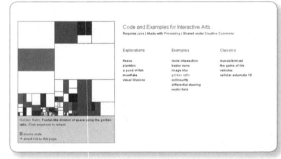

Metaphorical
www.metaphorical.net
You know how sometimes you read something or speak with someone and you can feel yourself getting dumber? Well this kind of does the opposite.

National Curriculum Online
www.nc.uk.net
The Government's definitive national curriculum site for teachers. For the Scottish curriculum, go to the LT Scotland Online Service:

www.ltscotland.org.uk

National Geographic Ed Net
www.ngsednet.org
Register (it's free) for access to world news digests, teaching resources and forums & communities.

National Grid for Learning
www.ngfl.gov.uk
This site is the centrepiece of the Government's plans to harness the Net as the future of education. As you might guess, it's a bit of a sprawling mess, but there are sections devoted to just about every educational issue you can think of, as well as tons of links, a virtual teacher centre and so on.

National Union of Students
www.nusonline.co.uk
How to buy a pint if your grant runs out.

BBC/OU Open2.net
www.open2.net
A fascinating site from the BBC with features, essays, multimedia and discussion groups that tie in with Open University programming. Encompassing history, arts, literature, economics, science, philosophy, and more.

 ### Osborne Books
www.osbornebooks.co.uk
Bookseller specialising in business, accounting and finance education. Titles range from *Costing Reports* to the more mysterious *A Fiery Glow in the Darkness*. There's also a resource section of documents suitable for accounting courses that are free to download.

Profquotes
www.profquotes.com
They sure do say the darnedest things.

Show Me
www.show.me.uk
Fun site for kids with cool stuff from museums

around the UK, along with games, competitions, and resources for parents and teachers.

Study Abroad
www.studyabroad.com
Hop to grass that's greener.

The Teacher Network
www.theteachernet.co.uk
Resources, links, job-search for teachers.

Topmarks Education
www.topmarks.co.uk
This excellent and very easy-to-use site searches the Web for educational sites pertaining to your subject and appropriate age level, so if you're searching for sites to help you with GCSE revision it will weed out all the sites aimed at Key Stage 1 students. See also Schoolzone:
www.schoolzone.co.uk

UCAS
www.ucas.co.uk
Information on university courses, including admissions requirements and general facts and figures, from the University and Colleges Admissions Service.

Unofficial Guides
www.unofficial-guides.com
Get the real dope on the unis from the students themselves, not the marketing boards.

Up My Street
www.upmystreet.com
Type in your postcode and get quick access to the performance tables of local schools.

Word Central
www.wordcentral.com
A site designed to broaden kids' vocabulary by introducing them to the joys of wordplay. There's also a section for teachers with lesson plans and a history of the English language.

Electrical

Buying electrical equipment can be a bit of a headache. With so many different products on offer, making an informed decision to suit your pocket usually involves a fair deal of head-scratching whilst peering at tiny images of characterless boxes and their accompanying jargon. Whether you know what you're looking for or not, it pays to start your search by visiting a price comparison site such as Kelkoo or Price Runner. Some of these even feature comparison charts with pop-up explanations that'll help you decide whether the spec you're comparing has any elevance to your needs. Others have user reviews to give you opinions from other real-life human beings about the products and retailers that could help steer you away from picking a lemon.

Shopping.com uk.shopping.com
Electrical Comparison www.electricalcomparison.co.uk
Kelkoo www.kelkoo.co.uk
Price Runner www.pricerunner.co.uk
Unbeatable www.unbeatable.co.uk

Rent or buy?

For those of you who'd prefer to sidestep the looming cost of repairs on appliances like washing machines or want to stay up-to-date with the latest in home entertainment without any expensive outlay, renting could be the way forward. There are now a number of companies online ready to lease you plasma screens, DVD recorders, washing machines, dryers, fridges and dishwashers…

Teleview Direct
www.teleview-direct.co.uk

Box Clever
www.boxclever.co.uk

R&M Rentals
www.rmtv.co.uk

General

247 Electrical
www.247electrical.co.uk
247 has departments for just about every aspect of home electricals, it even has gardening and DIY sections. Regular special offers make it well worth a visit.

AJ Electronics
www.ajelectronics.co.uk
A well-liked online trader that has an excellent selection of audio-visual equipment at prices consistently below the rest.

Argos
www.argos.co.uk

Argos has a fair selection of products with perhaps not as generous discounts as some of its online competition but there is some security in knowing they're just down the road if you need to return anything.

Comet
www.comet.co.uk

Cookers, fridges, washer-dryers – all the usual wares. The best prices are not the best on the Net but Comet is a name that won't disappear overnight.

Dixons
www.dixons.co.uk

High-street priced DVDs, videos etc. Basically, just the virtual equivalent of their bricks and mortar outlets, with similar products, prices and discounts.

Electrical Discount UK
www.electricaldiscountuk.co.uk

Has a strong selection of appliances across the board from all the leading brands with some massive savings off the high-street price.

Empire Direct
www.empiredirect.co.uk

A cornucopia of white goods and small appliances and a decent selection of TVs, DVD players and other audio/visual equipment, all with hefty discounts.

Pop Gadget
www.popgadget.net

Innovative lifestyle technologies for women.

Hi-fi

Hi-Fi Collective
www.hificollective.co.uk

An audiophile's dream site selling home-build kits and a considered selection of audio-grade

Enough is enough

While we'd all like megamoney systems, drawing on electronics and speakers with five-figure price-tags, the whole purpose of buying a system is to listen to music. Isn't it? If you're constantly worrying whether a new amplifier or that piece of black sponge you put under a CD player would make all the difference, you're not enjoying the music – just indulging in electronic masochism. So what's the answer? A large part of it is to buy right in the first place: when you're auditioning a system or a component, only buy something that blows your socks off with the improvement it makes to the music. We're often asked what is the best single upgrade anyone can make to their system, and the answer is invariably more music. Music is relatively cheap – especially if you buy online – and the thrill of discovering something new via that system on which you spent all that money is hard to explain. But one thing's for sure: it beats hearing a CD player just a tad better than your current one any day.

*Source: www.whathifi.com

components should you wish to upgrade your existing system. If you know your paper-in-oil capacitors from your tantalum beads this is the site for you. For more esoteric home-build kits visit: www.worldaudiodesign.com

Hi-Fi Store
www.hifistore.co.uk

Well-stocked online store with detailed product information that gives it the edge over similar outlets.

Hi-Fi World
www.hi-fiworld.co.uk
This magazine site has useful guides to buying second-hand and a snappy review section that's invaluable if you're looking for a new cartridge or speakers. A similar guide can be found over at Hi-Fi Choice.
www.hifichoice.co.uk

Matrix Hi-Fi
www.matrixhi-fi.co.uk
Purveyors of new & secondhand hi-end audio.

Retro Hi-Fi
www.retrohifi.co.uk
If you can get past the retro layout this site has a wealth of detailed information about various old-school separates.

Richer Sounds
www.richersounds.com
Select a section on this warehouse site and scroll through. Many items are either not in stock or are only available in store but every pocket is covered. Best of all, the price reductions come thick and fast.

What Hi-Fi
www.whathifi.com
This well-known consumer magazine's site offers a Sound Advice section to help you get the best out of your system.

In-car systems

Blue Spot
www.bluespot.co.uk
In-car CD players and navigation rub shoulders with Blaupunkt multimedia systems here. The range is limited yet covers most brands and prices. Plenty of explanations for those confused by the technical info; if you're still struggling, head for the specification comparison chart. Most systems are reduced substantially.

Car Audio Direct
www.caraudiodirect.com
Let's face it, if you've seen one car stereo you've seen them all. Most of us distinguish one from another using the fine art of counting the number of dials on a model. Car Audio not only offers a huge store, but also a useful, simple advice section. Once you know what Bass Engine Plus and Rotary Control mean and do, you can browse the offering of top brands including Pioneer, Maystar, Blaupunkt and Alpine.

MP3

Advanced MP3 Players
www.advancedmp3players.co.uk
Who would have thought there were so many MP3 players? Begin with the news, reviews and beginner's guide to get you started, then move on to the online shop. Latest models displayed include Sony, Mobi, i-With, iRiver and the Diamond Rio, each with reviews, spec sheets and images.

Satellite

The Association of Professional Satellite Installers
www.ukapsi.com
A nationwide collective of experienced, professionally qualified installation engineers who got together to try to inject some simple, common-sense standards into the industry. Worth a look if you're worried about inadvertently hiring a cowboy to fit your dish.

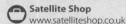

Satellite Shop
www.satelliteshop.co.uk
Detailed spec sheets, product guides and downloadable manuals, plus discounted prices to boot.

Satellites
www.satellites.co.uk
Useful forum for anyone experiencing installation or reception problems.

Wizard Satellite
www.wizardsatellite.co.uk
Wizard Satellite has everything you need for satellite reception: dishes & mounts, receivers, cables, upgrades, and a whole host of other things.

MP3 Player Deals
www.mp3playerdeals.co.uk
Dedicated MP3 store stocking mostly flash memory players but with some amazing deals on featured products.

Radios

Simply Radios
www.simplyradios.com
The older it looks, the more expensive it probably is. Search by brand – Roberts, Grundig, Freeplay, Pure – or select by design and function, including an array of wind-up rechargeable models.

Radio Craft
www.radiocraft.co.uk
Antique radio and TV specialists. They offer an excellent repair & restoration service and their site also includes a valuing guide and classifieds section. More here:
www.vintage-radio.com

Televisions

Krish Audio Visual
www.krishav.co.uk
Detailed product descriptions of a variety of audiovisual goods are the order of the day here, with the emphasis on TVs and DVD recorder/players.

Remote Controls
www.remotecontrols.co.uk
No prizes for guessing what this site sells. With thirty thousand replacement remote control units to choose from, the one you lost down the back of your sofa with the hamster should be there somewhere. Select the manufacturer and model number or code, and you're now completely rid of the need to indulge

in your last remaining form of physical exercise – stumbling to the set to change channels.

Web Electricals
www.webelectricals.co.uk

Comprehensive yet to the point. Search for TVs, videos and DVD players, or read the 'tech talk' guides with their glossary of all those manual terms that have meant nothing to you thus far.

White goods

Appliances.co.uk
www.appliances.co.uk

Exceptional site that has dedicated itself to monitoring prices exclusively on household appliances. You can search by brand or product type and be presented with a gargantuan list of available goods. It'll even recommend the best place to buy, although how impartial that recommendation is is anyone's guess.

Biasco
www.biasco.com

Biasco are a major company in the kitchen appliance market offering special prices on the world's leading appliance brands. They offer a price-match service and finance deals.

Co-op
www.coopelectricalshop.co.uk

The e-Co-op undercuts the bricks-and-mortar stores by substantial amounts in most cases and has all the big names.

Electrical Direct
www.electricaldirect.co.uk

Hundreds of pounds' worth of discounts across the board here. Electrical Direct offers kitchen appliances at trade prices with delivery throughout mainland UK

Farthing and Short
www.farthingandshort.com

Farthing and Short supply and fit built-in kitchen appliances. There's nothing to buy on their site but you'll find links to all the major manufacturers, a useful springboard if you're doing a bit of investigating.

Kitchen Science
www.kitchenscience.co.uk

For all your cooking, washing, and refrigeration needs. You can search by product, brand, or serial number, and there are extensive buyer guides for every type of appliance.

Miller Bros
www.millerbros.co.uk

Worth a look for discounts on many top-name brands including Zanussi, Belling, AEG and Ariston.

QED
www.qed-uk.com

QED offers a wide range of household products from kitchen appliances to audio-visual to computing with some great bargains to be found around the site.

Trade Appliances
www.trade-appliances.co.uk

Massive savings on all the top kitchen brands can be found right here.

We Sell It
www.we-sell-it.co.uk

Wordy and jumbled, We Sell It is nevertheless recommended for its range of ever-trendy Smeg appliances. Fridges, freezers and cookers are all available: read the specs and place your order.

Be Direct
www.bedirect.co.uk

Worth a visit to their Bargain Basement, where you'll find heavily discounted goods from the likes of AEG, Zanussi, Sony, and others.

Small appliances

Comet Clearance
www.clearance-comet.co.uk

Comes across as somewhere between eBay and online equivalent of a liquidation sale. Bid on ex-display and end-of line products from this reputable high-street retailer.

O'Gormans
www.ogormans.co.uk

Professional catering supplier making its services available to the public at bargain prices. You'll find stuff here you don't come across much on other sites, such as soup kettles, meat slicers and turbo toasters.

Pots and Pans
www.pots-and-pans.co.uk

Collossal bargains to be found on toasters & coffee makers and mixers – Dualit, Kenwood, Magimix, Briel, and others.

Vacuum cleaners

Dyson
www.dyson.co.uk

When you're through with this stylish site you'll know everything there is to know about vacuum cleaners. You can read all the specs to learn what the funny nozzles do, and buy, or not.

Vacuum World
www.vacuumworld.co.uk

Find tools, bags, belts and rollers to fit your machine from the biggest range of vacuum-cleaner accessories online. Just select the brand and scroll away. Also worth visiting Argos Spares and Vacuum Bags 2 U:
www.argosspares.co.uk
www.vacuumbags2u.co.uk

Employment

If you're looking to move on up, be aware that if you post your CV online your boss could find it – embarrassing at the very least. The same situation could also arise if you leave it online once you're hired. Most job agencies have sites these days, and the better ones update at least daily, so there are far too many to attempt to list here. Bigger isn't always better, as you'll find yourself competing with more applicants. On the other hand, your prospective employer isn't likely to restrict their job search to a site that isn't well known. Whether you're looking for a job or to fill a vacancy, try:

Career Builder www.careerbuilder.co.uk
Fish4Jobs www.fish4jobs.co.uk
Go Job Site www.jobsite.co.uk
Gradunet www.gradunet.co.uk
Guardian Jobs Unlimited jobs.guardian.co.uk
Job Search www.jobsearch.co.uk
Monster www.monster.co.uk
Overseas Jobs www.overseasjobs.com
People Bank www.peoplebank.com
Reed www.reed.co.uk
Stepstone www.stepstone.com
Total Jobs totaljobs.com

Many of these sites will send you email updates based on criteria you can set, which saves you from remembering to trawl through them all every day in case you miss something

All Jobs UK
alljobsuk.com
This recruitment portal claims to give access to every job vacancy on the Internet – all two million of 'em.

A–Z Guide to British Employment Law
www.emplaw.co.uk
Get the upper hand on your boss.

Brilliant Careers
www.channel4.com/brilliantcareers
Channel 4's employment site is a no-nonsense guide to the job market, with advice, support, vacancies and personality tests. It also has a regular online magazine and video interviews with people from all kinds of professions explaining how they got where they are today.

Buzzword Bingo
www.progress.demon.co.uk/Fun/Buzzword-Bingo.html
When your boss says something like, "proactive" or "quality management system", check it off on your card – you're a winner if you complete a row.

Connexions Direct
www.connexions-direct.com
Government organisation aimed at providing career advice for 13-19 year-olds. You can also apply for a connexions card, which is something like a reward-

points scheme for learning, work-based training and voluntary activities. These can be exchanged for discounted and free goods and services and other rewards. More info at:
www.connexionscard.com

Cool Works
www.coolworks.com
Seasonal jobs in US resorts, national parks, camps, ranches and cruise lines.

Despair Inc.
www.demotivators.com
Take the mickey out of your boss and colleagues with a range of sardonic calendars and mugs.

Doctor Job
www.doctorjob.com
Graduate career site with advice, forums, jobsearch and other resources.

Exec2Exec
www.exec2exec.com
An executive recruitment vehicle focusing on senior-level appointments.

Freelance

There are surprisingly few sites aimed at freelancers in the UK so finding work on the net can be quite a task. Here are a few worth taking a look at.

Elance
www.elance.com
Questionable site where prospective employers encourage professionals to outbid each other in order to win contracts.

Freelancers Network
www.freelancers.net
Probably the best place to look for freelance work and resources in the UK.

Freelance UK
www.freelanceuk.com
Advice and resources for freelancers, including tips on getting a mortgage, filing your tax return, running your business, etc.

Freelancers in the UK
www.freelancersintheuk.co.uk
Helpful site which aims to provide space for freelancers to advertise their services.

Expat Network
www.expatnetwork.co.uk
Overseas employment resource for working globetrotters.

Free Skills
www.freeskills.com
Expand your skills and then use them to find a better job with links to hundreds of free online courses.

FT Career Point
career.ft.com/careers
Advice from the suits at the *Financial Times*.

Guardian Jobs Advice
jobsadvice.guardian.co.uk
A good set of articles relating to job hunting techniques and strategies. Homeworking
www.homeworking.com
Useful support site for people working from home.

HRM Guide
www.hrmguide.co.uk
HRM Guide is a series of links to hundreds of free Human Resource Management-related articles and features.

I-resign.com
www.i-resign.com
Quit now while you're ahead.

Learn Direct
www.learndirect.co.uk
Learn Direct offers online business courses and impartial career advice.

Music Jobs
uk.music-jobs.com
Fancy yourself as the next Phil Spector? After all, who wouldn't want to hold the Ramones at gunpoint? For musicians, managers, teachers, administrators, PR, a selection of glamorous and less glamorous vacancies in the music industry.

Pay Scale
www.payscale.com
Accurate analysis comparing your job profile to the salary and benefits of people in your location with similar skills and experience.

Production Base
www.productionbase.co.uk
From runners to producers, this is a networking resource for people and companies working in the UK screen industries, tv and film.

The Riley Guide
www.rileyguide.com
Messy but massive directory of job-hunting resources.

Second Post
www.secondpost.com
Jobsite helping young professionals move up the ladder.

UK Jobs Sites
www.transdata-inter.co.uk/jobs-agencies
An excellent resource for the jobseeker, this directory lists and ranks all the major British online headhunters and ranks them by number of vacancies, services, regions and industries they serve.

Working Wounded
www.workingwounded.com
Get back at your boss and your co-workers without getting fired.

Yahoo! Careers
uk.careers.yahoo.com
As ever, Yahoo! is in on the act, and as ever, does it superbly, with careers articles, top 100 job sites for women, workplace advice, and of course an excellent search engine.

Ethical living

If you're the sort of person who worries about the impact that your life has on people and environments around the world, then the Web is an invaluable source of information – and a great place to shop. Try the following sites, or for more information check out *The Rough Guide to Ethical Shopping*.

British Association for Fair Trade Shops
www.bafts.org.uk
Locate your local fair-trade shop, for ethically sourced gifts, cards, jewellery, clothes, handmade papers, ornaments, quilts, etc.

Buy Nothing Day
www.buynothingday.co.uk
Take part in the annual celebration of non-consumerism.

Climate Care
www.climatecare.org
Offset your greenhouse-gas emissions by paying for new trees.

Clipper
www.clipperteasshop.com
More ethical hot drinks than you could shake a teaspoon at.

Divine Chocolate
www.divinechocolate.com
The finest Fairtrade chocolate.

Ecological Footprint Quiz
www.myfootprint.org
Calculate the total area of the earth needed to support your consumption habits. Expect a major guilt trip.

Esthwaite Water Trout Fishery
www.organicfish.com
Once you've read about the horrors of intensive fish farming, you'll want to get all your salmon from here. And for meats:
www.graigfarm.co.uk

Ethical Consumer
www.ethicalconsumer.org
The social & environmental records of the companies behind the brand names. Also has in-depth buyer's guides with ratings tables so you can compare the virtues of various products.

Ethical Investment Research Service
www.eiris.org
Background and links on all elements of ethical finance.

Ethical Trading Initiative
www.ethicaltrade.org
Find out which UK companies have (and haven't) signed up to the ETI, a UK organization working to stamp out sweatshops.

ethical living

Ethiscore
www.ethiscore.org
You have to subscribe to view all their information but doing so will reveal a complete database of companies, rated against environmental, animal welfare and human rights issues and various sustainability criteria.

Fairtrade Foundation
www.fairtrade.org.uk
Find out all about the Fairtrade label – from products to principles – from the organization that administers it in the UK.

Farmers' Markets
www.farmersmarkets.net
Explore the aims and ideas of farmers' markets and find your local.

Fish Online
www.fishonline.org
Find out which fish you can eat without worrying about falling stock levels, seabed destruction and dead dolphins, turtles and seabirds.

Forest Stewardship Council
www.fsc-uk.info
Locate wooden products certified as having been ethically sourced.

Freecycle
www.freecycle.org
A great way to recycle unwanted items from your home, list them here and other freecyclers can come & get them. Obviously it works the other way around, too.

Gooshing
www.gooshing.co.uk
Price comparison search engine relevant to the ethical consumer.

Gossypium
www.gossypium.co.uk
Nicely cut clothes in fairly traded cotton. More ethical threads at:
www.hug.co.uk
www.ptree.co.uk

Grist
www.grist.org
Snappy informal news & commentary site that attempts to present environmental journalism in a less austere format.

HippyShopper
www.hippyshopper.com
Tongue-in-cheek Ethical consumerism blog.

NFU Little Red Tractor
www.littleredtractor.org.uk
Read about the NFU's Little Red Tractor logo, which claims to ensure decent standards of animal welfare.

OneVillage
www.onevillage.co.uk
A huge range of ethically sourced homeware.

Responsible Travel
www.responsibletravel.com
Buy holidays from companies screened for ethical soundness. If you're just after flights, drop in to this charitable agent:
www.northsouthtravel.co.uk

Seat 61
www.seat61.com
Provides details of how to travel throughout Europe by rail & sea – avoiding air travel.

Smile
www.smile.co.uk
Brilliant online banking from the ethically right-on Co-op Bank.

Boycott campaign sites

At any time there are scores of consumer boycotts underway – some serious and widely observed, others silly and obscure. Following are a few campaign sites – to be treated, of course, as only one side of the argument. For more, visit: www.ethicalconsumer.org/boycotts/boycotts.htm

Adidas www.viva.org.uk
For using kangaroo skin in its football boots.

Bacardi www.ratb.org.uk
For using Cuban imagery while allegedly plotting to have Castro overthrown.

Drugs www.huumeboikotti.org

Why you shouldn't rail about oil firms while doing a line of Charlie.

Esso www.stopesso.com
Taking aim at the "global warming villain".

Gap www.gapsucks.org
For its owners' links to the felling of old-growth American forest in the US.

George W Bush's corporate donors www.boycottbush.net
You'd be amazed who bankrolls the US's simplest-ever president.

Gillette www.boycottgillette.com
For "using spy chips" to stop Mach 3 razor-blade theft

Nestlé www.babymilkaction.org
The breast-milk issue keeps on raging,

albeit less fiercly than before.

Tiger prawns www.ejfoundation.org
Read this and you'll never again order your favourite king-prawn bhuna.

Tropical timber www.foe.co.uk
Why not to purchase that mahogany sleigh bed.

Burma www.burmacampaign.org.uk
Find out which companies have links to the brutal Burmese junta. More country boycotts at:

    Canada www.boycott-canada.com

    China www.boycottmadeinchina.org

    Israel www.bigcampaign.org

    US www.krysstal.com/democracy_whyusa_boycott.html

Soil Association
www.soilassociation.org.uk
The UK's best-known organic certification body. The background articles are a bit one-sided, but the directory of organic suppliers (ox schemes to is unmatched. If you'd rather grow your own, head to: www.organicgardening.org.uk www.redtractortruth.com

Tourism Concern
www.tourismconcern.org.uk
Campaign which work with the tourist industry and communities in destination countries to reduce social and environmental problems connected to tourism and benefit local communities.

Traveline
www.traveline.org.uk
Index of public transport services across the UK.

Veg Oil Motoring
www.vegoilmotoring.com
Find out how to run your car on recycled chip fat.

Environment

The Centre for Alternative Technology
www.cat.org.uk
Primarily an education and research organisation, CAT's online shop is a virtual treasure trove of everything a person could need in order to live an environmentally-friendly life. Lots of gift ideas for children to get them interested in eco-concerns, like a paper-making press and a kit to help them construct their own solar-powered models.

Eco-Fibre
freespace.virgin.net/eco.cellulose
A fibre from recycled paper that has several industrial uses like soundproofing panels and loft insulation.

ethical living

Environmental Defense
www.environmentaldefense.org
In-depth site of problems, issues, solutions and links.

Environmental Organization Directory
www.eco-portal.com
Find primary production and green-minded sites.

Enviro-Roll
www.enviro-roll.com
Ingenious attempt to create a toilet roll you can go camping with that is impregnated with the seeds of endangered native flora.

 Ethical Junction
www.ethical-junction.org
An entire high street of fair-trading, earth-conscious retailers, with neatly categorised links to help guide you towards ethical products and retailers. See also: www.ethicalshopper.co.uk

Friends of the Earth
www.foe.co.uk
The homepage of the environmental pressure group features information on local, national and international campaigns, and related information.

Greenpeace
www.greenpeace.org
In addition to the charity's campaigns, the Greenpeace homepage covers genetic engineering, ocean preservation, toxic waste and the transport of nuclear materials.

Lycos Environment News
www.ens-news.com
A good source for unbiased environmental news.

The Natural Collection
www.greenstore.com
Catalogue of products for home use that have minimal impact on the environment. A brilliant place to come for unbleached cotton bed linen or magnetic water softeners for your washing machine. The hemp section is packed with items from socks to soap.

Rainforest Information Portal
www.rainforestweb.org
News from the frontline against deforestation. Also try:
www.rainforest-alliance.org
www.rainforest.org

The Recycled Bottle Glass Centre
www.rbgc.co.uk
Using a patented process, old bottles are turned into recycled glass in a variety of colours which you can purchase for your own project, or commission a unique stained-glass piece.

SEA and SKY
www.seasky.org
Explore the deep ocean and deep space with this excellent educational resource for kids of all ages.

UK National Air Quality Information Archive
www.airquality.co.uk
Worried about chemical factories or diesel emissions? Check the air quality for your area here. To feel guilty about the amount of carbon dioxide you are responsible for, check out the Carbon Calculator:
www.clearwater.org/carbon.html

United Nations Environment Programme
www.unep.org
Visit these pages to find out how the United Nations is planning to make a difference.

Events & entertainment

Ananova – Going Out
www.ananova.com
Comprehensive and nationwide general entertainment listings which you can have sent to your WAP phone.

British Arts Festivals
www.artsfestivals.co.uk
Keep tabs on the UK's highbrow festivals from Brighton to Edinburgh on this comprehensive site.

eFestivals
www.efestivals.co.uk
If you can't get enough of playing your bongos in the mud, point your virtual caravan to this site which contains ticket information, line-ups, rumours and reviews of all the major music festivals.

Ents Web
www.entsweb.co.uk
A directory of entertainment and leisure industry contacts, bringing together performers, agents, venues and suppliers to help them promote their services more effectively.

Last Minute
www.lastminute.com
Plenty of last minute bargains to be had in theatre tickets, meals, and other nights out.

London Theatre Guide
www.londontheatre.co.uk
This venerable site boasts not only excellent theatre listings but regularly updated cast news and seating plans. See also What's On Stage for regional as well as London listings:
www.whatsonstage.com

This Is London
www.thisislondon.co.uk
The *Evening Standard*'s site includes film, theatre, comedy and clubbing listings for the capital, as well as a visitor's guide and reviews of pubs and restaurants.

Time Out
www.timeout.com
Definitive London listings from the venerable magazine, as well as global city guides if you're planning to venture abroad.

Webflyers
www.webflyers.co.uk
Guide to clubbing in just about every corner of this green and pleasant land.

Regional listings

Most UK events sites can seem like a Big Smoke screen with all the emphasis on London. Itchy City (www .itchycity.co.uk), **Britinfo** (www.britinfo.net) an My Village (www.myvillage.com) have a growing number of city entertainment guides worth taking a look at. Or check one of the sites below:

Birmingham www.birmingham-alive.com
Bournemouth www.bournemouth.co.uk
Brighton www.brighton.co.uk
Bristol www.whatsonbristol.co.uk
Cardiff www.bigcardiff.co.uk
Chester www.chestercc.gov.uk/asp/events
Coventry www.cwn.org.uk/whatson
Edinburgh www.edinburghguide.com
Hampshire www.hants.gov.uk/whatson
Leeds www.leeds365.co.uk
Manchester www.manchesteronline.co.uk
Newcastle www.visitnewcastlegateshead.com
Sheffield www.sheffnet.co.uk/events/events.asp

Where Can We Go?

www.wherecanwego.com
Nationwide events-search by category. Everything from music and dance performances to pottery classes and passion plays.

Tickets

 Aloud

www.aloud.com
Ticket site offering a comprehensive list of music, comedy, theatre, fashion shows and other events. They also sell discounted magazine subscriptions and an array of merchandise and T-shirts to cater for all your needs. The theatre section also offers some dinner and show packages, to cater for your catering needs.

 Bigmouth

www.bigmouth.co.uk
A simple, alphabetical directory makes this site easy to search for information about tours, venues and travel. Postage is priced per total buy, not per ticket, so it may work out cheaper than a number of its competitors (some sites charge up to £4 per ticket).

 Keith Prowse

www.keithprowse.com
In addition to tickets for every kind of event in the UK, Keith Prowse also sells tickets for events world-wide, from a Niagara Falls by night tour to a contemporary jazz in Prague.

 Premier Events

www.premierevents.co.uk
Yep, they sell tickets too. See also: www.seetickets.com

 Ticket Finders

www.ticket-finders.com
Specialists in sourcing tickets to sold-out and hard to get sporting, musical, and theatre events worldwide; post an enquiry and they'll track them down for you.

Ticket Master

www.ticketmaster.co.uk
The Ticketmaster site is simple and well categorised, offering sports, music, arts and family events.

Film

Britinfo.net
www.britinfo.net/cinema
Full UK cinema listings searchable by town, with links to reviews of the films listed.

Easy Cinema
www.easycinema.com
UK cinema listings and charts.

Music

 Raymond Gubbay
www.raymondgubbay.co.uk
Gubbay is a leading promoter of classical music, opera and ballet. There are extracts of reviews of the shows on offer, and also a mailing list you can join.

 Ticket Web
www.ticketweb.co.uk
Ticket Web is a safe bet for all your UK gig and club tickets. If you're reluctant to pay their high postage charges, you can pick up your tickets at the venue.

Sport

6 Nations
www.6nations.co.uk
Buy tickets for 6 Nations rugby events here.

Epsom Derby
www.epsomderby.co.uk
Epsom racecourse, along with Kempton and Sandown Park, offers a simple system from which you can buy tickets for race meets throughout the year.
Kempton Park www.kempton.co.uk
Newmarket www.newmarketracecourses.co.uk

Euro Team
www.euroteam.info
Good source for hard to get sporting tickets.

Football Ticket Shop
www.footballticketshop.com
Your one stop-shop for Premier League tickets.

Just Tickets
www.justtickets.co.uk
For world-wide motor racing tickets.

Theatre

TheatreNet
www.theatrenet.co.uk
Invaluable resource for for all things performance related, with links to everything from festivals and city guides to agents and casting.

What's On Stage
www.whatsonstage.com
This dedicated theatre shop is one of the few to offer extra info about each performance, with news, reviews and regular thespian features. See also:
www.britishtheatreguide.info
www.thestage.co.uk

Fashion & beauty

Unless it entirely erodes your reading time, the Net isn't likely to cut your guilty expenditure on glossy mags. While there's a spree of fledgling style zines and something from nearly all the big rack names, nothing compares to getting it in print. Nonetheless it will certainly supplement your vice. What you will find the Net better for is researching products, checking out brands and saving money on consumables such as cosmetics at stores such as:

Drugstore www.drugstore.com
Gloss www.gloss.com
HQ Hair www.hqhair.com
iBeauty www.ibeauty.com
Perfumania www.perfumania.com
Perfume Shop www.theperfumeshop.com
Sephora www.sephora.com
Think Natural www.thinknatural.com

Buying clothes online is tough but popular nonetheless. They're out there, if you know what you're doing, but you'll soon see why **Boo.com** failed. Label sites are sometimes interesting for new season looks, stockists and direct ordering.

Bad Fads Museum
www.badfads.com
Revisit your past fashion mistakes.

BK Enterprises
www.b-k-enterprises.com
The only place to get that authentic 1970s Elvis jump suit. Prices range from $900 to $5000. Also has links to boot dealers, glasses shops and the place to get show scarves to complete the look.

Debenhams
www.debenhams.com
Indulge in some retail therapy at the site of everyone's favourite department store.

Diesel
www.diesel.co.uk
Browse their latest catalogue, hear music, and lots more – a very cool site. Also find time to check out the DieselKids games site, at:
www.protokid.com

Fashion Icon
www.fashion-icon.com
Irreverent New York fashion zine.

Fashion Net
www.fashion.net
Handy shortcut to high-profile shopping, designer, magazine, modelling and fashion industry sites, with enough editorial to warrant an extended stopover.

Fashion UK
www.fuk.co.uk
Minimal but fresh vanity monthly from London.

Figleaves.com
www.figleaves.com
Online underwear superstore for both men and women. And the chaps can find a whole lot more at:
www.hom-fashion.co.uk

Fragrance Direct
www.fragrancedirect.co.uk
It may look like a site for kids, but this etailer offers tremendous bargains on a good range of perfumes, cosmetics and skincare products.

Hats of Meat
www.hatsofmeat.com
Next season you won't be able to throw a brick without hitting someone wearing a hat of meat. Throw it hard.

Hint
www.hintmag.com
Hip online fashion magazine with columns, reviews, interviews and more.

Kookai
www.kookai.com
This high street fashion house's site decodes and reveals the influences behind current trends; you can also browse their catalogue.

Moda Italia
www.modaitalia.net
Patch through to the Italian rag traders.

Net-à-Porter
www.net-a-porter.com
Can't get to Harvey Nicks? Try here for posh frocks and accessories: Bottega Veneta, Clements Ribeiro, Missoni, Fake London and Paul & Joe are some of the cult labels this site stocks. Plus there's no snooty attitude. For Marc Jacobs, Fendi and Louis Vuitton, try:
www.eluxury.com
www.yoox.com

fashion & beauty

Mullets

The Kentucky Waterfall, the Soccer Rocker, the Missouri Compromise, Business Up Front/Party In The Back, Neck Blanket, Ape Drape – whatever you want to call it, no hairstyle in the history of the civilized world has generated so much scorn, derision or passion as the mullet. Here are a few sites where you can mull over "the hairstyle of the gods":

Mullet Junky www.mulletjunky.com
Mullet Lovers www.mulletlovers.com
Mullet Madness www.mulletmadness.com
Mullets Galore www.mulletsgalore.com
Rate My Mullet www.ratemymullet.com

Organization for the Advancement of Facial Hair
www.ragadio.com/oafh
Includes an archive of classic beard styles and a library of grooming tips. For more advice on beard trimmers and how to keep your hulihee at its best (or just to see pics of guys who look like 1970s country singers), try these other hirsute sites:
www.beards.org
www.menwholooklikekennyrogers.com

osMoz
www.osmoz.com
They haven't invented scratch'n'sniff technology for the Web yet, but this French site (in English) is the next best thing. A fragrance test will tell you whether floral or hesperide scents suit you best, and if you register they will send you free samples.

Salonweb
www.salonweb.com
Frizzy, flyaway, mousy, permed hair? Try this haircare portal for all the tips and advice you'll ever need. And for products visit:
www.4yourhair.co.uk

www.ehaircare.co.uk
www.hairways.net

Sixteen 47
www.sixteen47.com
A stylish and fun range of clothes for women over size 16, created by Dawn French and Helen Teague.

Studs And Spikes
www.studsandspikes.com
Relive those glory days with your old leather jacket.

Style.com
www.style.com
With an impressive archive of images from all the major catwalk shows of the past two years, the online home of American *Vogue* is one of the best resources for fashionistas. If you're after a more standard magazine approach, try the British equivalent:
www.vogue.co.uk

Style Maven
www.stylemaven.com
Your guide to hip boutiques in London, New York, LA and San Francisco.

Textile Dictionary
www.ntgi.net/ICCF&D/textile.htm
Don't know your buckram from your qiviut? Check here.

Victoria's Secret
www.victoriassecret.com
Order online or request the catalogue preferred by nine out of ten teenage boys.

Zoom
www.zoom.co.uk

Portal for the Arcadia group shops (Dorothy Perkins, Top Shop, Principles, Burton Menswear, etc), allowing you to recreate your high-street experience on the information superhighway.

Zoozoom
www.zoozoom.com

The online equivalent of a glossy magazine, with catwalk videos, fashion shoots, comment and more.

Accessories

Billy Bag
www.billybag.com

You can't buy yourself a Billy online but you can do everything but – seek out your nearest store, view the latest collection and if you just can't wait for your next trip to John Lewis, you can ring to order.

 Sunglasses 2000
www.sunglasses2000.com

Based in the US, this is the ultimate sunglasses warehouse. Designer ranges include Gucci, Ray Ban, Fendi and Nike, at more affordable prices. Each brand holds 40 to 50 different designs, with clear images, a choice of colours and precise measurements so you can find the perfect fit.

Catalogues

 Boden
www.boden.co.uk

Online version of the hugely successful catalogue selling upmarket family clothes. The range spans sturdy trousers for busy fathers to pretty velvet cardigans for women looking for a little glamour. The Mini Boden section has kids' styles you'll find irresistible.

 Brora
www.brora.co.uk

There's nothing like the feel of cashmere and this site will tempt you to feel it just a little more often. There are gorgeous and colourful cashmere designs for men, women and kids (who, quite frankly, don't deserve it) and there are some bargains to be had in the Sale section.

 Cotton Traders
www.cotton-traders.co.uk

If you live in your rugby shirt, you'll know this name. Specialists in super-tough sporty shirts, CT also stocks a range of other quality cotton gear like chinos, fleece jackets and shorts at excellent prices.

 Freemans
www.freemans.com

The trusted catalogue has had a style overhaul in recent years and now features wearable and affordable ranges from labels like Whistles and Betty Jackson. The menswear section has clothes ranging from Pierre Cardin to Red or Dead.

 James Meade
www.jamesmeade.com

High quality, conservative classic clothes from a company owned by an ex-Coldstream Guardsman. There's an alteration service on trouser and skirt lengths and they will even monogram and recuff and collar your shirts for you.

Kays
www.kaysnet.com
You're unlikely to set the world on fire with these clothes, but the selection is good and the prices are keen. Kays still offers the option to spread your payments over 20 weeks to make budgeting easier.

 Lands' End
www.landsend.co.uk
UK website for the US clothing catalogue giant. If you're looking for long-lasting cotton T-shirts and wrinkle-resistant chinos, you'll find them here. The stock is all good value for money, with regular sales and special offers.

 La Redoute
www.redoute.co.uk
Even catalogue shopping is more chic in France. Given the design and quality of the clothes, this site is excellent value for money.

 Long Tall Sally
www.longtallsally.co.uk
Wide range of stylish clothes for women over 5ft 8in from leather skirts to a formal worksuit. There's also a swimwear section for the long-bodied and maternity wear for high-held bumps.

 Lounge Lizard
www.loungelizard.com.au
This site shows details of the Lounge Lizard clothing range from Australia and it's vehemently anti-fit. If it's baggy you're looking for, you'll get it here.

Racing Green
www.racinggreen.co.uk
A good, clear version of the men's and women's casual clothing catalogue, this features high-quality products, good clearance offers (available only online) and a Fast Find service.

 Sweaty Betty
www.sweatybetty.com
Dance-and-sport inspired streetwear aimed to appeal to hard-bodied young things. There's a limited range on the website, but the snow-wear range is on its way.

Children

 Children's Warehouse
www.childrens-warehouse.com
Once you've found Caroline Bunting's neat, west London-based site you'll find yourself returning again and again. Her clothes are well designed and great quality; there's every item you could want, in sizes from babies to 12-year olds, and from cuddly fleeces to cute pyjamas.

 Giant Peach
www.giantpeach.co.uk
Truly adorable kidswear ranging from the traditional to the very funky indeed for little people up to the age of eight. Packed with good ideas like laminated paint smocks for messy young artists, plus a range of gifts and nursery accessories.

 Patricia Smith
www.psdesigns.demon.co.uk
Cornish clothing company making and selling traditional children's garb. Lots of smocked party dresses in cotton, and there's even a sailor suit if you really want to torture your son, although there are more up-to-date clothes as well.

 Poppy
www.poppy-children.co.uk
Bright and pretty crease-resistant cotton dresses, with jackets and hats to match. The printed fabrics are designed by local artists so you won't find the fabric being used elsewhere. Prices are not cheap but

the quality is good, and there's little in the high street to match the designs.

School Uniforms Online
www.schooluniformsonline.co.uk

Standard school uniform items like duffel coats and polo shirts are available on this straightforward site at much lower prices than on the high street, plus you don't have to depress the kids by taking them to the school outfitter while they're still on summer holidays. They also stock a range of Scout and Guide uniforms.

Spirit of Nature
www.spiritofnature.co.uk

Organic, unbleached and mostly undyed clothing for those babies with advanced environmental concerns. Cuteness has not been sacrificed in the pursuit of purity and where dyes have been used they are non-toxic and formaldehyde-free. Accessories include organic bedding and toys and even environmentally-friendly disposable diapers if reusable is too unbearable.

Designer

Brown Bag Clothing
www.bbclothing.co.uk

Armani, Moschino and Versace are among the designers with ranges on this chi-chi clothes site for men and women. They promise to have the latest styles at discount prices, not just last year's overstocks.

Brown's
www.brownsfashion.com

One of London's most valued fashion landmarks, offering clothes that have been individually hand-picked from the world's top designers.

Designer Discount
www.designerdiscount.co.uk

Like most designer discount sites, the catalogue is restricted to sportswear ranges. The reductions on many items reduce designer clothes to high-street prices.

Haburi
www.haburi.com

Massive reductions available here on names such as Diesel, DKNY, Bruuns Bazaar, Hilfiger, and others.

Net-à-Porter
www.net-a-porter.com

Sharp, sleek and sophisticated, and that just covers the site itself. Search by product or your favourite designer, flavours of the month include Matthew Williamson, Paul & Joe, Jemima Khan, and fetishists will drool over the Jimmy Choo shoes.

Yoox
www.yoox.com

Arty designer store where you can find an infinite mix & match of styles and trends that are not currently available in traditional stores. They offer exclusive products from international designers, end-of-season clothing and accessories at accessible prices, vintage collectibles and an original selection of books, magazines, music and art.

High street

French Connection

www.frenchconnection.com
As well as the online store, this site offers video downloads of films and debates about fashion.

H&M
www.hm.com
Create a virtual 3D model of yourself here to try on the clothes for you..

Next
www.next.co.uk
Web version of the popular directory, with clear and enlarged images, fabric details and easy ordering.

Arcadia
The high street wouldn't be the same without Arcadia names such as Top Shop, Dorothy Perkins and Principles, and now they're embracing the Net. Each store has its own site but all follow a similar set-up. Style-wise each is vibrant, colourful and easy to follow. Arcadia has adopted the whole package with multiple ways to shop including casual browsing and quick shopping, online magazines with news, reviews and competitions, and specialist sections, including maternity wear, petite and larger sizes. There are washing guidelines, fitting-room help and packed sale sections. Most of all, the comprehensive site does make you want to buy online.
www.burtonmenswear.co.uk
www.dorothyperkins.co.uk
www.evans.ltd.uk
www.hawkshead.com
www.principles.co.uk
www.topman.co.uk
www.tops.co.uk

River Island

www.riverisland.com
Nicely designed store with good detailed views of the clothing on offer.

Labels

Abercrombie & Fitch
www.abercrombie.com
Having been eulogised in many an American rap song, Abercrombie & Fitch clothes have become a must-have with those in the know. Skate and urban wear dominates. Inexpensive compared to the UK market, though you should always bear in mind the added costs of importing.

AW Rust
www.awrust.co.uk
A fresh and simple site selling all things leather from bags to coats to shirts to trousers. No pants though. There are good discounts on some items.

Boxfresh
www.boxfresh.co.uk
British streetwear outlet. Not much in the way of descriptions but pricing is fair.

Fat Face
www.fatface.co.uk
Surfer bods fill the homepage so it's not hard to recognise the young, fit and funky target audience. Despite their swank status, the clothes are relatively inexpensive. The online catalogue sells men's, women's and kids' clothes, plus accessories.

Ted Baker
www.tedbaker.co.uk
Not a site for those in a hurry. Standard men's and women's categories apply but it's a mystery why Lentil and Danish are used as names for skirts, or why Kiwi refers to a stone-coloured pair of trousers. On the plus side are laundry instructions and size charts for each item.

Toby Pimlico
www.tobypimlico.com
You might not be familiar with the name, but Toby's range of designs should ring a few bells. All the hot young television stars are shouting about his T-shirts, baseball shirts and underwear blazoned with every slogan from Eat Me Whole to Dirty Girl.

Zoo Village
www.zoovillage.com
Sick of wearing the same, tired, old labels as every other Tom, Dick and Harry? This Swedish outfit can put you back at the forefront of urban and street fashion. Names to watch out for include Acne,

Dispensary and Kulte. Prices are good, principally in Euros but GB pounds are also listed.

Menswear

SPRING/SUMMER 2006 COLLECTION

Crombie
www.crombie.co.uk
Crombie has been in business for nearly 200 years, and shows the attention to detail that has kept them going. In addition to their coats, the site offers a good range of shirts, ties, knitwear and accessories for the discerning traditional lady or gent.

Hector Russell
www.hector-russell.com
A Highland fling can be yours. Kilt-making being a serious business you can't just click and have one sent out, but you can e-mail for details and there are excellent photos and guidelines to the different styles. Secure shopping using an order form is available for accessories like sporrans and clan ties.

Shirt Press
www.shirt-press.co.uk
The answer to all our prayers: shirts that never need to be ironed. Add to this a well thought-out website

fashion & beauty

with button cuffs, double cuffs, dress shirts and ties in every possible colour.

Thomas Pink
www.thomaspink.co.uk
Thankfully Mr Pink's shirts are slightly more interesting than the site itself, but only just.

Underwear

Agent Provocateur
www.agentprovocateur.com
If the current Agent Provocateur range at your local Marks & Spencer is a little tame, you can buy the real thing here. Both the lingerie and the site are stylish and risqué.

Ann Summers
www.annsummers.co.uk
The Ann Summers' site holds an extensive online catalogue with something for every taste. This is a useful site for lingerie that's a little bit different but not beyond the average budget.

Hom GB
www.hom.gb.com
If you don't mind pictures of men's groins thrusting at you from your terminal, Hom GB is worth a look with its large selection of men's underwear and swimwear.

Kiniki Direct Male
www.kiniki.com
More a peep show than a shopping site. Search through a selection of boxers, briefs, thongs or swimwear and you may be somewhat intimidated. Tamer items include the Charmer boxers in black satin, or for the more adventurous, Jungle boxers in leopard print that come with a matching short satin robe.

Midnight Express
www.midnightexpress.co.uk
Selling well-known brands and designers, this very user-friendly site has gone to some length to make buying online pain-free, with bargains to be had all over the store.

Nile Trading
www.nile.co.uk
Not exactly the sexiest gear going, but doubtless a godsend in the deep midwinter: a complete range of lightweight, thermal underwear. All the tights, vests and pants in the collection are made in Britain and since you're buying direct from the manufacturer, the prices are excellent.

Victoria's Secret
www.victoriassecret.com
The online version of the US catalogue phenomenon, Victoria's own-brand underwear and lingerie is so popular she can afford to have supermodels on her website. Get your indulgence fix with Deluxe, Miracle, second skin and T-shirt bras to name just a few, or search for wardrobe essentials in the Bra Salon. They also offer an e-zine section on what's happening in the bra world. Hosiery and clothing also available.

Shoes & boots

Barratts
www.barratts.co.uk

The footwear from Barratts and Saxone is exactly what you'll find in the shops with no discounts and a delivery charge. On the plus side they offer a range from Tall & Small where you can buy similar fashionable designs in different sizes and at no extra cost.

Cox The Saddler
www.saddler.co.uk

Smarten up for the local gymkhana with smart riding boots galore here.

Danceworld
www.danceworld.demon.co.uk

Salsa, flamenco, tap, ballet, le roc or rock 'n' roll are all catered for. Online ordering is a little clunky but worth a look for the sheer quantity of footwear to choose from.

Faith
www.faith.co.uk

If fuchsia kinky boots and baby-blue go-party shoes are the sort of thing you're looking for, Faith stocks all the backache-inducing footwear you could ever want. After revamping its image, Faith now sells some of the best designer replicas on the high street.

John Norris of Penrith
www.johnnorris.co.uk

The Rolls-Royce of Wellington boots is sold here at a reasonable price. We even found a special offer which lowered the cost of Hunter boots further.

Jones the Bootmaker
www.jonesbootmaker.com

Despite being awkwardly placed at the higher end of the high-street price bracket, you can't help but love Jones and the sophisticated range of men's, women's and children's footwear on this refined site. Better than the high-street equivalent.

Office
www.office.co.uk

High heels, mid heels, low heels, ankle boots, knee boots: Office and its casual sporty partner, Offspring, have a shoe for every occasion. Bright, blazing graphics match polka-dot kitten heels and pink snakeskin boots. Trainer brands include Adidas, Nike and Converse.

Regalos Country & Western Store
www.linedancing.co.uk

Can't shake the line dancing bug? Regalos sells suitably tasselled and fringed boots.

Shoe Shop
www.shoe-shop.com

With labels DKNY, Duffer, Red Or Dead and Diesel all at reduced prices, it's a great place to buy your designer kit. They also have perfect shoes for the wider foot, and those that are larger or smaller.

Sports Shoes Unlimited
www.sportsshoes.com

Alongside the usual trainers there are useful sub-categories like pool shoes.

Tim Little
www.timlittle.com

Upmarket shoes as worn by Robbie Williams, Tina Turner, John Lee Hooker, and Jeremy Irons, and you never hear them complaining about their feet hurting, do you?

Vegetarian Shoes
www.vegetarian-shoes.co.uk

A large selection of vegetarian footwear in a variety of styles and finishes, including canvas, fake suede and fake leather. Check their bargain basement for items under half price.

Film & DVD

When it comes to movies, one site clearly rules:

The Internet Movie Database www.imdb.com

To say that it's impressive is an understatement. You'll be hard-pressed to find any work on or off the Net as comprehensive as this exceptional relational database of screen trivia from over 100,000 movies and a million actors. It's all tied together remarkably well – for example, within two clicks of finding your favourite movie you can get full filmographies of anyone from the cast or crew and then see what's in the cooker. Still, it's not perfect, or without competition. You'll find a similar service with superior biographies and synopses at:

All Movie Guide www.allmovie.com

Or for more Chan, Li and Fat:

Hong Kong Movie Database www.hkmdb.com

For cinema listings:

Cinemas Online www.cinemas-online.co.uk
Cineworld www.cineworld.co.uk
Odeon www.odeon.co.uk
Picture House www.picturehouses.co.uk
UCI Cinemas www.uci-cinemas.co.uk
Virgin Net www.virgin.net/movies
Vue Cinemas www.myvue.com

The following sell a range of films on video and DVD, plus other items like books and CDs. Their catalogues may not be extensive, but if you stick to the mainstream, they're certainly worth checking for price comparisons:

Amazon www.amazon.co.uk
Game Play www.gameplay.com
Tower Records uk.towerrecords.com/Video
WHSmith www.whsmith.co.uk

Ain't It Cool News
www.aintitcool.com
The movie news and gossip site that has Hollywood execs quaking in their boots. Founder Harry Knowles has been blamed several times when movies have tanked at the box office, and *Premiere* magazine has ranked him as one of Hollywood's most powerful people. More production gossip can be overheard at:
www.chud.com
www.darkhorizons.com
www.imdb.com/Sections/Inproduction

American Film Foundation
www.americanfilmfoundation.com
The AFF makes and sells DVDs of independent features and short documentaries which often pop up at the Oscars. Based in California they will ship abroad – but make sure the region codes are compatible with your DVD player.

 **asSeenonScreen**
www.asos.com
Buy stuff you've seen on TV or in movies. For more, try:
www.movieprop.com

The Astounding B Monster
www.bmonster.com
Excellent resource for fans of Mamie Van Doren, Rondo Hatton and other cult 1950s and 1960s drive-in/late-show fodder. For fans of more modern fare like *Cannibal Women in the Avocado Jungle of Death*, there's:
www.stomptokyo.com/badmoviereport
www.badmovies.org

Atom Films
www.atomfilms.com
Watch entertaining short films.

Bad Movie Night
www.hit-n-run.com
Invite a couple of mates over to your house, get in a few beers, rent an aggressively mediocre movie and hurl invective at the screen. More snide remarks available at:
bigempire.com/filthy
www.mrcranky.com
www.thestinkers.com

Lo-tech film remakes

Who needs a £20 million special effects and pyrotechnics budget when you've got a couple of Lego sets? The Spite Your Face site has Lego remakes and pastiches of 2001, Star Wars, Spiderman, and others.
www.spiteyourface.com

It's also worth checking sites like Video Bomb for homages to the Hollywood greats and hilarious recut and deconstructed movie trailers:
www.videobomb.com

Or check below for a small selection of what's out there.

Being Puffy www.urbanentertainment.com
The Fountainhead – A Parody www.jeffcomp.com/faq/parody
Shark Attack www.exposure.co.uk/eejit/3act/sharkattack.html
Titanic Legos at Sea www.legosatsea.cjb.net htm

 BBC Shop
www.bbcshop.com
Find your favourite Beeb programmes here, whether it's EastEnders or I Claudius.

Blaxploitation.com
www.blaxploitation.com
Superfly guys and gals stickin' it to the man. More Afros and dashikis at BadAzz Mofo:
www.badazzmofo.com

Bollywood World
www.bollywoodworld.com
Massive portal for the Indian film industry, with everything from production news to ringtones for your mobile.

 Britannia Video Club
www.britannia-video.co.uk
This site offers the same deal as those Britannia pamphlets which cascade from your paper – though, online, there are far more videos to choose from and an immediate contact point to resolve any problems.

DVD rental

Loads of companies are starting to do this now, even biggies such as **Amazon**. The basic idea is simple: you choose what you want to watch online, they post it to you, you watch it, you post it back…easy. Some firms offer a flat-rate monthly membership which gives you a certain number of films each month, which could be a little restricting, so shop around for a deal that suits you or compare services at uk-dvd-rentals.co.uk. Here are a few of the best:

Amazon www.amazon.co.uk
Blockbuster www.blockbuster.co.uk
Easy Cinema www.easycinema.com
ITV Movie Club www.itvmovieclub.com
LoveFilm.com www.lovefilm.com
Screen Select www.screenselect.co.uk
Sendit www.sendit.com

British Film Institute
www.bfi.org.uk
Reviews, features and loads of great content, including NFT interview transcripts, a selection of articles from current editions of *Sight & Sound* and access to the National Film and Television Archive.

Carfax-Abbey Horror Film Database
www.carfax-abbey.com
Splatter-flick Central, with loads of info on gore masters such as Dario Argento and Wes Craven. More zombies and fake blood at:
www.joblo.com/arrow
www.dune12.demon.co.uk
www.sexgoremutants.co.uk

The Cube Cinema
microplex.cubecinema.com
Truly independent co-operative cinema based in Bristol, hosting unique events including music performances, open film screenings and exhibitions. Also commissions short films to screen before the main features. Micro cinemas in other areas include:

Cinematheque, Brighton www.cinematheque.org
Curzon, London www.curzoncinemas.com
Exploding Cinema www.explodingcinema.org
Fact, Liverpool www.fact.co.uk
The Horse Hospital, London www.thehorsehospital.com
ICA, London www.ica.org.uk
Side Cinema, Newcastle www.sidecinema.com

Docspace
www.docspace.org.uk
A UK network of digitally equipped cinemas providing opportunities for the screening of new films.

Documentary Filmmakers Group
www.dfglondon.com
Useful site for documentary makers, offering forums, training, advice and their own in-house production company.

Dogme95
www.dogme95.dk
Homepage of the Danish film movement led by Lars Von Trier, including the manifesto, a how-to page and the latest news from the film vanguard.

Drew's Script-O-Rama
www.script-o-rama.com
Hundreds of entire film and TV scripts. Need help writing or selling your own? Try:
www.scriptfly.com

DVD File
www.dvdfile.com
All the latest UK DVD release news and reviews. For more on DVD hardware and software:
www.dvdtimes.co.uk

DVD Street
www.dvdstreet.infront.co.uk
This site claims to sell the biggest online selection of DVDs and also has an outstanding technical guide to the issues of aspect ratio and DVD territory codes. There are also loads of good special offers which change every week.

DVD World
www.dvdworld.co.uk
This site claims to stock every DVD available in the UK, with some prices heavily discounted.

E! Online
www.eonline.com
Daily film and TV gossip, news and reviews.

Empire Magazine
www.empireonline.co.uk
Reviews of every film showing in the UK.

555-LIST
home.earthlink.net/~mthyen
Useful catalogue of fake telephone numbers used in TV and film.

Film Site
www.filmsite.org
Plenty of links, resources and recommendations here, including links to many other sites' 'greatest film' lists.

Four Word Film Review
www.fwfr.com
Very concise film reviews.

Future Movies
www.futuremovies.co.uk
Reviews, news and features. Also has an archive section with analytical reviews of films, plus a useful set of articles on filmmaking, including interviews with directors and writers.

Golden Raspberry Award Foundation
www.razzies.com
The Oscars in an alternate universe.

HMV
www.hmv.co.uk
HMV both online and offline is always a good bet for bargain videos and DVDs. You'll be hard-pressed to find a time when there isn't a sale going on, so one to bookmark.

Hollywood Reporter
www.hollywoodreporter.com
Tinseltown tattle, loads of previews and reviews daily, plus a flick biz directory.

Home Cinema Choice
www.homecinemachoice.com
In-depth reviews of DVD players, LCD screens and the kind of entertainment hardware that would negate the need ever to leave your house again.

Melon Farmer's Video Hits
www.dtaylor.demon.co.uk
Challenges British screen censorship.

Monsters In Motion
www.monstersinmotion.com
For all your monster requirements.

film & DVD

Movie Cliches
www.moviecliches.com
Nothing unfamiliar.

MovieFlix
www.movieflix.com
Download hundreds of movies, some free but most require a monthly subscription.

Moviemags.com
www.moviemags.com
Directory of film print and e-zines.

Movie Mistakes
www.movie-mistakes.co.uk
Archive of screw-ups and inconsistencies from Hollywood's finest. More continuity errors at:
www.nitpickers.com

Movie Review Query Engine
www.mrqe.com
This specialist search engine, dedicated to finding film reviews on the Web, has a database of more than 25,000 titles and does a great job of finding info on obscure movies. Or perhaps you'd prefer a summary:
www.rottentomatoes.com
film.guardian.co.uk
www.formovies.com

Movies.com
www.movies.com
Preview box-office features and trailers direct from the major studios. Loads more to be streamed at:
www.universalstudios.com
movies.real.com

Mr Kiss Kiss Bang Bang
www.ianfleming.org
A worryingly complete and obsessive guide to the shaken, not stirred universe of James Bond, with daily news and rumour updates.

My Movies
www.mymovies.net
Huge film site with production news, gossip, reviews, competitions, shopping, trailers and movies on demand.

Science Fiction Continuum
www.sfcontinuum.com
Where else could you find Dr Goldfoot And The Girl Bombs? This site has a spectacular B-movies section alongside the more conventional sci-fi fare and UFO documentaries.

SciFi.com
www.scifi.com
Science fiction news, reviews and short films. More of that sort of thing here:
scifi.ign.com
www.cinescape.com

Screenit
www.screenit.com
To really unveil box-office evil and discover the reasons behind the censors' certificate ratings on the latest releases. More to be found at:
www.capalert.com

The Script Factory
www.thescriptfactory.co.uk
Site aimed at finding and developing new screen-writing talent.

Sendit
www.sendit.com
Exemplary home video and DVD site with a huge catalogue to help you find that movie. Each film has a mini-synopsis to help. Prices are excellent and they offer a competitive home rental service. Other video and DVD etailers worth checking out are:
www.bensonsworld.co.uk
www.dvdworld.co.uk

Senses Of Cinema
www.sensesofcinema.com
An online journal devoted to the serious and eclectic discussion of cinema.

Shooting People
shootingpeople.org
In their own words, "the fastest growing UK online filmmakers' community"; whether you're a director without a crew, or a runner with nowhere to run, look here first.

Shorts International
www.britshorts.com
If you've got broadband access you can watch trailers and short films. For more shorts and trailers:
www.movie-trailers.com

Silent Era
www.silentera.com
This great online journal devoted to silent film is certainly one of the best film sites on the Web, even if you don't know Fatty Arbuckle from ZaSu Pitts.

Smoking List Movie Reviews
SmokingSides.com/asfs/m
A history of smoking on the silver screen. Non-smokers might want to try Soup at the Movies:
www.soupsong.com/imovies.html

Variety
www.variety.com
Screen news fresh off the PR Gatling gun.

VCR Repair Instructions
www.fixer.com
How to take a VCR apart and then get all the little bits back in so it fits more easily into the bin.

Viaduc Video
www.viaducvideo.com
This European documentary video site sells films in English, German or French. Prices are shown in French francs and euros, but the site is secure so you can let your credit card do the maths.

Warning6
www.cinepad.com/warning6.htm
If you don't want to know the twists at the end of *The Usual Suspects* or *The Crying Game*, don't you dare visit this site.

WildestWesterns.com
www.wildestwesterns.com
A great site for fans of classic oaters.

Woolworths
www.woolworths.co.uk
You just can't beat Woolworths when it comes to finding a bargain; prices are always good, particularly on classic films.

World Cinema Online
www.worldcinemaonline.com
Exhaustive selection of arthouse and foreign language movies and documentaries. Rent DVDs or download the whole film to own.

Flowers & gifts

Cards

Clinton Cards
www.clintoncards.co.uk

You know the drill. Browse through the collection and either have the card sent directly to the recipient, or have it delivered to you to add your message.

Cyber Card
www.cybercard.co.uk

Search Cyber Cards' extensive range of images to create your own card for whatever occasion and have it posted to the recipient.

Moonpig
www.moonpig.com

Your chosen card with message can be delivered anywhere in the UK by the following day.

Sharp Cards
www.sharpcards.com

Easy to shop and fun to browse. Prices vary but are generally reasonable.

Flowers

Expressions
www.expressions.co.uk

This easy-to-use flowers and gifts site can be a bit pricey for bouquets but the balloon in a box option is a cheaper and more original alternative.

Flower Card
www.flowercard.com

Flower cards – cards sprouting fresh flowers – are an unusual alternative to your typical bouquet.

Interflora
www.interflora.co.uk

Comprehensive site where you can search by occasion, price, type and colour. As you would expect from Interflora, there's a concise description of each arrangement, along with an enlarged image.

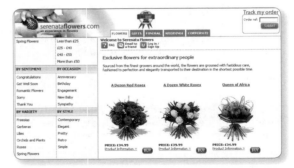

Serenata Flowers
www.serenataflowers.com

Well laid-out florist site where, again, you can browse by occasion, flower type, sentiment, style, or colour. Delivery is inexpensive and you can specify the delivery date from the next day to months in advance.

Gifts

Gift Inspiration
www.giftinspiration.com

Selling both luxurious (see the Sari Photo Albums), and fun items (check out the Cat Napping Cushion & Pyjama Case), here's a shop that offers something a little more interesting than his'n'her chrome pens. Lots of original ideas and easy to use.

The Gift Store
www.giftstore.co.uk

Categories include run-of-the-mill chocolates, flowers and balloons, alongside magic sets, juggling equipment and Majorcan Pearls. A Cornish clotted cream tea or a saffron cake are among the best gift items.

Go Bazaar
www.gobazaar.co.uk

Go Bazaar see their wares as the perfect alternative gift. Kitsch in other words. What you'll find are the usual array of neon lights, UFO lamps, cigarette cases and board games, oh and how could we forget, "Babes of the Week" posters.

Bears by Mail
www.bearsbymail.com

Offers furry friends old-style, and has teddies galore to suit every pocket. Each comes with a brief description and character reference.

Oxfam
oxfam.org.uk/shop

You're unlikely to find Ghanaian clay pots or Mankind Vases from El Salvador just anywhere. Divided into standard food, home and gift categories, the range is limited but not pricey.

Presents Direct
www.presentsdirect.com

Search by category or personality through an adequate selection of both refined and fun gifts.

Top items include pet robots, fish radios, weather stations, and for those a little less gadget-obsessed, floral photo albums and cufflinks.

Rennie Mackintosh
www.rennie-mackintosh.co.uk

This site offers a large range of jewellery and home-wares inspired by the famous architect and designer. For those who want to recreate that Willow Tea Rooms ambience at home, an Argyle chair will put quite a dent in your pocket. If you'd just like a little piece of Mackintosh, the jewellery range includes affordable rings and bracelets.

Weird gifts

City Morgue
www.citymorguegiftshop.com

"Welcome to the best place for gothic, mortuary, forensic and death-related gifts" this site greets you cheerily. Enter a strange world of skull maracas, model guillotines and celebrity death certificates.

Love Hearts
www.lovehearts.com

It's definitely unusual, we'll give it that. What you find are gift boxes filled with Swizzels Matlow sweet treats, everything from Drumsticks to Parma Violets. Not everyone is likely to jump at the chance to ask their loved one to marry them with a personalised Love Heart, but it's a good site for silly gifts.

Kitsch
www.kitsch.co.uk

There is so much tack here that you can't fail to be impressed. But it's worth a try.

Pushin Daisies
www.pushindaisies.com
More macabre gift ideas here, from coffin luggage to an anatomically correct chocolate human heart.

Gadgets

Adventure Kit
www.adventurekit.co.uk
Gadgets of all kinds from electronic gizmos to outdoor survival kits.

Barmans
www.barmans.co.uk
Barmans has gadgets, games and accessories to keep you amused from flocked wallpaper to match that in your local to authentic pub signs to create a home from home.

Boy's Stuff
www.boysstuff.co.uk
The most remarkable feature of this site is its unashamed targeting of men. When you click to confirm an order the phrase "Don't listen to her" appears.

EFX Design
www.efx.co.uk
Gadgets for people with everything – except a Titanic salt and pepper set.

Gadget Shop
www.gadgetshop.com
Click around the store whilst practising a surprised smile and saying "Oh! you shouldn't have!" semi-convincingly.

Gadgets UK
www.gadgetsuk.com
A speedy way to determine whether a gadget site is any good is to check out any 'Cool Stuff' category. You'll soon know if their cool is your dull. Gadgets UK's cool stuff includes novelty items like the Stress Shooter, the Cheering Basketball Basket and the Truth Machine.

Initial Ideas
www.initialideas.co.uk
The Initial Ideas site includes unusual items such as spider catchers, racing snails, and a satanic rubber duck.

Innovations
www.innovations.co.uk
This is the website from the people who make the catalogue that you love to receive. Fortunately the well-defined categories mean you don't have to read all about "walking your way to a healthy lawn". Unless you want to.

I Want One of Those
www.iwantoneofthose.com
More bizarre gadgetry, including chocolate fountains, robotic guinea pigs and inflatable sumo suits.

Obsessions
www.obsessions.co.uk
Finding what you want is easy and there are plenty of suggestions. A bonus is the gift-wrapping service but even Austin Powers would shy away from the choice of paper.

Pinball Heaven
www.pinballheaven.co.uk
The site itself is rudimentary but there are enough images and additional information for you to convince your partner that this oversized toy is an absolute necessity.

Simply Sports
www.simplysports.co.uk
Gadgets with a sporting theme.

Food & drink

101 Cookbooks
101cookbooks.com
Excellent recipe / magazine / blog site with cookbook reviews, bustling forums and food travelogues.

African Studies Cookbook
www.africa.upenn.edu/Cookbook/about_cb_wh.html
A frighteningly comprehensive database of African recipes.

All Recipes
allrecipes.com
Look no further; actually, okay, look here too:
www.recipesource.com

Al Mashriq
almashriq.hiof.no/general/600/640/641/recipes/misc.html
No-nonsense list of Middle Eastern recipes.

BBC Food
www.bbc.co.uk/food
A very branded site (there are lots of familiar faces) but with a good database of solid recipes that you can be sure will have been tested properly.

Beershots
micro.magnet.fsu.edu/beershots
Beers of the world put under a microscope.

Bevnet
www.bevnet.com
"The beverage industry's source for product reviews, news & more."

 ### Butler's Cheese Shop
www.butlerscheeses.co.uk
This site focuses on a small range of quality cheeses, with descriptions and strength levels for favourites like crumbly Lancashire through to more exotic vintage varieties.

 ### Carmichael Meats
www.carmichael.co.uk
Click on Estate Farm Meats to visit this Scottish site selling traditionally farmed beef and lamb products and top-quality venison. Although not fully organic, Carmichael prides itself on humane farming methods.

 ### Chandos Deli
www.chandosdeli.com
This Bristol deli offers delivery of its range of treat foods and store-cupboard essentials for keen cooks.

food & drink

The recipe section has links to suitable wines to enjoy with your meal, and some really quite obscure ingredients can be tracked down here.

Cheese
www.cheese.com
Excellent cheese information site with an exhaustive list of cheeses and detailed info on composition.

Cheeseburger in Paradise
www.fdu.com/cburger.htm
Stranded in Alabama or Helsinki and jonesing for a cheeseburger? Check here for your nearest vendor.

Chile-Heads
www.exit109.com/~mstevens/chileheads.html
Get 'em while they're hot; more belly-burners at:
www.ringoffire.net

Chinatown
www.chinatown-online.co.uk/pages/food
Good site for Chinese recipes, information on ingredients and contextual stuff.

Chocolate & Zuccini
www.chocolateandzucchini.com
Entertaining food blog encompassing thoughts, recipes, musings, cookbooks, ideas, inspirations & experimentations. More great food blogs at:
www.amateurgourmet.com
www.holyshitake.com
glutenfreegirl.blogspot.com
chubbyhubby.net
www.obsessionwithfood.com
www.accidentalhedonist.com

Cigar Aficionado
www.cigaraficionado.com
Archives, shopping guides and tasting forums from the US glossy that sets the benchmark in cigar ratings.

Cookability

www.cookability.biz
No food here, but everything you could possibly need in order to prepare it. Kit your entire kitchen out with everything from cutlery to pasta machines.

Cooks Delight
www.organiccooksdelight.co.uk
Food shop offering a worldwide service, so you can buy your fruit, veg and biscuits wherever you happen to be.

Cook's Thesaurus
www.foodsubs.com
Look no further if you want to find substitutes for fatty, expensive or hard-to-find ethnic ingredients.

The Cook's Thesaurus

Cucina Direct
www.cucinadirect.co.uk
Excellent online kitchen equipment site with a solid bricks-and-mortar business behind it.

Curryhouse
www.curryhouse.co.uk
Make the perfect vindaloo or look up your nearest balti house if you're too lazy. For more masala matters, try:
rubymurray.com

Curry Pages
www.currypages.com
Don't know your paneer from your paratha? Then the Curry Pages dish glossary will put you straight on all intricacies of Indian cooking, as well as find

you the nearest curry house in a hurry. Some of the restaurant reviews, which come from real punters as far as we could glean, are worth reading and features include a review of readymade curries.

Delia Online
www.deliaonline.com
A double-header of a site: lots of good recipes and useful tips plus the alarming Delia diary for true fans who really want to know about her life. And to see where all the site's ideas came from, go to:
www.marthastewart.com

Dolce Vita
www.dolcevita.com/cuisine
Life is sweet at this Italian cookery site.

 ### Edible.com
www.edible.com
Fancy something a bit different? How about a crocodile meat curry, coffee beans harvested from civet droppings or aphrodisiac honey with a giant hornet floating around in it. Check here for all these delicious items and more.

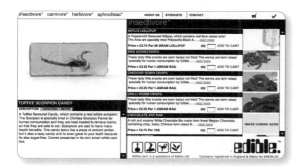

The Empty Bowl
www.emptybowl.com
"The definitive source for all your cereal needs."

Epicurious
www.epicurious.com
The best food website there is. Online marriage of Condé Nast's *Gourmet*, *Bon Appetit*, and *Traveler* magazines, crammed with recipes, culinary forums and advice on dining out worldwide.

Fair Trade
www.fairtrade.org.uk
Complete information about the full range of fair trade approved products and where to get them.

Famers' Markets
www.farmersmarkets.net
Find your nearest farmers' market and start buying local food.

 ### The Fish Society
www.thefishsociety.co.uk
With categories ranging from Everyday to Luxury, this site can be great fun. There's an emphasis on special offers and last-chance buys, while books, recipes and cooking accessories are also on offer.

Food Allergy and Anaphylaxis Network
www.foodallergy.org
All the news and developments from the nut intolerance frontline.

Food 411
www.food411.com
Useful site that scours the rest of the web for good food sites. Well worth a look.

Foodlink
www.foodlink.org.uk
Your complete guide to food safety. But if you can't remember anything unless it's set to music, go to:
foodsafe.ucdavis.edu/music.html

The Food Timeline
www.foodtimeline.org
Did you know that popcorn was invented in 3600 BC?

food & drink

Obviously they then had to wait a few millennia for cinemas to be invented but that's beside the point.

The Fresh Food Company
www.freshfood.co.uk

This award-winning organic supermarket has a good specific product or recipe search facility, or you can just browse the site to see the full range. There are many organic items you may not easily find elsewhere.

Fruitarian Site
www.fruitarian.com

The joys of chomping on raw fruit and the chance to make new fruitarian friends.

Galloway Smokehouse
www.gallowaysmokehouse.co.uk

Smoked Scottish Salmon is the main draw on this independent smokehouse site. Since you're buying direct the prices are excellent. It also sells smoked trout, venison and duck.

Generic Mac and Cheese Gallery
www.geocities.com/macandcheesebox

Gawp in wonder at the diet of the American student.

Good Pub Guide
www.goodguides.com

Offers a good pub locator for the UK, as if you needed help.

Grayson & Starts Sausages By Post
www.sausagesbypost.co.uk

Pork, beef, even venison sausages made by a family butcher and delivered to your door. Reasonable prices given some products' prizewinning status.

Gourmet World
www.gourmet-world.com

If you're trying to avoid artificial flavours and colourings as well as genetically modified ingredients, but you still want outstanding quality and taste in your food, this site could be the answer to your prayers. With lots of tip-top foods from around the world, all made with natural ingredients, you can stock up your larder or put together a gift box for a hungry friend.

Harpers Food
www.harpersfood.co.uk

Tasty, solid British food without a hint of lemon grass or balsamic vinegar to be found. Meat pies, game, fruit puddings and a variety of Christmas staples will keep any gastro-Brit happy.

Inverawe Smokehouses
www.smoked-salmon.co.uk

Inverawe Smokehouses offers over eighty different smoked products – covering Scottish fish and game. The product descriptions are mouth-watering, and the prices are reasonable.

Internet Chef
www.ichef.com
Over 30,000 recipes, cooking hints ("Ground Beef Meals"), kitchen talk and more links than you can jab a fork at.

Jamie Oliver
www.jamieoliver.net
The most overexposed man on TV – but he makes a pucker salad.

Lakeland
www.lakelandlimited.co.uk
Everything you could and couldn't possibly need in the kitchen.

Martins Sea Fresh Local Fish
www.martins-seafresh.co.uk
Live lobster and crabs, along with other fish and shellfish from a Cornish fishmonger, delivered direct from the boats to your door. If it's freshness you're after, this is the service you're looking for, and it supports responsible practice to help the UK's beleaguered fish stocks. Availability on most items depends on the day's catch.

McSweeney's Reviews of New Food
www.mcsweeneys.net/links/newfood
Hilarious food reviews emailed in to this well-liked humour site.

Meals For You
www.mealsforyou.com
A decent American recipe search engine – each listing includes the details of the fat and cholesterol present in each recipe.

New York Seafood
www.nyseafood.org
Great site for loads of piscine information. To get cod and haddock delivered to your door, try The Fish Society:
www.thefishsociety.co.uk

An Ode to Olives
www.emeraldworld.net/olive.html
You'll never look at an olive ambivalently again.

Organic Delivery
www.organicdelivery.co.uk
Another London-only vegetable box scheme that has expanded to include more general organic groceries such as milk and bread.

Organics Direct
www.organicsdirect.co.uk
Weekly or fortnightly deliveries of super-fresh organic vegetables save you money in the long term, or choose from the excellent selection for a one-off delivery of organic groceries, from breakfast cereals to baby food.

Our Food
www.ourfood.com
An excellent collection of scientific articles pertaining to food science and food safety.

Proper Cornish
www.propercornish.co.uk
Cornish pasties made to an authentic recipe supplied either cooked or ready to cook.

Ray's List of Weird and Disgusting Foods
www.weird-food.com
How many have you tried?

food & drink

Real Beer
www.realbeer.com
None of the usual beer yarns like waking up in a strange room stark-naked with a throbbing head and a hazy recollection of pranging your car. Here beer is treated with the same dewy-eyed respect usually reserved for wine and trains. Like to send your chum a virtual beer? Stumble over to:
www.pubworld.co.uk

Recipe Link
www.recipelink.com
Points to more than ten thousand galleries of gluttony.

Recipe Search
www.birdseyefoods.com/birdseye/recipes
Cast your line into the fishfinger king's own recipe database or trawl through hundreds of other Net collections. See also:
recipes.alastra.com
www.mealsforyou.com

Restaurant Row
www.restaurantrow.com
Key in your dining preferences and find the perfect match from hundreds of thousands of food barns worldwide.

Riverford Organic Vegetables
www.riverford.co.uk
One of the largest organic vegetable home delivery schemes in the UK. Choose from 4 sizes of box brimming with veg or a variety of fruit options.

Room Service
www.roomservice.co.uk
Restaurant delivery, catering, and even dry cleaning available from this swish home service

Scope GM Food
scope.educ.washington.edu/gmfood
Forums, FAQs, links and reference library concerning mutant seeds.

ScotchWhisky.com
www.scotchwhisky.com
Excellent site with loads of info on whisky, plus a shopping facility.

Simply Recipes
www.elise.com/recipes
Enough mouthwatering ideas here to keep you going for the rest of the year.

Somerset Organics
www.somersetorganics.co.uk
A group of West Country farms have got together to provide an organic site where you can get a variety of quality meats delivered anywhere in the country. Since you're buying direct prices are lower than buying organic in a supermarket so on bulk orders the savings can be huge.

Spice Advice
www.spiceadvice.com
Encyclopedia of spices covering their origins, purposes, recipes and tips on what goes best with what.

Swaddles Green Farm
www.swaddles.co.uk
Selling their own naturally raised meat as well as other organic groceries, Swaddles Farm is devoted to promoting the cause of good food for all. There's a fabulous ready-prepared meal selection for dinner party cheats, as well as children's meals to satisfy both parent and offspring.

Take It From Here
www.takeitfromhere.co.uk
This online deli stocks all the essentials you need to produce a traditional Italian meal – fresh pasta, pesto sauces and Amaretti biscuits for dessert.

Tasty Insect Recipes
www.ent.iastate.edu/misc/insectsasfood.html
Dig in to such delights as Bug Blox, Banana Worm Bread, Rootworm Beetle Dip and Chocolate Chirpie Chip Cookies (with crickets).

Tea & Sympathy
pages.ripco.net/~c4ha2na9/tea
For more, try the Tea Council or, to buy tea, the English Tea Store:
www.teacouncil.co.uk
www.englishteastore.com

The Teddington Cheese
www.teddingtoncheese.co.uk
You can almost smell the goods on this beautiful site brimming with British and European farmhouse cheeses. It also runs a Cheese Club where you can sign up to receive a selection of their finest goods throughout the year.

Thai Recipes
www.importfood.com/recipes.html
Order fresh Thai produce, buy Thai cookware, dive in to recipes such as Volcano Chicken or Frog with Chilli Paste, and sign up to a recipe newsletter.

Tokyo Food Page
www.bento.com
Where and what to eat in Tokyo, plus recipes. More at:
www.thesushibar.com
www.sushilinks.com

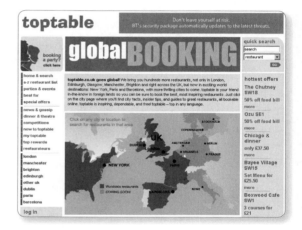

Top Table
www.toptable.co.uk
This free service will book you into a restaurant in your area within your budget. Backed by Gary Rhodes and Sir Alex Ferguson, all the restaurants have been visited so you can trust the info. Sign up for the newsletter to stay informed of special deals in your area. Also visit:
www.5pm.co.uk

Top Secret Recipes
www.topsecretrecipes.com
At least one commercial recipe, such as KFC coleslaw, revealed each week. Many are surprisingly basic. Also investigate Copykat.com:
www.copykat.com

Tudocs
www.tudocs.com
Rates cooking links across the web. Search under "fruit", for instance, and get linked to such ever-useful sites as 104 Things to Do With a Banana.

The Ultimate Cookbook
www.ucook.com
Pinch recipes from hundreds of popular cookbooks. More food porn unplugged at:
www.cook-books.com

Vegetarian Society of the UK
www.vegsoc.org
Support for veggies. And to find out where to eat without meat, try:
www.veggieheaven.com

Webtender
www.webtender.com
Guzzle your way to a happier home. Drink recipes, forums, and a supplies store. More here:
www.barmeister.com
www.drinkboy.com

Wine Spectator
www.winespectator.com
Research your hangover.

Chocolates & sweets

Chocolate Lover's Page
chocolocate.com
The good gear: where to find recipes and dealers.

And if just looking at that site doesn't make you pile on the pounds, visit:
www.chocolate.co.uk
www.divinechocolate.com
www.hotelchocolat.com

Chocolate Store
www.chocolatestore.com
To shop here you just need to decide whether you prefer Swiss, Belgian or English truffles and chocolate. With pictures of most products and a brief description of each.

Cooks of Swanton
www.cooksofswanton.com
Luxury handmade chocolate delicacies. Descriptions and images to tantalise your taste buds are limited, but the no-nonsense pricing makes ordering simple.

Cybercandy
www.cybercandy.co.uk
Bizarre sweets and foods from around the world. Where else are you going to get a snake venom lollipop or coffee beans vomited up by weasels?

Fudge Kitchen
www.fudge-kitchen.co.uk
Who couldn't be tempted by rocky road, Belgian chocolate swirl, lemon meringue or Christmas cake

fudge, and that's just the tip of a huge list of traditional and speciality flavours at this fabulous site.

Hotel Chocolat
www.hotelchocolat.co.uk

Browsing according to personality may not always be that successful but it's fun. Useful info includes the number of chocolates in a box rather than just the weight, so it's easier to determine value for money.

Montezumas
www.montezumas.co.uk

Montezumas sells organic and vegan-friendly chocolate delights. Choose from a vast selection – from your everyday bars to occasion gifts. The more adventurous can opt for the specialist selection with more interesting choices like lemon and apple, cinnamon, nutmeg or even chilli.

 Roly's Handmade Chocolates
www.handmade-chocolates.com

A well-thought-out and mouth-watering selection of handmade chocolates and truffles. Many sites assume you'll buy anything as long as it's chocolate, but Roly is happy to reveal exactly what's in the box.

Coffee & tea

Clipper Teas
www.clipper-teas.com

Masses of information on the company, and tea in general. The selection in the store is good, with a definite ethical bias in favour of fair trade and organic teas.

Coffee Compass
www.coffeecompass.co.uk

Those who struggle when faced with making choices could be in trouble here, given the 45 different single-varietal coffees on offer including the hard-to-

come-by Australian Skybury. No online ordering but worth the effort for the product.

Coffee Geek
coffeegeek.com

Everything caffeinated. For essential espresso links, take a peek at:
www.espressotop50.com
And for even more of the brown stuff:
www.coffeeuniverse.com
www.coffeefest.com

Coffee World
www.realcoffee.co.uk

A staggering selection of coffee and tea, including fair trade and organic varieties. They also green beans you can roast at home.

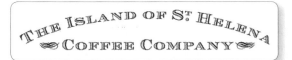

St Helena
www.st-helena-coffee.sh

Buy direct from the island by the pound or half-pound. It's pricey but maybe you like pricey.

Tea 4 Health
www.tea.co.uk

Everything you need to know about the nation's favourite drink, including the health benefits of drinking four cups a day, a directory of the best tea houses, and instructions for making the perfect brew, with a timing chart for different varieties.

Whittard of Chelsea
www.whittard.co.uk

Whittard's site is easy on the eye and contains an

impressive range of products and some nice essays on various aspects of tea, coffee and the like.

Wines

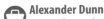
Alexander Dunn
www.alexanderdunn.uk.com
Celebrating an anniversary or looking for a present for your fussy uncle? Here's your answer: personalised wine gift sets, port or champagne. A calligrapher will hand-inscribe the name and message on the label. The wines and spirits are good to vintage quality, and shipping (within mainland UK) is included in the price.

Berry Bros & Rudd
www.bbr.co.uk
Can you serve red wine with salmon? Well, yes, as long as it's dry and fruity like the selection recommended here in the hugely useful food and wine matching section. This is a top class wine merchant where you can find delicious vintages or simply outstanding everyday wines, as well as learn more about your choices and the site's own recommendations before you buy. Try also:
www.oddbins.co.uk
www.virginwines.com

Discount Champagne
www.discount-champagne.com
Good champagne, including a number of vintages, sold in cases at knock-down prices. The site is basic, as is the customer service set-up, but all this means is that their overheads are low and the savings are passed on to the customer.

French Regional Wines
www.french-regional-wines.co.uk
Buy wines by region or grape. There's also a wine-tasting event calendar and a guide to grape variet-

ies if you don't know your Pinot Noir from your Gewurztraminer.

Grapeland UK
www.grapeland.uk.com
Offers a great range of wines from around the globe. Select a region, Chile, South Africa and France included, to view simple yet effective descriptions that won't make you think you're about to buy a bottle of perfume or furniture polish.

Hot Wines
www.hotwines.co.uk
Bottles are clearly illustrated for you label fans, and brief but relevant info like best serving temperature and top flavour are noted.

Laithwaites
www.laithwaites.co.uk
This site sells wines from all over the world. If you don't like the wine, for whatever reason, they will replace it or give you a refund. A user-friendly site that aims to take the fear out of buying wine. Also has regular bin-end offers worth checking out.

Nick Dobson wines
www.nickdobsonwines.co.uk
The emphasis is on fine wines from the southern Burgundy region, with some German, Swiss and Austrian plonk thrown in for good measure.

Original Wine
www.originalwine.com
A large variety of exciting quality wines you won't find on the high street, sourced from family run wineries where tradition and quality matter.

Rouge & Blanc
www.rouge-blanc.com
This French-based site sells wine from all over the world and offers plenty of advice and special offers for the unsure. The bargains section has some excellent everyday drinking tips on offer, or you could

And for the morning after

Ever since man first woke up with a mouth that felt like it had been cleaned with a toilet brush, he's been searching for the ultimate answer to the morning after. Here's what the online gurus recommend:

 Estronaut
www.estronaut.com/a/hangovers.htm
Prevention intervention and cures – alcohol advice for women who can't remember how they got home.

Sob'r – K
www.hangoverstopper.com
Miracle pills said to cure even the hairiest of hangovers. Only drawback is that you have to remember to take them while you're still drinking…

Wrecked
www.wrecked.co.uk
Prevention being better than cure, one look at this drinking information site will put you off the sauce for life. Go on, have a peek, you owe it to your liver.

consult their wedding service if you need advice on what to serve on your big day.

 Vinceremos
www.vinceremos.co.uk
Specialising in organic wines and spirits, Vinceremos

offers a large selection of vintages, with everything from Hungarian to Portuguese. Sold by the case, prices are good for specialised choices and such a vast selection ensures every palate is catered for.

Spirits

Alcohol Reviews
www.alcoholreviews.com
Reviews of wines, spirits and accessories.

Black Mountain Liqueur
www.celticspirit.co.uk
And people say there isn't anything to do in Wales. Black Mountain Liqueur is a traditional cordial that is brewed in the Wye valley from local apples and blackcurrants and packs a comforting punch served after meals or over ice.

Drink Finder
www.drinkfinder.co.uk
If your chosen tipple is whisky or wine you'll love this site, with hundreds of bottles from around the world to choose from.

Drinx
www.drinx.com
The spirits section is comprehensive, with even a section devoted to fruit schnapps for the very brave.

Whisky Shop
www.whiskyshop.com
From familiar blends to rare single malts (how about a bottle of 40-year-old Bowmore for £4,000?), this site will keep any whisk(e)y drinker more than happy. It's well-designed with lots of info on the products and how to shop.

Free stuff

Yes, there really is free stuff on the Net (even if it doesn't yet extend to lunch). Whether it's worth having is another matter and, like the real world, there's always a catch…

Discounted or Free
www.discountedorfree.co.uk
A whole slew of companies desperate to give you stuff right here.

Freebie List
www.freebielist.com
Neatly categorized list of freebies. Mostly services & software as opposed to tangible goods.

Freebies Club UK
www.freebiersclub.co.uk
Claims to be the UK's biggest and best free stuff site. You have to register (it's free though, duh), to get access to free samples, competitions, services, and all the usual stuff. They also offer a downloadable Freebie Alert program which they claim is "the world's only program to alert you to the latest freebies" right from your desktop.

Free Channel
www.freechannel.net
A fairly comprehensive directory of links to all the stuff to be had for free on the Net. Why do companies give all this stuff away? Because they want you to fill in the form and become part of their database. And a healthy database equals advertising revenue. So you'll find that you have to register to get your mitts on that free baby formula or colouring book, and then tolerate tons of junk e-mail. Your choice.

Free Stuff Junction
www.freestuffjunction.co.uk
Some of the stuff here is just cheap, but again, lots of links to free offers and the like.

Free stuff UK
www.freeukstuff.co.uk
An essential gateway for the aspiring British free-loader. Of course the reality of what you can get free over the Net isn't always as glamorous as the idea. The pick of this crop is probably the free software and free webspace.

Free Shares UK
www.free-uk-shares.co.uk
Here you get a financial twist.

Freebie Site UK
www.adsenger.co.uk
Thankfully broken down into categories, from competitions to freebies and offers. The clothing section had free gloves, a "free" backpack once you got ten others to sign up, a free T-shirt for joining. The adult section had lots of free (plain and flavoured) condoms and lubricants.

Net Cash back
www.netcashback.co.uk
Register to recieve a small percentage cashback on

your online purchases from participating vendors.
See also:
www.greasypalm.co.uk

Charity

Charity Café
www.CharityCafe.com
Go to your favourite search engine via this link and
money will be donated to charity every time – it even
tells you how much. Add it to your favourites and you
could be feeding that family in Somalia in no time.
It's not actually possible though to find out which
charities actually receive the loot.

Easy Donations
www.easydonations.net
Plenty of tips and tricks here for donating to charity
just by changing your webmail provider or search
engine, or when you buy products and services
online.

Fight AIDS at Home
fightaidsathome.scripps.edu
Donate your computer's unused resources to help
AIDS research. You'll need to download a small application that will run in the background downloading
packets of data and processing them. It won't slow
your computer or internet connection down as it
only runs while your machine isn't busy doing something else. Or if you're more concerned with climate
change visit Climate Preduction.net.
www.climateprediction.net

The Hunger Site
www.thehungersite.com
Free food for the hungry! Sounds too good to be true
but for once it isn't. Just visit the site, make a couple
of clicks and someone in need gets 1.1 cups of staple
food. This site also has tabs for similar sponsored
donation sites including breast cancer, child health,

Free iPod?

Most of the stuff you really want to get your mitts on
requires a little more effort than just filling in your details.
There is now an ever growing number of sites offering
free gadgets such as iPods if you participate in one of
their offers and then persuade a handful of friends to do
the same. The offers themselves vary but usually include
spending a bit of money. Occasionally you can find an
offer that you can cancel and still get credit for. The whole
thing looks and feels like a scam, but apparently it isn't.
digitalcameras.freepay.com
digital.freestuff-uk.com
www.pcgrab.co.uk
www.freeipodnanouk.co.uk
www.freeipoduk.co.uk
www.ipodgrab.co.uk

literacy, rainforest, and animal rescue. See also:
geocities.com/dailyfreedonation/
www.freedonation.com
www.clickforwolves.com

Competitions

My Offers
www.myoffers.co.uk
New competitions every week; win everything from
an iPod to your weight in chocolate to a car, simply
fill in the questionnaires to be entered into the prize
draw. Then sit back and wait for the spam to hit your
inbox with your finger poised over the delete button.
For more prize draw madness visit:
www.win4now.co.uk

Loquax
www.loquax.co.uk
Competition portal with links to competitions being
run by vendors, magazines, TV & radio, etc.

Games

Most multiplayer games can be played across the Net. There are also thousands of simple table, word, arcade and music games as diverse as Chess, Blackjack, Connect 4, and Frogger that can be played on the Web courtesy of Java and Shockwave. In some cases you can even contest online opponents for prizes. Peruse the selection on offer at:

Coffee Break Arcade www.coffeebreakarcade.com
Flipside www.flipside.com
FreeArcade.com www.freearcade.com
Gamesville www.gamesville.com
Playsite www.playsite.com
Pogo.com www.pogo.com
Shockwave.com www.shockwave.com
The Station www.station.sony.com
Yahoo! Games games.yahoo.com

For reviews, news, demos, hints, patches, cheats, downloads and other console, PC and Mac game necessities, try:

Absolute Playstation www.absolute-playstation.com
Avault www.avault.com
Gamers.com www.gamers.com
Games Domain www.gamesdomain.co.uk
Games Spot www.gamespot.com
Games Spy www.gamespy.com

HappyPuppy www.happypuppy.com
Hot Games www.hotgames.com
MacGamer www.macgamer.com
Old Man Murray www.oldmanmurray.com
PSXExtreme www.psxextreme.com
XBox xbox.ign.com

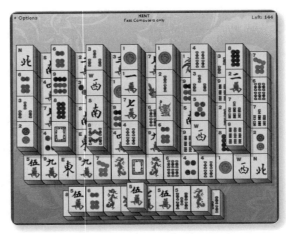

1001 Online Games
www.1001onlinegames.com
We haven't counted them but there are quite a few, we even found a flash version of mah-jong. More at:
www.miniclip.com

Amazon.co.uk
www.amazon.co.uk
Amazon has well structured games section with a cross-referenced database and some charts to give you ideas. Practical info on availability and age restrictions is clearly marked, but what sets Amazon apart is the number and quality of its reviews written by real people.

 Argos
www.argos.co.uk
Argos stocks a fair selection of consoles and games, usually with a few special offers in the mix.

Blues News
www.bluesnews.com
Keep up with what's Quakin'.

Cheat Station
www.cheatstation.com
Get Sonic to do what you want him to do. For more devious tricks, try The Codebook:
www.codebook.se

 Chipsworld.co.uk
www.chipsworld.co.uk
Chipsworld carries a decent range of games, consoles and accessories. New prices are fairly normal but they list secondhand goods in tandem so you'll be able to find plenty of bargains.

Classic Gaming
www.classicgaming.com
Take a trip down memory lane with the console and game museum. Affectionate and witty write-ups of first and second generation game platforms.

 Computer Exchange
www.cex.co.uk
Cex buys and sells computer and game electronic equipment. On the site you'll find prices for the game or console you're looking for, plus the price they'll give you for it if you want to sell, and a slightly higher part-exchange price. Handy if you want shot of your old PS2.

Croft Times
www.cubeit.com/ctimes
More news about the Tomb Raider bombshell than you could ever want. For the truly smitten, you can download a customized version of Internet Explorer featuring Lara's likeness everywhere.

Emulators Unlimited
www.emuunlim.com
Revive old-school arcade games such as Xevious on your home PC. For more 1980s fun, try:
www.smiliegames.com

Ferrago
www.ferrago.com
Intelligent and in-depth gaming features & reviews.

File Planet
www.fileplanet.com
Free games, downloads demos and patches.

Flash Games
en.t45ol.com
Play a variety of flash games from around the world. More at Mix Arcade:
www.mixarcade.com

Game
www.game.uk.com

You would expect to find a good online store when you're dealing with one of the best games retailers in the real world and you won't be disappointed. There are excellent descriptions of each title complete with nice large screen shots. The charts and featured titles offer plenty of ideas.

GameFAQs
www.gamefaqs.com

Stuck on a level or just want to know more?

Game Girlz
www.gamegirlz.com

Team up with other game girls and prepare to kick dweeb-boy butt right across their own turf. More reinforcement at:

www.womengamers.com

Gameplay
www.gameplay.com

Fifteen years old and still going strong, this is certainly the best British gaming portal, with an excellent magazine, shop and loads of online gaming options.

 ### Gamesstreet
www.gamesstreet.infront.co.uk

Run-of-the-mill gaming retail with a few quid off most releases and free delivery on orders over £19.

Game Tab
www.gametab.com

Game news & reviews, organised by platform.

Gaming Age
www.gaming-age.com

All the latest news from the gaming frontline, plus interviews with designers and previews of big games before they hit the shops.

Little Fluffy Industries
www.littlefluffy.com

Links to the best flash games on the web. More great links and reviews over at Jay is Games:

jayisgames.com

Orisinal
www.orisinal.com

Simple but compelling and very very cute online games, usually involving tiny pastel-coloured animals.

 ### PC World
www.pcworld.co.uk

A good selection of games here, including some classics at low prices.

Pointless Games

pointlessgames.com

A selection of games that are actually worse than Pong.

Popex

www.popex.com

Similar to Fantasy Football or Fantasy Shares, but with pop bands.

RPG Planet

www.rpgplanet.com

Popular role playing and fantasy game news, updates tips, cheat, forums and more. You can also join a game or set up your own for others to join.

RPG Vault

rpgvault.ign.com

Role Playing Gamers' heaven.

 Simply Games

www.simplygames.co.uk

Fun, nicely designed site that offers nothing but gaming products at good prices.

Spooks

www.spooksmi5.info

Nifty online game from the BBC. Can you make it as an MI5 Officer?

 Toys "R" Us

www.toysrus.co.uk

This famous high-street toyshop has a section dedicated to video games on all the major platforms, as well as some hardware. There's a lot of choice and the selection of kids' games (such as Rugrats, Spongebob, Scooby Doo) is particularly good.

 WHSmith

www.whsmith.co.uk

A fairly average selection at fairly average prices but worth a look for their deal of the week, 2-for-1 on PS2 games when we visited.

Traditional games

 Big Game Hunters

www.gardengames.co.uk

Traditional garden games like croquet and skittles are joined here by oversize lawn chess and Snakes and Ladders sets. The stand out is the Hi-Tower, a large-scale version of the table game Jenga, which comes very smartly presented in its own wooden box. All items are durable and beautifully made.

 The Chess Shop

www.chess-shop.co.uk

It's chess and chess accessories only from this Scottish site. They range from wood and stone carved sets to an expensive novelty set depicting characters from the battle of the Alamo.

 Games on Board

www.gamesonboard.co.uk

Purveyors of quality traditional board games and accessories. The place to go for all your backgammon, cribbage, roulette, chess and poker needs.

Green Knight Games
www.greenknightgames.co.uk
An unusual selection of board games from children's puzzles and party games through to complex strategy and development games. A slightly more obvious selection available at:
www.farscapegames.co.uk

 Intense Games
www.intensegames.co.uk
For air hockey, table football, snooker tables, bouncy castles and trampolines.

 Jigsaws R Us
www.jigsawsrus.co.uk
Jigsaws R them. Even more at:
www.alljigsawpuzzles.co.uk
www.jigsawpuzzlesdirect.co.uk

Kasparov vs. The World
classic.zone.msn.com/kasparov
Take tips from the Russian master.

 Kevingston Boardgames
www.kgames.demon.co.uk
Very basic site with only a few items but worth mentioning because of a brave effort to support small independent games manufacturers who make the kind of board games your gran used to have. The vastly underrated Flibble, for example. Orders are by cheque only.

 Leisure Games
www.leisuregames.com
For all your role-playing and strategy gaming needs, including miniature figures, paints and brush sets, dice, rule books and the games themselves.

 Masters Traditional Games Shop
www.mastersgames.com
If you can play it in a pub, you can buy it here. Loads of traditional table-top games like Shove Ha'penny

(the set includes a set of old halfpenny pieces), outdoor games, chequers, and table bowls. They're all made to a very high standard and likely to last a lifetime.

 The Real Games Company
www.realgamescompany.com
Wonderful selection of nicely crafted and ingenious games for all ages. Whether you're into card games, table games, garden games, board games or adult games, you'll find some interesting and unusual things here.

Traditional Games
www.tradgames.org.uk
Provides history, useful links and current information about traditional games from around the world.

Gardening

Birstall Garden & Leisure

www.birstall.co.uk
Everything you would expect to find at a large garden centre, plus a garden diary.

The Botanical Dermatology Database

bodd.cf.ac.uk
Why you should wear gardening gloves.

British Trees
www.british-trees.com
Dedicated to the preservation of British woodland.

Capital Gardens
www.capital-gardens.co.uk
Online store for a south-east chain has equipment including fencing, mowers and composters, they also have a selection of bulbs and seeds. There's a comprehensive array of eco-friendly products and tips on cultivation and on gardening problems.

The Carnivorous Plant FAQ

www.sarracenia.com/faq.html
Novel solutions for garden pests.

CMS Gardens
www.cmsgardens.co.uk
Everything for the serious gardener, from propagators and watering systems to greenhouses, with excellent savings to be made in the 'Specials' section.

Crocus

www.crocus.co.uk
The main draw of this online garden centre is that plants are delivered by trained gardeners who will help bolster your borders. There are also sections devoted to plant finding, jargon busting and news and advice on organic gardening.

Debby's Garden Links
www.debbysgardenlinks.co.uk
Decent links page with connections to everything from hammocks to rabbit-resistant plants. More at:
www.gardenlinks.co.uk

Dig It

www.dig-it.co.uk
Good gardening store with plenty of bargains. Also has a pet section.

English Country Gardening
www.suite101.com/welcome.cfm/english_country_gardening
Jane Hollis's site devoted to the grand old art of

gardening

English country gardening includes discussion groups, articles, virtual tours and flower show and garden reports.

 E-seeds
www.eseeds.com

There are plants to buy here too, but since this site is based in Canada you're more likely to have a few packets of their unusual seeds delivered to your door. There are excellent photos of most plants and seed packs, plus comprehensive links to information on plant care. For cactus, bonsai, palm, and other exotic seeds from a UK supplier, visit nothing but seeds:
www.nothing-but-seeds.co.uk

Exhibition Seeds
www.exhibition-seeds.co.uk

North Yorkshire company specialising in vegetable and herb seeds via mail order. Lots of lovely ideas like a seed mixture for a wild flower meadow, but since the quantities they sell can be fairly large, you either have to have a large garden or be sharing with a friend.

Garden Forum
www.gardenforum.co.uk

All the latest news, views, advice, job postings and gossip from the gardening community.

Garden Guides
www.gardenguides.com

Has most of the features you should expect from the better general gardening sites (plant guides, discussion forums, advice), but this site sets itself apart with its lengthy book extracts on topics like choosing bulbs and designing herb gardens.

 The Garden Shop
www.thegardenshop.co.uk

Turn your patio into an additional room with some fancy seating, outdoor heaters and lanterns. This beautifully designed site sells quality garden furnishings at outstanding prices.

Garden Visit
www.gardenvisit.com

Maps of gardens open to the public around the world and a history of garden design.

Garden Web
www.gardenweb.com

One of the best horticultural resources on the Web, this site hosts a multitude of regional and specialist forums (roses, wild flowers, kitchen gardens), plus a glossary, plant database, calendar of events, plant and seed exchange, plenty of articles and shopping areas.

 Greenfingers
www.greenfingers.com

The Ground Force of the Internet world is probably the best way to describe this busy, yet well-organised site. If you're looking to shop you can buy everything from plants and trees to decking and garden sheds, and benefit from hundreds of discounts. Beyond this you'll find step-by-step workshops, from how to plant a bulb correctly to how to plant a tree, and ideas for giving your garden a particular look or feel. A good all-round gardening resource.

 Indian Ocean Trading Company
www.indian-ocean.co.uk

Quality garden and patio furniture including chairs, benches, lounges, tables and parasols, all individual designs, made from quality teak.

Just Gardeners
www.justgardeners.com

Pleasant little gardening hub with discussion forums, articles, and plant descriptions. More useful forums, guides and links to garden centres and shops can be found at the UK Garden Directory:
www.gardeners.co.uk

Kitchen Gardener
www.taunton.com/finegardening
Online presence of *Kitchen Gardener* magazine, dedicated to foodies who grow their own produce. For a more organic perspective, check out:
www.thevegetablepatch.com

Open Directory Gardens
dmoz.org/Home/Gardens
The Open Directory Project's comprehensive set of links.

The Organic Gardening Catalogue
www.organiccatalog.com
One-stop shop for all your organic gardening needs, including organic seeds for vegetables, heritage and modern varieties, herbs, flowers and green manures, organic composts and fertilisers, biological pest controls, organic gardening books and gifts.

Postcode Plant Database
www.nhm.ac.uk/science/projects/fff
This excellent resource from the Natural History Museum allows you to find the right native trees, shrubs and flowers for your area.

R.K. Alliston
www.rkalliston.co.uk
Stylish garden accessories from wicker bird houses to ceramic wasp catchers, trugs, and garden clothing.

Royal Botanic Gardens
www.rbgkew.org.uk
Featuring access to its enormous academic database, the homepage of Kew Gardens is one for the real horticulturalist.

Royal Horticultural Society
www.rhs.org.uk
The online presence of the RHS includes plant databases, seasonal advice and a garden finder.

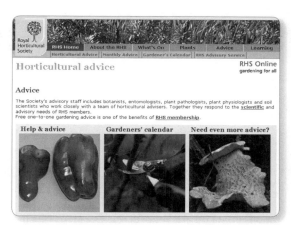

Thrive
www.thrive.org.uk
UK-based charity encouraging the therapeutic use of gardening for disabled people.

Gay & lesbian

AEGIS
www.aegis.com
Claiming to be the largest HIV/AIDS-related site on the Web, AEGIS is an amazing resource filled with the latest news from the treatment front, bulletin boards, a law library of judicial cases and an archive of publications from organizations such as Gay Men's Health Crisis and Act Up, and from the Government. For more news, advice and dispatches from the activist front, try:
www.gmhc.org
www.actupny.org

The AIDS Memorial Quilt
www.aidsquilt.org
View the quilt online, find out how to become involved with the project, and contribute to the memory book.

Gay.com UK
uk.gay.com
The British version of the enormous American portal has a huge array of channels for everyone from scene queens to those not yet out of the closet. Also see:
www.planetout.com
www.queertheory.com

Gay Britain Network
www.gaybritain.co.uk
Homepage of the network that hosts sites such as UK Gay Shopping, UK Gay Guide and Gay Video Shop.

Gay & Lesbian Alliance against Defamation
www.glaad.org
Stand up against media stereotyping and discrimination against those deviating from the heterosexual norm.

Gayscape
www.gayscape.com/gayscape
Probably the best gay search engine on the Web. See also the Queer Resource Directory, the Gay Index and Larry-bob's:
www.qrd.org
www.gayindex.co.uk
www.io.com/~larrybob/hotlist.html

Gay to Z
www.gaytoz.com
Directory of gay-friendly hotels, bars, clubs, builders, plumbers, electricians and erotica in London, Manchester and Brighton. Give them your email address and they'll send you more complete guides on the above cities plus Paris.

Gay Travel Guide
www.gaytravel.co.uk
This excellent site has detailed guides to destinations such as Mykonos, Benidorm, Ibiza, New York and Amsterdam, plus a good search facility for gay-friendly hotels in more exotic locales. Also see:
www.gayhotel.co.uk

Holy Titclamps
www.holytitclamps.com
Homepage of San Francisco's fab queer zine which features fiction by the likes of Sarah Schulmann and Steve Abbot plus comics, poetry, rants and humour from some of the best writers and artists on the scene.

Lesbian UK
www.lesbianuk.co.uk
A list of resources for Britain's lesbian community.

The Old Dyke
www.rowfant.demon.co.uk
Essays devoted to lesbian and women's history.

OUTintheUK
www.outintheuk.com
Fantastic, non-profit networking site for gay men who want to meet other gay men socially.

Out UK
www.outuk.com
UK-based gay men's guide, with advice, links, personals, travel listings and more.

Pink Passport
www.pinkpassport.com
A site with all the usual features, but it does have one of the best gay venue selectors on the Web, covering the entire world.

Positive Finance
www.positivefinance.com
Helpful site offering financial advice to HIV people, including life cover and mortgages.

Rainbow Network
www.rainbownetwork.com
Bustling gay & lesbian site with channels for news, features, culture, film & TV, music, nightlife, travel, and more. Also has forums, classified ads, finance and health news.

Rictor Norton
www.infopt.demon.co.uk
Essayist on gay and lesbian history, politics and culture, including a history of homoerotica and a history of homophobia. Some interesting articles worth a look.

Stonewall
www.stonewall.org.uk
The homepage of the lesbian and gay rights organization may strike some as dull and worthy, but it's a good source of information on British activism and issues like the age of consent.

Techno Dyke
www.technodyke.com
Part of the Indie Gurl Network (www.indiegurl.com) of zines, this fun e-zine has drag king galleries, horoscopes, articles on sex and relationships and a "Biosphere" section.

UK Gay Guide
www.gayguide.co.uk
The design is slightly irritating, but this site features excellent guides to UK gay-friendly services plus advice and personals.

Genealogy

Don't expect to enter your name and produce an instant family tree, but you might be able to fill in a few gaps.

1901 Census for England and Wales
www.1901censusonline.com
Search for your ancestors from over 32 million people and discover a person's address, age, occupation, place of birth and who else they lived with. To travel even further back in time, visit:
www.1837online.com

Ancient Faces
www.ancientfaces.com
Picture your ancestors.

British Genealogy
www.british-genealogy.com
Useful resources, forums and links to help you trace your family history.

Cyndi's List
www.cyndislist.com
Twenty million users can't be wrong. With just about 100,000 links, the genealogy resource you're after is undoubtedly here. For Brit-specific links, try:
www.ukgenealogy.co.uk

Ellis Island Records
www.ellisislandrecords.org
If your family had a stopover in the US in the past 150 years or so, their records will be here.

Family History
www.familyhistory.com
This site, a section of the massive Ancestry.com umbrella, hosts some 130,000 message boards organized by surname or location. You can also set up your own family website here for free.

Family Relatives
www.familyrelatives.org
Offers very comprehensive facilities allowing you to search the databases for Civil Registration records from 1866-2002 for Births, Marriages and Deaths.

FamilySearch
www.familysearch.org
If you're going to be doing family research on the Web you'll come here at one stage or another. This site (also known as the LDS Resource) is run by the Mormons, who believe it is their duty to record the ancestry of every living soul. The religious aspect is played down in favour of sheer information.

Free Surname Search
www.freesurnamesearch.com
A global database of surnames that might be of some use. Also see:
www.surnameweb.org

Genes Runited
www.genesreunited.co.uk
Register for free and build your family tree online.

Historical Text Archive

historicaltextarchive.com

A very useful resource for people with Caribbean and African ancestry, including a Caribbean ancestry newsletter and a database of slave names. Also check the Christine's Genealogy site:

ccharity.com

My Heritage

www.myheritage.com

Applies advanced facial recognition technology to personal photos and family history. Upload elusive old photos that no one in your family knows who is in them and let MyHeritage.com try to recognize these people. If some other member contributed another photo with one of your mystery people, the site will make the facial connection, show you the similar faces and allow you to get in touch with them.

One Great Family

www.onegreatfamily.com

Free trial available for this subscription site which allows you to enter as much of your family tree as you know. It then searches for links with other users

worldwide (their database has over 190 million unique entries) and matches up the connections, exponentially increasing your ancestral knowledge.

Public Record Office

www.nationalarchives.gov.uk

If you need to approach the Public Record Office or National Archive for materials this site gives you the lowdown on how to go about it. For more information visit the Government's Family Records site:

www.familyrecords.gov.uk

RootsWeb

www.rootsweb.com

The oldest, largest and probably the best free genealogy site on the Net. It features a very good search engine, links to resources and lots of humour preventing things from getting too dull. More gene gardening can be done at:

www.ancestry.com

www.familytreemaker.com

www.genhomepage.com

www.genealogytoday.com

UK BMD

www.ukbmd.org.uk

Provides links to 412 web sites that offer on-line transcriptions of UK births, marriages, deaths and censuses.

Health

While the Net's certainly an unrivalled medical library, it's also an unrivalled promulgator of the twenty-first-century equivalent of old wives' tales. So by all means research your ailment and pick up fitness tips online, but as the pill bottles say, check with your doctor before putting them to work. And while you're with your GP, ask if they use the Net for research and if so, which sites they recommend.

Don't expect to go online for first-aid advice. If it's an emergency, you won't have time. The Net is better for in-depth research and anecdotal advice, none of which comes quickly. But once you've spent a few sessions online studying your complaint, you'll be fully prepared to state your case. To find a doctor, dentist or specialist, try:

NetDoctor www.netdoctor.co.uk.

Or for a phone, fax or email response that could save your life on the road, try:

WorldClinic www.worldclinic.com

It's hard to say where to start your research. Perhaps a directory, or you could try one of the specialist health portals:

Health on the Net www.hon.ch
MedExplorer www.medexplorer.com

Patient UK www.patient.co.uk
SearchBug www.searchbug.com/health

Or a government gateway:

NHS Direct www.nhsdirect.nhs.uk
World Health Organization www.who.int

You'll find tons of excellent self-help megasites, though the presence of sponsors may raise ethical questions. Their features vary, but medical encyclopedias, personal health tests and Q&A services are fairly standard fare. Starting with the former US Surgeon General's site, try:

Dr Koop www.drkoop.com
HealthAtoZ.com www.healthatoz.com
HealthCentral www.healthcentral.com
HealthWorld www.healthy.net
Mayo Clinic www.mayoclinic.com
Netdoctor.co.uk www.netdoctor.co.uk
Surgery Door www.surgerydoor.co.uk
24Dr.com www.24dr.com
WebMD www.webmd.com
Yahoo! Health health.yahoo.com

But for serious research go straight to **Medline**, the US National Library of Medicine's database. It archives, references and abstracts thousands of medical journals and periodicals going back to 1966. You can get it free at **PubMed**, but the subscription services may have access to more material. These are aimed more at health pros and students:

Medline Plus www.nlm.nih.gov/medlineplus
Medscape www.medscape.com
Ovid www.ovid.com
PubMed www.ncbi.nlm.nih.gov/PubMed

Despite first appearances, **Martindale's** maintains an outstanding directory of medical science links:

Martindale's www.martindalecenter.com/HSGuide.html

If you know what you have and you want to contact other sufferers, use a search engine (www.google.com) or directory (dmoz.org) to find organizations and personal homepages. They should direct you to useful mailing lists and discussion groups. If not, try **Google Groups** (groups.google.com) to find the right newsgroups.

Acne Regimen
www.acne.org
Out, damned spot! Out…

Alex Chiu's Eternal Life Device
www.alexchiu.com
Live forever or come back for your money.

All Nurses
www.allnurses.com
Springboard to chat groups, research data, professional bodies, jobs and other nursing resources.

Ask Dr Weil
www.drweil.com
Popdoctor Andrew Weil's eagerness to prescribe from a range of bewildering and often conflicting

alternative therapies has seen him called a quack in some quarters, but not by Warner. *Time* put him on the front cover and gave him a job peddling advice beside vitamin ads. Whether or not you believe in food cures, his daily Q&As are always a good read.

Biopharm Leeches
www.biopharm-leeches.com
Cure your ailments the old-fashioned way.

The British Chiropractic Association
www.chiropractic-uk.co.uk
Don't get bent out of shape: this is a good introduction to chiropractic health care.

Calorie Counter
www.caloriecounter.co.uk
Diet sensibly. For more dieting advice, check out the Open Directory's Weight Loss pages:
dmoz.org/Health/Weight_Loss

CancerHelp UK
www.cancerhelp.org.uk
Jargon-free guide to living with the disease, plus information on treatments, ongoing studies and trials.

Alternative therapies

Association of Reflexologists
www.reflexology.org
Take the link from this US site to learn about reflexology in the UK and how your natural healing process can be stimulated by specialist foot massage.

British Acupuncture Council
www.acupuncture.org.uk
Get details of accredited training courses or find a registered acupuncturist for this ancient healing method. And needle-phobes don't fret: it doesn't hurt.

British Homeopathic Journal
www.homeopathyhome.com
Read cutting-edge articles like 'Homeopathic E-Mail: Can the "memory" of molecules be transmitted via the Internet?' Links to online suppliers too.

Foundation for Traditional Chinese Medicine
www.ftcm.org.uk
Plenty of articles and news about specific research projects undertaken to strengthen the position of Chinese Medicine alongside conventional practice.

 Home Herbs
www.homeherbs.com
Good source for herbal remedies, categorized by ailment.

International Federation of Aromatherapists
www.int-fed-aromatherapy.co.uk
Smell your way to good health with essential oils and soothing massage. This site has details of courses and accredited aromatherapists throughout the UK.

 Magnetic Therapy
www.magnetictherapy.co.uk
Magnetic Therapy is credited on this site with the ability to help any number of health-related conditions from arthritis to seasickness. In addition to all kinds of bracelets and wraps with magnets in to there's a range of books about magnets and even a section on therapeutic products for your pets.

Osteopathy in the United Kingdom
www.osteopathy.org.uk
If someone's going to manipulate your back and neck, you want to be sure they know what they're doing. Find a properly trained osteopath through the search facility, and learn about how they can help more than just bad backs.

National Institute of Ayurvedic Medicine
niam.com/corp-web
A good, low BS guide to balancing your life energies with the ancient Indian practice.

 Neal's Yard Remedies
www.nealsyardremedies.com
Browse their health products or their remedy finder for a homeopathic fix for what ails you.

 Planet Botanic
www.planetbotanic.com
Planet Botanic sells a wide range of herbal remedies, backed up by well-written and comprehensive fact sheets. There are also a number of appealing environmental and spa products on sale here, such as de-stressing bath-oil concoctions.

Shirley's Wellness cafe
www.shirleys-wellness-cafe.com
Holistic health and self-treatment information site for people and their pets.

The Society of Teachers of the Alexander Technique
www.stat.org.uk
Learn about how FM Alexander's methods can improve your posture and your health. The site offers guidelines for choosing a teacher, how much you should pay and information on courses in your local area.

Specialist Herbal Supplies
www.herbalsupplies.com
Simmonds has been busy making its own herbal formulae since way back in 1982 and a very good range of them is on offer here. The site also goes out of its way to provide heaps of sensible advice and information on natural health, using those remedies, and other lifestyle tips.

Tai Chi – Qigong Health Centre
www.taichi-qigong.net
Brief introduction to the art of Qigong, so you too can attain natural health and harmony in body, mind and soul. Step-by-step videos can also be bought online.

Cancer Nutrition Info
www.cancernutritioninfo.com
Dietary advice for cancer patients, with recipes, news about clinical trials, and nutrition information.

ConsumerLab
www.consumerlab.com
An independent testing authority which publishes its studies online. It tests herbal remedies, vitamins, supplements, sports products and functional foods for effectiveness, purity, potency, consistency and bioavailability (ie, whether the body can deal with the product properly).

The Diabetes Quiz
www.diabetes.co.il
How much do you know about the condition? If you suffer from diabetes and need some encouragement, pay a visit to the diabetes mine blog at: diabetesmine.com

Dr Squat
www.drsquat.com
Avoid getting sand kicked in your face through full squats. Also see: www.weightsnet.com

Embarrassing Problems
www.embarrassingproblems.co.uk
Dr Margaret Stearn has hit onto a great idea. Simply select the A-Z directory to view facts, guidance, including diagrams, and remedies (where possible), for a host of embarrassing ailments – everything from hairy backs and sweat patches to condom selections and impotence.

E-med
www.e-med.co.uk
Despite the disturbing thought that a doctor's bedside manner could well soon be a thing of the past as it is superseded by good e-mail etiquette, you can't deny the appealing nature of never having to set foot in a doctor's surgery again – particularly with all those sick people around. E-med is just one of the many online surgeries emerging. An annual membership charge will get you immediate access to Dr Julian Eden, a prescription service, consultations, diagnosis and general advice. Additional charges are

of course made for each service, but your time is your own and you'll no longer feel the pressure to explain your most intimate problems in a 10-minute time slot.

Garden Pharmacy
www.garden.co.uk
The online store of London's Garden Pharmacy, this site offers a comprehensive range of products, but no prescription medicines. You can, however, buy hair-loss treatments, contraceptives and anti-smoking aids, as well as a wide variety of cosmetics and toiletries. Complementary treatments include vitamins, minerals, homeopathy, Bach flower remedies and herbs.

Goodness Direct
www.goodnessdirect.co.uk
Online shop for Leicester-based healthfood store, selling a standard range of vitamins and minerals at high-street prices, with regular special offers. The site's strength is in classifying its products to show which are safe for diabetics, or are kosher, gluten-free or dairy-free. It also has a good selection of sports drinks and supplements for athletes.

Gyro's Excellent Hernia Adventure
www.cryogenius.com/mesh
Holiday snaps from under the knife.

HandHeldMed
www.handheldmed.com
Arm your pocket computer with medical software and references. There's even more to be found at:
medicalpocketpc.com

www.pdamd.com

Health Fitness Tips
www.health-fitness-tips.com
Ironically, the site itself is somewhat flabby, but hopefully the exercise tips, low-fat recipes and motivational quotes will help you shed the inches.

HIV Stops With Me
www.hivstopswithme.org
Aims to reduce the stigma associated with HIV and to acknowledge the powerful role that people who are positive have in ending the epidemic.

Holland & Barrett
www.hollandandbarrett.co.uk
Web version of the high street health store, with detailed information of all the products on offer,

simple online ordering and regular reductions. More supplemental bargains at.
www.healthydirect.co.uk

Intellihealth
www.intellihealth.com
Consumer health information from the Harvard Medical School.

International Society for the Enhancement of Eyesight
www.i-see.org
Resources for people wanting to improve their vision, with information about the Bates method, nutrition, glaucoma, and more.

Internet Health Library
www.internethealthlibrary.com
Information on complementary therapy from the University of Essex.

Lab Tests
www.labtestsonline.org
Get inside your sample.

Leukaemia Busters
www.leukaemiabusters.org.uk
Who you gonna call?

Life Expectancy Calculator
www.livingto100.com
Find out if you'll still be around to witness all that exciting climate change and global catastrophe. Best stock up on popcorn now while they can still grow it.

Mental Health
www.mentalhealth.com
It's guaranteed that you'll come out of this site convinced there's something wrong with you. Worry your way along to:
www.anxietynetwork.com

The Merck Manual Online
www.merck.com/mmhe/index.html
Access an online version of the well-known book,

which explains disorders, who is likely to get them, their symptoms, how they're diagnosed, how they might be prevented, and how they can be treated.

Museum of Questionable Medical Devices
www.mtn.org/quack
Gallery of health-enhancing products where even breaks weren't bundled free.

mynutrition
www.mynutrition.co.uk
Offers users a free personal consultation and then provides nutritional advice tailored to their needs.

19th-Century Medical Curios
www.zoraskingdom.freeserve.co.uk
The Elephant Man, bearded women and other strange Victoriana.

Nutritional Supplements
www.nutritionalsupplements.com
First-hand experiences with vitamins, body-building supplements, and other dubious health-shop fodder. For the real deal, go to the British Nutrition Foundation:
www.nutrition.org.uk

Quackwatch
www.quackwatch.com
Separating the docs from the ducks. Don't buy into any alternative remedies until you've read these pages.
www.ncahf.org
nccam.nih.gov

Reuters Health
www.reutershealth.com
Medical newswires, reviews, opinion and reference.

The RSI Association
www.rsi.org.uk
Essential resources for repetitive strain injury sufferers, with factsheets, support groups and information on how to minimise the risk of developing RSI.

RxList
www.rxlist.com
Look up your medication to ensure you're not being poisoned.

Spas Directory
www.thespasdirectory.com
Locate a British spa or health resort.

Talk Surgery
www.talksurgery.com
Discuss your operation with people who appear interested.

ThinkNatural.com
www.thinknatural.com
ThinkNatural scores highly as an attractive, easy-to-use online store which offers thousands of natural health products. The shop is backed by an excellent Health File, packed with information from expert contributors.

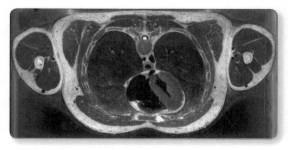

Travel Health
www.travelhealth.co.uk
Come back in one piece.

The Virtual Hospital
www.vh.org
Patient care and distance learning via online multimedia tools such as illustrated surgical walkthroughs.

Recreational drugs

Everything you ever wanted to know about the pleasure, pain and politics of psychoactive drugs and the cultures built around them:

Erowid www.erowid.org
Lycaeum www.lycaeum.org
Neuro Pharmacology www.neuropharmacology.com
Drug Library www.druglibrary.org

The Visible Human Project
www.nlm.nih.gov/research/visible
Whet your appetite by skimming through scans of a thinly filleted serial killer, and then top it off with a fly-through virtual colonoscopy. For higher production values, see the Virtual Body:
www.medtropolis.com

Vitamin Shoppe
www.vitaminshoppe.com
Vitamin junkies can save a fortune on all their supplements with this comprehensive US site. All the usual health-helpers are here, along with some you won't have heard of yet, at prices far lower than you'll find anywhere in the UK. Remember, overseas delivery will bump up the costs, so you'll need to buy in bulk if you're going to make any real savings.

Web Direct Condoms
www.condoms.co.uk
Top of the list of modern health and safety products has to be the humble condom, but keeping stocked up can be pricey. Then, of course, there's the girl-in-the-chemist or slot-machine trauma of buying them. Solve your problems in one go with this straightforward site. Prices are excellent, delivery is speedy (often overnight) and free, and your order arrives in a plain brown package. As if it was anything to be ashamed of.

Women's Health
www.bbc.co.uk/health/womens_health
A refreshingly relatively unbranded site from the Beeb.

World Wide Online Meditation Center
www.meditationcenter.com
Connect with your essence.

Drugs

The legal variety. For illegal ones you'll have to buy a different kind of guide book. Prescription and over-the-counter medicines are popping up all over the Web, and despite dire warnings, there are plenty of reputable sites which don't allow customers to flout the rules.

Academy Health
www.academyhealth.com
Stylish and calming, this site has a wide variety of products on sale: vitamins and supplements, sports nutrition, herbal remedies, skin and body care, family planning, and some over-the-counter medicines such as aspirin, and, oddly enough, fine wines.

Allcures.com
www.allcures.com
This is currently the UK's only full-service online pharmacy, dispensing both private and NHS prescription medicines. Also on offer are the usual beauty products, toiletries, herbal remedies and vitamins, and even films. There are comprehensive sections on health information, plus news and FAQs.

Wellbeing
www.wellbeing.com
Wellbeing has joined up with high-street retailer Boots to offer an overall health site featuring not only pharmaceutical products but lifestyle items as well,

Online prescribing

Prescribing drugs over the Net can be easily abused but the Royal Pharmaceutical Society of Great Britain has laid down a code of practice to ensure the public receives the same quality care from online pharmacies as from a high-street chemist. (Obviously the RPSGB assumes you get high quality care from its members. You may not agree.) The main points are:

• Security and confidentiality of patient information has to be assured by encryption of data transmission.

• The e-pharmacist must advise when a patient's symptoms suggest a face-to-face consultation would be better. (Most of the e-pharmacy business is for repeat prescriptions where you often don't need to see a doctor.)

• A questionnaire must be filled in if you want a pharmacy medicine (the ones kept behind the counter in the chemist's shop).

• The online pharmacy must keep proper records of medicines prescribed.

• An online pharmacy can only operate from registered premises open to inspection by their officers.

Meanwhile, the tricky issue of online doctor consultations (where you e-mail your symptoms to a doctor who prescribes in response) is under debate at the British Medical Association. Some say there's no substitute for a face-to-face consultation (although this could be achieved with videoconferencing technology) and there's a danger of missing a serious condition if e-mail replaces a trip to the surgery. But for people waiting up to a week for an appointment, you can see why e-mail is an appealing option.

---

many not available from the offline shop. Ranges include the usual beauty and health products plus nutritional supplements, a mother and baby section and fitness equipment. There are also plenty of articles, a discussion forum and even a Wellbeing television station. A recent addition is an online magazine. The Boots brand lends credibility, and you can earn Advantage points on some items as you shop, with special online-only deals.

 Direct Response Marketing
www.propecia.co.uk

Offering Viagra, Propecia and Xenical (the latter two being for baldness and weight loss respectively, the former for you-know-what troubles), this bold and brash site has all the info you need right up front. To order, you fill in a medical questionnaire, including the name and address of your doctor, who will be informed by DRM.

 Getfit
www.1getfit.com

You may be in need of a lot more drugs than you originally thought after browsing this site which has

vitamins and supplements to halt the ageing process, give you the body of a god(dess) and the stamina of a Duracell bunny. If you don't already know how Gen Dhea halts the ageing process you won't find out here, but you can buy it online. At a very high price.

Pharmacy2U
www.pharmacy2U.co.uk

Sells prescription medicines plus the normal range of personal care products. Attractive and easy-to-use, this site even offers e-mail advice from trained phar-

History

The Archive
www.archive.org
An expanding digital library of Internet sites and other cultural artefacts (moving images, audio, text etc) in digital form.

ArchNet
archnet.asu.edu
Digital directory to online archaeology sites with an academic leaning. See also the Archaeological Resource Guide to Europe:
odur.let.rug.nl/arge

BBC Online – History
www.bbc.co.uk/history
As you'd expect, the Beeb's history pages are a good place to start. They're well designed and informative. Channel 4's history site is also worth a look:
www.channel4.com/history

Britannia
britannia.com/history
One of the best British history sites on the Web, with biographies of the "bravest knights of the fourteenth century", virtual tours of Sussex churches, a history of Welsh royalty and an electronic version of the Anglo-Saxon Chronicle.

Children's Compass
www.thebritishmuseum.ac.uk/childrenscompass
Interactive kids' guide to the collection at the British Museum, with guided tours of everything from mummified animals to the history of badges. For an adult version point your browser to:
www.thebritishmuseum.ac.uk/compass/

History Buff
www.historybuff.com
A collection of press clippings through the ages.

History Channel
www.historychannel.com
Perhaps too much of an American slant for most British users, but it does have some great features, such as an amazing archive of great speeches, both as text and as RealAudio documents:

History House
www.historyhouse.com
Dedicated to rescuing history from the historians, this excellent American site tells the stories of real people who have had an impact on the world's major and not-so-major events. A necessary corrective to the "great man of history" myths.

History in Focus
www.history.ac.uk/ihr/Focus
Provides original articles on subjects like the holocaust, gender, the sea, medical history, etc. Also book reviews, and links to historical resources.

History Ring
members.tripod.com/~PHILKON/ring.html
Homepage of the history ring, linking you to hundreds and hundreds of non-commercial history sites.

History World
www.historyworld.net
NIcely presented world history site. The timelines feature is particularly useful, it even allows you to edit and make your own historical timeline from their existing resources.

Internet History Sourcebooks Project
www.fordham.edu/halsall
A fantastic resource for students of history, with links to thousands of articles on women's history, Jewish history, Islamic history, African history, lesbian and gay history, medieval studies and the more standard ancient and modern cultures.

Journal for Multimedia History
www.albany.edu/jmmh
Academic history journal with hyperlinked bells and whistles.

The Lemelson Center
invention.smithsonian.org
The history of invention and innovation.

London's Past Online
www.history.ac.uk/cmh/lpol
Find everything relating to the history of the capital, from counting house to music hall; from the Fire to the Blitz; from Whittington to Livingstone.

Regia Anglorum
www.regia.org
Relive the age of the Vikings.

School of History
www.schoolhistory.co.uk
Historical learning and teaching resources, with online lessons, revision help, and interactive tours, quizzes and games. All helpfully classified by age group. For more history links visit History Mad:
www.historymad.com

Victoria County History
www.englandpast.net
The greatest publishing project in English local history. Since 1899 the VCH has presented the authentic history of English places and their people, written county by county from original documents.

Hobbies & craft

Hobbies

All Magic Guide
www.allmagicguide.com
Your passport to the world of illusion.

Balloon HQ
www.balloonhq.com
Become a part of pop culture.

The Contortion Home Page
www.contortionhomepage.com
"Hey, Stretch, how do you do that?"

Discovering Fossils
www.discoveringfossils.co.uk
Where to go and what to look for and what you need to take. More at:
www.juniorgeo.co.uk

The Doll's House
www.thedollshouse.biz
Large selection of houses, furniture and figures available here in a range of sizes & styles from classic to modern.

Experimental Aircraft
exp-aircraft.com
Online resource for lunatics interested in building their own planes.

Firewalking.com
www.firewalking.com
The official website of Tolly Burkan, the father of fire-walking.

Hobbies Plus
www.hobbies-plus.co.uk
Hobby and craft superstore. Whatever your interest is you're likely to find it here, model kits, marbles, gnome moulds, doll's houses, needlecrafts, marquetry, oil painting and much more besides.

Hobby Club
www.hobbyclub.co.uk
Specialists in working steam engine models and remote-controlled planes, cars and boats.

Home Sewing Association
www.sewing.org
Pick up hints from a bunch of sew and sews.

International String Figure Association
www.isfa.org
Perfect your cat's cradle technique.

Joseph Wu's Origami Page
www.origami.vancouver.bc.ca
Gateway to the wide world of paper folding, including diagrams, galleries and links. To make your folds fly, see:
www.paperairplanes.co.uk

Juggling Information Service
www.juggling.org
If you can't keep your balls up, this site has just about everything any sane human could ever want to know about juggling. There's a collection of juggling software so you can see how the pros do it, a history of juggling and other arcane stuff. For the "best bean-bag kit on the market", try the Juggling Store:
www.jugglingstore.com

 ### Kites
www.kiteshop.co.uk
The selection varies from beginners' kites all the way up to the "easy to assemble and virtually indestructible" Flexifoil range of power kites. For tips & advice check the resources section at Into The Wind:
www.intothewind.com

Kitez
www.kitez.com
Go fly a kite at this dedicated search engine for kite-surfers.

 ### Lock-picking
lock-picks.com
If lock-picking is one of your hobbies it suggests, at best, that you are congenitally forgetful. But if picking locks is important to you, this US site is the place to be.

Metal Detecting
ukdetectornet.co.uk
It's a fascinating world, metal detecting, at least so this site claims, which helps you enter its world with a link to a selection of shops that can help you get kitted out and set you on the path to buried treasure. Plenty of other info for the wannabe detector too.

Model Mart
www.modelmart.co.uk
Model online community for modellers.

NMRA Directory of World Wide Rail Sites
www.cwrr.com/nmra
The National Model Railroad Association's vast site of model railway links across the world.

Potato Cannon Fun Page
www.geocities.com/Yosemite/Rapids/1489
Charm and delight your parents for years to come.

The Puppetry Homepage
www.sagecraft.com/puppetry
The ups and downs from the world of puppetry, from animatronics to ventriloquism.

Rocketry.org
www.rocketry.org
Send your worst enemy to the Moon.

TreasureNet
www.treasurenet.com
Exchange tall tales and learn about metal detection.

Crafts

About Hobbies
www.about.com/hobbies
Your first portal of call for any crafts search should be About's impressive hobbies page which contains links to their basketry, beadwork, candle-making and

woodworking sites as well as twenty other crafts sites that they host.

Art Education

www.art-education.co.uk
This is a shockingly inartistic site for a business that specialises in art tuition videos, but worthwhile if you're dying to master airbrushing, oils, drawing, pastels, watercolours etc.

Candle Makers Supplies

www.candlemakers.co.uk
Europe's largest candle-making supply store. Experts, novices, adults and kids are all catered for. Prices are good and there are plenty of hints to help you create more intricate designs.

Classic Stitches
www.classicstitches.com
The homepage of *Classic Stitches* magazine includes some 150 downloadable charts to set your needles working.

Crafts Council
www.craftscouncil.org.uk
News on and listings of craft shows, events, exhibitions, seminars and workshops. The Crafts Council also provides a regional list of shops selling contemporary crafts as well as buying guides.

Crafts Unlimited
www.crafts-unlimited.co.uk
Over 1100 cross-stitch patterns to buy, plus downloadable beginner's and advanced guides to cross-stitch technique. Also check out Cross-Stitch Design: www.maurer-stroh.com

Economy of Brighton

www.economyofbrighton.co.uk
Specialising in decorative rubber stamps and hole punches, this site also sells a vast range of other art supplies including powder paint, modelling clay and Plaster of Paris at excellent prices.

Encaustic Arts

www.encaustic.com
Large site full of tips and ideas for projects involving heating wax to make pretty pictures. It sells a rainbow of coloured wax blocks plus card, rubber stamps and even the right sort of iron for creating the best result.

Heaton Cooper

www.heatoncooper.co.uk
Site run by Cumbrian artists selling high-quality paints and art supplies, including specialist items like gold leaf.

Hobbicraft

www.hobbicraft.co.uk
A huge range of hobby and craft supplies here. Glass engraving equipment, beads, and painting-by-number kits to mention just a few.

Hobby's

www.hobby.uk.com
Online version of weighty craft supplies catalogue specialising in model-making, but now featuring other creative kit like glass cutters and doll's houses.

Home Sewing Association

www.sewing.org

An essential bookmark for budding Gallianos and hopeless bachelors alike. The site is packed with sewing lessons for beginners and tips and trends and advanced techniques for more experienced seamstresses.

Internet Craft Fair

www.craft-fair.co.uk

Put a stitch in time at this massive online community for the UK's crafts scene.

Planet Patchwork

www.planetpatchwork.com

Blocks and vectors of info devoted to the mystique of quilting.

 ### Scottish Wood Craft

www.scottishwoodcraft.co.uk

Simple but effective site selling woodworking tools as well as delightful handmade wooden items from chairs to bird mobiles.

Sunflower Fabrics

www.sunflowerfabrics.com

Specialises in quilting and other needlework supplies, and offers a lovely selection of patterns and complete quilt kits.

 ### Sybilla Davis Designs

www.sd-designs.com

A limited range of cross-stitch designs displaying picturesque scenes from Devon and Cornwall.

 ### Wells Models

www.wellsmodels.com

Huge selection of airfix, die-cast, matchstick, wood and other types of model available here.

Wool Works

www.woolworks.org

Containing an archive of more than 250 patterns, an extensive hints and tips section on making socks and knitting for dolls, and a comprehensive links page – this is a darn good knitting site.

Home improvement

Alaris Avenue

www.alarisavenue.co.uk
High-quality contemporary home improvement products for the whole house. Bathrooms, kitchen, furniture, lighting, windows and more.

Art 2 Wall

www.art2wall.com
Nice little site selling modern art prints (with or without your choice of frame) if you spend a lot of time sitting around staring at the wall and fancy a change of scenery.

Ask the Master Plumber
www.clickit.com/bizwiz/homepage/plumber.htm
Save a small fortune by unblocking your own toilet.

BBC Homes
www.bbc.co.uk/homes
Plenty of advice and inspiration from the BBC with practical DIY guides (including a handy paint calculator to help you figure out how many tins to buy) alongside colour and style guides, safety tips, and more.

Blinds Bar

www.blinds-bar.co.uk
Custom made-to-measure quality window blinds in a variety of styles, with free samples and free delivery.

Chandeliers

www.chandeliers.co.uk
Glamorous chandeliers at reasonable prices, delivered

direct from the Czech Republic. The designs are fairly traditional and they also supply wall sconces and lamps to match if you want the complete bordello look.

Direct Doors

www.directdoors.com
A healthy selection of doors, frames, hinges and locks available here, with a useful section that walks you through every aspect of door installation and care.

Ewindows

www.ewindows.co.uk
Get an online quote for having your windows done.

Fig

www.fig.co.uk
Fig combines stylish ideas and design with the practicality that every consumer craves. You can find yourself a Swedish-style mirror or a piece of abstract art, or if you're more of an antique hunter the events calendar and guide should keep you up to date. The shop itself offers a wide selection of furniture and home accessories, obviously pricier than your average Ikea but far more interesting.

Find a Builder
www.findabuilder.co.uk
Enter your postcode to find Federation of Master Builders approved tradesmen in your area and wave goodbye to the cowboys. The site also provides advice to help your build run smoothly and a free

plain English building contract that you can apply to most jobs.

Fix it now
www.fixitnow.com
Battling with a washing machine or microwave? Help is at hand from the Samurai Appliance Repair Man. Also see:
www.repairclinic.com

Home Repair Stuff
www.factsfacts.com/MyHomeRepair
Design-free site answering questions such as "Which caulk?" and "Squirrel in your belfry?", plus beginner's guides and basic tool kits.

Home Tips
www.hometips.com
Load your toolbox, roll up your sleeves and prepare to go in. Then retreat, have a cup of tea, and take another look online. Try also:
www.doityourself.com
www.naturalhandyman.com

How to Clean Anything
www.howtocleananything.com
Just add elbow grease.

Improveline
www.improveline.com
Peruse the latest design ideas and find someone to do the job. You can even screen your local builders against public records and find the one least likely to quaff all your home-brew and sell your nude holiday snaps to the *National Enquirer*. Also see:
www.homepro.com

Mumford & Wood
www.mumfordwood.com
Makers of high-quality doors and windows, including conservation replacement sash and casement windows.

ThePlumber.com
www.theplumber.com
Includes tips and online repair handbooks plus the history of plumbing from Babylonia through the inventions of Thomas Crapper to waterworks in the White House. For more plumbing sites, try the Plumbing Web:
www.plumbingweb.com

Self Build
www.selfbuildanddesign.com
If you'd rather build your own house than visit an estate agent, click here. Also try:
www.ebuild.co.uk
www.self-build.co.uk

Skills Register
www.skills-register.com
Thinking of hiring a plumber or handyman? Try this great service: a directory of British tradespeople who have passed site owner Will Stevens's stringent quality assurance tests.

This to That
www.thistothat.com
So what would you like to glue today?

Truss Loft Conversion
www.trussloft.co.uk
Complete UK-wide loft conversion service.

Wacky Uses
www.wackyuses.com
Using Coca-Cola to clean corrosion from batteries, pantyhose to polish furniture and other wacky household hints from Joey Green. TIP: you have to scroll down the page to find the SKIP INTRO button.

Catalogues

The Cotswold Company
www.cotswoldco.com
Wood and luxurious ethnic patterned fabrics do feature strongly, but you will find more than a hint of chrome lurking along the way. Design is middle-of-the-road but fairly contemporary.

Ikea
www.ikea.com
They still don't sell online but the Ikea site serves as a useful augmentation to their catalogue. Entire rooms are whittled down to individual pieces showing you how to create that Ikea experience in your own home. You then need to head for your nearest industrial estate to buy the things.

Lakeland
www.lakeland.co.uk
This Lake District family business publishes a range of hugely successful catalogues featuring stylish high-quality, great value-for-money household basics and accessories.

Past Times
www.past-times.com
There's not much in the way of contemporary design, but there are plenty of decorative and well-made accessories, including Art Deco, Art Nouveau, and Mackintosh-inspired designs.

Contemporary design

Blue Deco
www.bluedeco.com
Lovely homewares, many of them handmade, from a selection of modern designers. The oak furniture is particularly attractive, but even if you're only after placemats there's something here for you too.

Ochre
www.ochre.net
Ochre's collections of modern furniture, accessories and especially lighting, are truly outstanding.

Pepper Mint
www.pepper-mint.com
Purveyor of the Qube, a piece of plastic furniture that will remind you of the building blocks from your childhood. You can use it as shelving, seating, a display unit, a table, even a hostess trolley. They also sell a small range of lighting, including a flat-pack plastic chandelier.

White Company
www.thewhiteco.com
A tasteful store selling simply-designed furniture, accessories, and soft furnishings.

Decoration & DIY

B&Q
www.diy.com
The online version of the DIY giant offers everything from flooring and tools to gravel and the proverbial kitchen sink. It may look like a Sunday paper pull-out ad, but there's plenty here. Also see Homebase: www.homebase.co.uk

Coping With Winter

www.ag.ndsu.nodak.edu/coping

Building a ski house in the Alps or moving to Irkutsk? Follow these building and DIY tips from North Dakota State University.

Digital Home DIY

digitalhome.cnet.com

Some of the information on here is America-specific but worth a look anyway for the beautiful interface that'll show you how to set up various digital media products to work around the home.

DIY Fix It

www.diyfixit.co.uk

This decent UK home improvement encyclopedia is very informative, and one of the few that come from this side of the pond.

DIY Doctor

www.diydoctor.org.uk

Completely free Self build and DIY help from qualified tradesmen through an interactive question and answer service plus tips, tricks and projects. There's also a bookshop, links to suppliers and a facility to locate a specialist in your area. Very handy site. More projects and tips can be found at:

www.diydata.com

Fine Homebuilding

www.taunton.com/home

American magazine for real DIY enthusiasts.

House in Progress

www.houseinprogress.net

Aaron and Jeannie's charming blog about restoring their big old house. More at houseblogs:

www.houseblogs.net

MFI

www.mfi.co.uk

Redo your kitchen with some modular cabinets. For more chi-chi options, try Magnet and PS4 Kitchens:

www.magnet.co.uk

www.ps4kitchens.co.uk

The Old House Web

www.oldhouseweb.com

An excellent resource for those restoring the old money pit. Again, the site is American so the product info may not be entirely appropriate, but there are good articles on choosing the right primer and quick fixes for wallpaper repair problems.

Plumbing Pages

www.plumbingpages.com

Comprehensive heating, plumbing and bathroom installation advice, including sections on reducing heating bills, condensing boilers, water treatment, and legislation & regulations.

Stencil Library

www.stencil-library.com

Who needs wallpaper when you can go stencil crazy for a fraction of the price. The variety of stencils runs into the thousand with themes including art deco, flower garden, Celtic, Japanese and children's designs.

Tooled Up
www.tooled-up.com

Tools, tools, and more tools. All the top brands at better than high-street prices, with further bargains to be found in the special offers section. If your hunger for hardware persists there's even more at Screwfix and DIYtools:
www.screwfix.com
www.diytools.co.uk

Wallpaper Direct
www.wallpaperdirect.co.uk

A wide online selection of wall coverings. You can search by designer; alternatively browse according to the look of your home.

Furniture

Conran
www.conran.co.uk

Full range of designer items with detailed descriptions about their history. Did you know, for example, that the Karuselli chair was created by renowned Finnish designer Yrjö Kukkapuro after a vodka-fuelled night out ended with his sleeping in a surprisingly comfortable mound of snow?

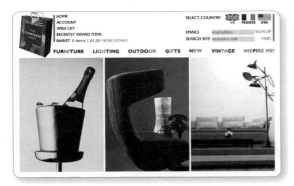

Feather & Black
www.featherandblack.com

Excellent sales site from a made-to-order bed retailer, with iron and wooden beds available. They also stock a nice range of bedding and accessories.

Furniture Web Store
www.furniturewebstore.co.uk

A huge variety of beds, mattresses and sofa beds, some at substantially marked-down prices

The Futon Shop
www.futonshop.co.uk

Handmade futons and contemporary beds you can buy online. If you live in Luton and you want a bed to rhyme with your town, more can be found at:
www.futonworld.co.uk

Habitat
www.habitat.co.uk

A nice stylish site where you can browse through their range or flick through an interesting year-by-year retrospective. No online ordering though.

Holding Company
www.theholdingcompany.co.uk

The Holding Company offers a vast collection of storage products with mesh, bamboo and chrome featuring prominently. It prides itself on being able to mould any fabric into anything you desire. Stylish yet practical and easy to manage.

Home Frenzy
www.homefrenzy.com

Modern furniture and lighting, with emphasis on fun contemporary items such as the Alessi range.

Just Click Beds
www.justclickbeds.com

Unfortunately you can't bounce up & down on them, which is the whole point of buying a bed, but if that doesn't bother you there are a whole range of beds a mattresses available here. More at Bed World: www.bedworld.net

Sofas And Sofa Beds
www.sofabeds.co.uk

A wide range of sofas also available as sofabeds. Choose your base, fabric, and then order online (at a discount from their shop prices) with minimum fuss.

Sträad
www.straad.co.uk

Offers art prints, lighting and executive gifts alongside furniture and home accessories. Pricey but unusual.

Urban Icons
www.urbanicons.com

Unusual designer furniture, mostly dealing in coffee tables and small household accessories.

Viva Sofa
www.vivasofa.co.uk

Sofas in every style, each available in a choice of colours. They also have some incredible offers (buy one get one free on some products).

Voodoo Blue
www.voodooblue.co.uk

Specialists in traditional, fair-trade natural wares from Kenya. Storage is generally the name of the game, with products in a variety of natural materials: soapstone, earthenware, wood and basket weaves.

Inspiration

Gilatimur
www.gilatimur.co.uk

Indian and Indonesian-inspired furniture and accessories, everything from dining suites to mirrors to ornate carvings is available. They also have a fair selection of more western pine furniture, including grandfather clocks. Check the Unusuals section for some really bizarre and unique pieces.

Interior Internet
www.interiorinternet.co.uk

Suppliers of designer furniture to interior designers and architects. It's a nice place to browse through thumbnails of exquisite pieces of furniture loosely grouped into categories such as 'chic and bleak' or 'fantasy furniture'. Well worth a visit, especially if you're planning a real household overhaul.

Wood for Good
www.woodforgood.com

A useful resource if you are already considering wood flooring, decking or you're just going for fancy beams throughout your house for that pub deco look. The site offers information on building and living with wood, as well as a directory of suppliers in your area.

Kitchens & bathrooms

Alba Tops
www.albatops.co.uk

Suppliers of hard-wearing kitchen worktops in granite, luxore, corian, and various hardwoods.

Kitchen design

All the designer tableware in the world is not going to help you if your kitchen has seen far better days. Kitchens are where everyone hangs out these days, so it's only polite to make it as cool and user-friendly as possible. Of course, few people have the serious cash it takes to completely remodel the whole thing, but with a few ideas nicked from the professionals, even the saddest of cabinets and mouldiest of fridges can be persuaded to have a new lease of life. The following kitchen design sites, ranging from the cheap and cheerful to the eye-crossingly pricey, might provide some inspiration for your own kitchen ambitions.

Chantry Kitchens
www.chantrykitchens.co.uk
Bespoke units at factory prices.

Magnet
www.magnet.co.uk
Affordable prices with a surprisingly stylish choice of designs.

MFI
www.mfi.co.uk
Low prices and special offers on a wide range of kitchen cabinetry.

Plain & Simple Kitchens
www.ps4kitchens.co.uk
Delicious contemporary and traditional designs.

Appliances Online
www.appliancesonline.co.uk
Plenty of stoves, washers, fridges and dryers to choose from. For more kitchen appliances take a look at the electrical section on page 66.

Bathroom Express
www.bathroomexpress.co.uk
A large range of bathroom suites, shower units and general bathroom accessories. Detailed descriptions and dimensions accompany clear images.

The Cook's Kitchen
www.kitchenware.co.uk
Competitive prices on a vast range of kitchen equipment from specialist utensils (such as crème brûlée torches) to picnic hampers. More kitchen equipment available at cookability:
www.cookability.biz

Culliners
www.culliners.co.uk
If you're following the trend for all things industrial, this site will help you kit out your kitchen with a range of professional catering equipment, whether it's oversize baking sheets or indestructible knives.

Doors Direct
www.doorsdirect.co.uk
Overhaul your old kitchen for far less than the cost of getting a new one by simply changing the cabinet doors. This site has a selection of both rustic and modern styles – choose from standard sizes or their made-to-measure service. There's also a good choice of handles.

Pots & Pans
www.pots-and-pans.co.uk
Not just pots and pans though, you can kit your whole kitchen out from this online store with a bargain around every corner.

Thomas Crapper & Co
www.thomas-crapper.co.uk
We couldn't leave this one out, could we? Traditional Victorian and Edwardian-style toilets and sinks from the sanitary-ware supplier to Edward VII and George V.

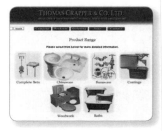

Furniture & interiors

BBC Good Homes
www.bbc.co.uk/homes
The BBC's interiors magazine has all the features you've come to expect, offering advice on everything from Moroccan living rooms to the good flooring guide.

DesignBoom
www.designboom.com
Massive site with details of loads of design events worldwide. There's also a wealth of articles and potted histories.

Design Gap
www.design-gap.co.uk
Directory of work by three hundred contemporary British designers and furniture makers that includes everything from tchotchkes to chests-of-drawers.

Design-Online
www.design-online.co.uk
A database of British interior designers, feng shui consultants, building services, soft furnishing companies and other providers of interiors essentials.

Dwell
www.dwell.co.uk
Get that modern designer look at a fraction of the cost. If chrome tubing is your thing you'll be right at home.

Furniture Wizard
www.furniturewizard.com
Tips on how to restore your Louis XIV chair after your cat pees on it.

Geomancy.Net – The Centre for Applied Feng Shui Research
www.geomancy.net
Harmonize Qi and recreate the ambience of a Chinese restaurant. For more wizard assistance, try Qi Whiz and Feng Shui Fanzine: www.qi-whiz.com

History of Furniture Timeline
maltwood.finearts.uvic.ca/hoft
Detailed history of furniture, with glossary and links.

Let's Go Retro
www.letsgoretro.com
Get a Space Invaders machine for your living room.

On-Line Furniture Style Guide
www.connectedlines.com/styleguide
Detailed guide to styles from Jacobean to Scandinavian.

Sotheby's Collecting Guides
www.sothebys.com
The venerable auction house's guides to collecting ceramics, furniture, prints, rugs, clocks and silver are well worth a gander.

Tribu-Design
www.tribu-design.com/en
A fascinating database of twentieth-century furniture and design.

Wallpaper Direct
www.wallpaperdirect.co.uk
Apparently wallpaper hasn't been this trendy since the 1970s, so stock up at this easy-to-use site, featuring a database of 20,000 papers, borders and fabrics.

The White Company
www.thewhitecompany.com
For all your home and furnishing needs in any colour you like, so long as it's white.

The Work of Charles and Ray Eames
lcweb.loc.gov/exhibits/eames
The Library of Congress's online exhibition of the work of the most influential designers of the twentieth century.

Horoscopes & fortune telling

American Federation of Astrologers
www.astrologers.com
Impress your hairdresser by becoming a fully accredited seer by correspondence course.

Astro Advice
www.astroadvice.com
Aside from its treasure trove of arcane astrological systems (like Nine Star Ki) and slightly dodgy advice (astrological financial forecasts, for example), this site's best feature is its free, in-depth astrological charts.

Astrology.com
www.astrology.com
Advice and predictions from just about every sooth-

saying system under the sun. Horoscopes both free and charged, past-life reports, celebrity horoscopes, self-empowerment guides, karmic profiles, crystal balls, Chinese astrological readings and plenty more.

Astrology – Atlas and Time Zone Database
www.astro.com
Know exactly what was happening upstairs the second of your birth. Or if you prefer your cold readings with a touch less pseudoscientific mumbo-jumbo, try:
www.skepdic.com/coldread.html
astrology.about.com
www.astrocenter.com

Astro Tea
www.tea.co.uk/astro.php
Ever wanted to learn how to read your own tea leaves? This site has a video explaining how to perform the incredible art of tassology (with a tea-bag even!). There's also a dictionary of tea symbols to help you along the way.

Biorhythm Generator
www.facade.com/attraction/biorhythm
A cyclical report that can double as a sick note.

Dreamstop
www.dreamstop.com
Analyse your night visions and jot them into a journal to share with your friends.

Metalog
www.astrologer.com
The Astrological Association of Great Britain and the Centre for Psychological Astrology's site is devoted to promoting quality astrology so that people can "discover the richness of their own unique chart and learn that they are more than 'just' their sun-sign."

Oracle of Changes
www.tarot.com/oracle
This site enables you to virtually consult the I Ching. The user casts coins into a pool six times which creates a hexagram that the oracle interprets according to the laws of ancient wisdom. See also:
www.facade.com/iching

Panchang
www.panchang.com
Get a personalized time-planner based on this ancient Indian astrological system.

Past Life Regression
www.pastlives.cc
Send your worst enemy back to the Stone Age.

RealAge
www.realage.com
Compare your biological and chronological ages.

Russell Grant Astrology
www.live-astro.com/horoscopes
Chirpy advice from the chubby prognosticator.

Sarena's Tarot Page
www.talisman.net/tarot
Look no further if you need help with your chandelier, fan or seven triplet spreads, and for the expert, a section on tarot spells. Also consult Tarot Magi:
www.tarot.com

Skyscript
www.skyscript.co.uk
Excellent astrology resource with details about the constellations and their relevance in the current epoch. They can also hook you up with skilled astrologers and even offer a phone consultation service.

Spirit Network
spiritnetwork.com
Portal for horoscopes, psychic readings, biorhythms, I Ching readings, paranormal activity and other New Age pursuits.

Psyche tests

There are plenty of sites out there offering psyche tests; these vary from glib what-breed-of-dog-are-you type quizzes to in-depth and revealing personality tests. Find out all about yourself with dating questionnaires, career finders, IQ and even ink blot tests from this selection of sources:

Psyche Tests www.psychtests.com
Emode www.emode.com
Keirsey.com www.keirsey.com
Queendom.com www.queendom.com/tests.html
Tickle uk.tickle.com

Stichomancy
www.facade.com/stichomancy
Type in your question and the site will choose a book and a passage at random that miraculously will apply to your query. See also Bibliomancy, which does the same thing using Bible passages:
www.facade.com/bibliomancy

Tarot Reading
www.tarot411.com/pkt/tarot0.htm
Free online tarot reading with detailed explanations of what your cards represent. The Tarot 411 site also offers a wealth of information with a pictorial key to the tarot, expert advice and free psychic readings.

The Voice of the Woods
www.pixelations.com/ogham
This is the site to visit if you wish to seek guidance from the Ogham, an ancient Celtic divination method.

What's in your name?
www.kabalarians.com
The Kabalarians claim names can be boiled down to a numerical stew and served back up as a character analysis. Look yourself up in here and see what a duff choice your parents made. Then blame them for everything that's gone wrong since.

Jewellery & watches

Argenteus
www.argenteus.co.uk
Contemporary designer jewellery at high-street prices.

Dejoria
www.dejoria.co.uk
Useful site specialising in diamond rings. They offer an online 'create your own ring' service and guarantee all their rocks to be conflict-free.

Gracia Amico
www.graciaamico.co.uk
Simple and stylish jewellery site. Prices are good for the quality.

Harriet Glen Design
www.hgd.co.uk
For golden horse, bird and wildlife jewellery.

Higuchi Inc
www.higuchi-inc.com/index-e.html
Get the latest Japanese watches ahead of the rest.

Ice Cool
www.icecool.co.uk
A broad range of diamond accessories, including toe rings and belly bars at excellent prices.

Icon
www.icon-jewellery.com
Each item here is handcrafted and you can regulate the expense according to which carat of gold or gem you choose.

Inspirals
www.inspirals.co.uk
Inspirals offers a varied selection of funky silver and gem-set jewellery pieces, all moderately priced.

Jewellers
www.jewellers.net
This catalogue-style site offers gold, silver and luxury items, along with cheap and cheerful fashion novelties.

Silver Chilli
www.silverchilli.com
A pleasant selection of fair-trade South American jewellery from this community-conscious retailer.

Stone Henge Stones
www.stonehengestones.com
A range of designs incorporating Preseli Bluestones, the same material that was used to build Stonehenge.

Tateossian
www.tateossian.com
This stylish site sells unusual and contemporary jewellery items. There's a small range of fibre-optic glass jewellery and silver and zircon designs.

Traser Watches
www.traser-uk.com
Watches guaranteed to glow in the dark for up to ten years, useful if you're into caving or deep sea diving, or reading under the covers.

Kids & teens

It's your choice whether to let them at it head-long or bridle their experience through rose-coloured filters. But if you need guidance or pointers towards the most kidtastic chowder, set sail into these realms:

Cybersmart Kids www.cybersmartkids.com.au
Kaboose www.kaboose.com
NetMom www.netmom.com
Open Directory: Kids dmoz.org/Kids_and_Teens
Scholastic International www.scholastic.com
Surfing the Net with Kids www.surfnetkids.com
Yahooligans (Yahoo! for kids) www.yahooligans.com

The search engines **Google** and **Altavista** can also be set to filter out adult content. For encyclopedias and dictionaries, see p.198.

Ask Dr Universe
druniverse.wsu.edu
Answers to all the big questions. Are worms animals? Does the universe have a shape? How many stomachs do horses have?

Babygadget
www.babygadget.net
Every wished you could have a CD set that would help your dog adapt in advance of a new arrival? How about Feng Shui dolls? Look no further.

Barbie
www.barbie.com
It's a huge, Flash-intensive site, but there's a massive amount of stuff here to keep any girl entertained for hours – so just give in to the inevitable. Your Little Madam might also like to visit:
www.care-bears.com
www.mylittlepony.com

Beat Bullying
www.bbclic.com
Helpful site aimed at helping kids deal with bullying. It offers information and advice in the form of a 'tool-kit'; a step-by-step guide for people who are or know someone who is being bullied. More at:
www.bullying.co.uk

The Belch Page
www.goobo.com/belch
Gross out your parents and your little sister.

The Bug Club
www.ex.ac.uk/bugclub
Creepy-crawly fan club with e-pal page, newsletters and pet care sheets on how to keep your newly bottled tarantulas, cockroaches and stick insects alive.

Remember these?

Show your kids what you were glued to back in the day... it's gotta be better than the nonsense they watch now.

Bagpuss www.smallfilms.co.uk/bagpuss
Battle Of The Planets www.akdreamer.com/botp
The Clangers www.bbc.co.uk/cult/classic/clangers
The Flumps members.lycos.co.uk/theflumps
Hector's House www.davethewave.co.uk/hector/hector.htm
He-Man www.he-man.org/cartoon/cmotu/index.shtml
Ivor The Engine www.smallfilms.co.uk/ivor
Jamie And The Magic Torch www.80snostalgia.com/classictv/jamie
Noggin The Nog www.smallfilms.co.uk/noggin
Pinky & Perky www.pinkyandperky.com
Smurfs www.smurf.com

And for everything else, including *The Littlest Hobo, Hear Bear Bunch* and even *Roger Ramjet*, see:

Catch Henderson
www.catchhenderson.com
Unusual interactive site where you can visit a derelict town and interact with the strange mechanical toys that live there.

CBeebies
www.bbc.co.uk/cbeebies
Auntie's portal for the little 'uns; there are loads of games, stories and things to colour in – a great site. Everyone from *The Fimbles* to *Pingu* gets a look in.

Censored Cartoons
www.toonzone.net/looney/ltcuts
Find out what was removed from your favourite classic cartoon.

Child Line
www.childline.org.uk
The 24-hour helpline for children has revamped its website with bright, bold colours and an easy to navigate interface. The search facility will let children search for information using their own words, colloquialisms, slang and misspellings. There's also celebrity interviews and stories, problem pages and interactive quizzes.

CIA for Kids
www.odci.gov/cia/ciakids/
The whole idea of this site is kind of strange, but it's nothing compared to the FBI for kids site: www.fbi.gov/fbikids.htm

Club Girl Tech
www.girltech.com
Encourages smart girls to get interested in technology without coming across all geeky.

Cyberteens
www.cyberteens.com
Submit your music, art or writing to a public gallery. You might even win a prize.

Decoding Nazi Secrets
www.pbs.org/wgbh/nova/decoding
Use World War II weaponry to exchange secret messages with your clued-in pals. Also see: www.thunk.com

Disney.com
www.disney.com
Guided catalogue of Disney's real-world movies, books, theme parks, records, interactive CD-ROMs and such, plus a squeaky-clean Net directory. For an unofficial Disney chaperone, see: laughingplace.com

The Flat Stanley Project
www.flatstanley.com
Interesting schools project where kids make a cut-out person and then send it with a letter to another school.

Funbrain
www.funbrain.com
Tons of mind-building quizzes, games and puzzles for all ages.

Funschool
www.funschool.com
Educational games for preschoolers.

Goofyface
www.goofyface.com
Gurning from the pros.

gURL
www.gurl.com
Aimed at teenage girls, this site has all kinds of tips and advice on a whole range of matters. Alongside the serious stuff there's a healthy balance of fun stuff, witch comics, forums, photos, polls, and an interactive 3D model you can make look like you and then try outfits on.

The History Net
www.thehistorynet.com
World history with emphasis on the tough guys.

I Used to Believe
iusedtobelieve.com
Confess your childhood phobias.

I Will Knot!
www.iwillknot.com
It's not what you know; it's what knots you know. This site has handy step-by-step video instructions. More at www.realknots.com

Kaboose
www.kaboose.com
Huge array of stuff here for kids and their parents: brain-builders, games (both online and download-able), tips on safe surfing, crafts, desktop icons, etc.

Kids Jokes
www.kidsjokes.co.uk
Reams of clean jokes, riddles and knock-knocks.

Kids-Party
www.kids-party.com
Ideas to prevent your child from crying at their own birthday party.

Kids' Space
www.kids-space.org
Hideout for kids to swap art, music and stories with new friends across the world.

Koclicko
www.koclicko.com
This excellent site sells European toys and games, everything from dolls and plushies to complex wooden town-planning kits. They also sell colourful and unusual furniture for children's rooms. Prices are in Euros but standard delivery to the UK seems to be free for orders over 100 euros.

The Little Animals Activity Centre
www.bbc.co.uk/education/laac
The second the music starts and the critters start jiggling you know you're in for a treat. Let your youngest heir loose here after breakfast and expect no mercy until afternoon tea. As cute as it gets.

kids & teens

Magic Tricks
www.magictricks.com
Never believe it's not so. More tricks at:
www.trickshop.com
www.magicweek.co.uk

The Muppets
muppets.go.com
Magical site with games, downloads, news, movie clips, character profiles and more. Take a peek inside Miss Piggy's trailer, make a remix of the Electric Mayhem Band or hang out with the Swedish Chef.

Neopets
www.neopets.com
Nurture a "virtual pet" until it dies.

Noggin
www.noggin.com
Beautiful site for pre-schoolers. Colourful animated characters walk you through fun activities and games connected with shows such as Miffy and Maisy.

Paper Dolls Online
collectdolls.about.com/od/paperdolls
Download 'em, print 'em out, colour 'em in – magic. Links to yet more paper dolls can be found at:
www.paperdollparade.com

Secret Languages
www.factmonster.com/ipka/A0769354.html
Learn Double Dutch, Pig Latin and Skimono Jive.

Seussville
www.seussville.com
The online home of the Cat in the Hat, Sam-I-Am, Horton, The Grinch and The Whos.

StarChild
starchild.gsfc.nasa.gov
NASA's educational funhouse for junior astronomers. See also:
www.starport.com

Star Wars Origami
www.happymagpie.com/origami.html
Graduate from flapping birds onto Destroyer Droids and Tie Fighters. For more paper folding, visit:
www.aricraft.com
www.origami.com

Teen Advice
www.teenadvice.net
This site has forums and expert advice on anything from acne to (surprise, surprise) sex. More help at:
www.embarrassingproblems.co.uk

The Unnatural Museum
www.unmuseum.org
Lost worlds, dinosaurs, UFOs, pyramids and other exhibits from the outer bounds of space and time.

Vocabulary
www.vocabulary.co.il
Great online word games.

What Is Happening to Me?
www.thehormonefactory.com
Find out what's throbbing in your glands.

The Yuckiest Site on the Internet
www.yucky.com
Fun science with emphasis on the the creepy-crawly. Get even more engrossed in the gross at:
www.grossology.org

Law & crime

For legal primers, lawyer directories, legislation and self-help:

Compact Law www.compactlaw.co.uk
Delia Venables www.venables.co.uk
FindLaw www.findlaw.com
InfoLaw www.infolaw.co.uk
UKLegal www.uklegal.com

For more on criminal activities, trends, arrests and law enforcement, rustle through the following guides:

About Crime crime.about.com
Crime Spider www.crimespider.com
Open Directory dmoz.org/Society/Crime

ADRnow
www.adrnow.org.uk
Strategies for resolving disputes before they end up in court.

A–Z Guide to British Employment Law
www.emplaw.co.uk
Get the upper hand on your boss.

The Absolute Worst Things to Say to a Police Officer
www.geocities.com/Heartland/Prairie/7559/copjokes.html
"Aren't you the guy from The Village People?"

The Anonymous Lawyer
www.anonymouslawyer.blogspot.com
Stories from the trenches, by a fictional hiring partner at a large law firm in a major city.

The Barrister
www.barristermagazine.com
Independent magazine for legal professionals.

Copyright Myths
whatiscopyright.org
Just because it's online doesn't make it yours. For even more clarity on the situation, see:
www.templetons.com/brad/copyright.html

The Court Service
www.courtservice.gov.uk
In amongst all the dull information and legalese is a collection of recent judgements handed down by the country's Justices.

Crime Library
www.crimelibrary.com
Stay up to date with the latest serial killers, criminal profiles and forensics news. More sensational news at:
www.courttv.com

law & crime

Famous mugshots

Lifestyles of the rich and famous. As well as naughty Mr Gates, you'll find the likes of Frank Sinatra, Charles Manson and Steve McQueen:

Famous Mugshots www.mugshots.com
The Smoking Gun www.thesmokinggun.com/mugshots

Crime Magazine
www.crimemagazine.com
Encyclopedic collection of outlaw tales.

Crimes Of Persuasion
www.crimes-of-persuasion.com
Don't get scammed.

Crimezzz
www.crimezzz.net
Non-sensational serial killer and forensics oriented site. Worth a visit for its forensic science timeline.

Cybercrime
www.cybercrime.gov
How to report online crooks. More snitching at: www.cybersnitch.net

Desktop Lawyer
www.desktoplawyer.net
Cut legal costs by doing it online.

Divorce Online
www.divorce-online.co.uk
DIY D.I.V.O.R.C.E. for residents of England and Wales.

Dumb Crooks
www.dumbcrooks.com
Let the masters teach you how not to do it.

Dumb Laws
www.dumblaws.com
Foreign legislation with limited appeal.

The Evidence Store
www.evidencestore.com
"Need a hand for your day in court? How about a foot or a skull?... Accident reconstructions? The Evidence Store's experts will create all the visual exhibits you'll need to educate even the toughest jury."

FBI Files
foia.fbi.gov/alpha.htm
Download the FBI's reports, released by the Freedom of Information Act, on the Black Panthers, Al Capone, Pablo Picasso, Elvis and Winston Churchill.

Freelawyer
www.freelawyer.co.uk
Ask a legal question and get a jargon-free response from a qualified solicitor with a list of local specialists as well as no-obligation estimates.

Gang Land
www.ganglandnews.com
This amazing site from former New York *Daily News* reporter Jerry Capeci has just about everything you could want to know about Salvatore "Sammy Bull" Gravano, John Gotti, Wing Yeung Chan and their ilk.

Guide to Lock Picking
www.lysator.liu.se/mit-guide/mit-guide.html
Never climb in through the window again.

Identity Theft Resource Center
www.idtheftcenter.org
Award-winning site that provides information and support to "people", if that is indeed their real name, who have had their identities stolen. They also provide prevention tips.

Law Centres Federation
www.lawcentres.org.uk
Providing free independent legal advice and representation to disadvantaged members of society.

Legal Services Commission
www.legalservices.gov.uk
Information on Community Legal Service and Criminal Defence Service from the public body that oversees their administration.

Out Law
www.out-law.com
Thousands of pages of free legal news and guidance, mostly centered around e-commerce and IT issues.

Police Officer's Directory
www.officer.com
Top-of-the-pops cop directory with more than 1500 baddy-nabbing bureaux snuggled in with law libraries, wanted listings, investigative tools, hate groups, special ops branches and off-duty homepages. To see who's in Scotland Yard's bad books:
www.met.police.uk

PursuitWatch
www.pursuitwatch.com
Get paged when there's a live police chase on TV.

Serendipity
www.serendipity.li
Interesting site offering detailed hypotheses for events surrounding 9/11, the London Bombings, the Iraq war, and other contentious issues.

The Smoking Gun
www.thesmokinggun.com
Exclusive legal documents and news on celebrities and their legal wrangles. The 'Backstage' section has over 200 rider contracts for everyone from Frank Sinatra to Jennifer Lopez.

Society of Will Writers
www.willwriters.com
Information on wills from the will writers' professional body.

UKSpeedtrap.com
www.ukspeedtraps.co.uk
A great resource for drivers who want to know, umm, where traffic flashpoints might occur.

Video Vigilante
www.videovigilante.com
If you lived in Oklahoma City, what else would you do but wander the city streets with a video camera looking for guys picking up prostitutes?

Money & banking

If your bank's on the ball it should offer an online facility to check your balances, pay your bills, transfer funds and export your transaction records into a bean-counting program such as Quicken or Money. If that sounds appealing and your bank isn't already on the case, start looking for a replacement. Go for one you can access via the Internet rather than by dialling direct. That way you can manage your cash through a Web browser whether you're at home, work or in the cybercafé on top of Pik Kommunisma. For help finding a true online bank:

Online Banking Report www.netbanker.com
Qualisteam www.qualisteam.com

If you can resist the urge to day-trade away your inheritance, the Net should give you greater control over your financial future. You can research firms, plot trends, check live quotes, join tip lists and stock forums, track your portfolio live, trade shares and access news. By all means investigate a subscription service or two – at least for the free trial period – but unless you need split-second data feeds or "expert" timing advice you should be able to get by without paying. Start here:

Yahoo! UK quote.yahoo.co.uk

Apart from housing the Net's most exhaustive finance directory, **Yahoo!** pillages data from a bunch of the top finance sources and presents it all in a seamless, friendly format. Enter a stock code, for example, and you'll get all the beef from the latest ticker price to a summary of insider trades. In some markets stocks have their own forums, which, let's face it, are only there to spread rumours. In other words, be very sceptical of anything you read or that's sent to you in unsolicited email.

Yahoo! is by no means complete nor necessarily the best in every area, so try a few of these as well:

Bloomberg www.bloomberg.co.uk
CBS MarketWatch cbs.marketwatch.com
Digital Look www.digitallook.com
Free Real Time Quotes www.freerealtime.com
Gay Financial Network www.gfn.com
Hemscott www.hemscott.net
Interactive Investor www.iii.co.uk
Microsoft MoneyCentral moneycentral.msn.com
Money Extra www.moneyextra.com
Raging Bull www.ragingbull.lycos.com
Sharepages www.sharepages.com

You'll no doubt be after a broker next. As with banking, any broker or fund manager who's not setting up online probably doesn't deserve your business. In fact, many traders are dumping traditional brokers in favour of the exclusively online houses. **E*Trade** (www.etrade.co.uk), for example, offers discount brokerage in at least nine countries (click on "International" to find your local branch). But traditional brokers are catching on. Many have cut their commissions, and offer online services in line with the Internet competition, so it pays to shop around. You might find you prefer to research online and trade by phone. Compare brokers at:

Gomez uk.gomez.com

For a British e-trading portal, try **E-Trader UK**:

E-Trader UK www.e-traderuk.com

A word of warning, though: some online brokers have experienced outages where they were unable to trade. So if the market crashes in a big way, it mightn't hurt to play safe and use the phone instead.

Advice Online
www.adviceonline.co.uk
Contact an independent financial adviser for help on everything from mortgages to PEP transfers.

Bank of England
www.bankofengland.co.uk
Keep tabs on financial policy decisions.

BigCharts
bigcharts.marketwatch.com
Whip up family-sized graphs of US stocks, mutual funds and market indices. More statistical wonders to be had here:
www.livecharts.com
stockcharts.com

Banks and building societies

Online banks

Cahoot www.cahoot.com
First Direct (HSBC) www.firstdirect.com
Intelligent Finance www.if.com
Smile (Co-op) www.smile.co.uk
Virgin One Account www.oneaccount.com

High-street banks and building societies – online

Abbey www.abbey.com
Alliance & Leicester www.alliance-leicester.co.uk
Co-operative Bank www.co-operativebank.co.uk
Halifax www.halifax.co.uk
HSBC www.hsbc.co.uk
Lloyds TSB www.lloydstsb.com
Nationwide www.nationwide.co.uk
Natwest www.nwolb.com
Barclays ibank.barclays.co.uk

And for a critical look at who's offering the best deals, see:

BillPay
www.billpayment.co.uk
Pay your electricity, gas and water bills over the Net with this service from Alliance & Leicester.

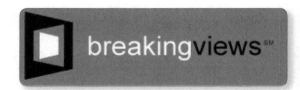

Breaking Views
www.breakingviews.com
Up-to-the-minute financial news and pithy commentary. They also provide daily email updates, instant notification and other features.

money & banking

British Bankers' Association
www.bankfacts.org.uk
Review the Banking Code, find a cash machine, convert currency and consult a glossary of banking terms.

Buy.co.uk
www.buy.co.uk
Tracks and ranks utility prices and finance rates across every UK market. Also links to hundreds of banking sites and investment products. For more rates, try:
www.moneygator.com
www.moneynet.co.uk

Clearstation
clearstation.etrade.com
Run your stock picks through a succession of gruelling obstacle courses to weed out the weaklings, or simply copy someone else's portfolio.

Compare Online
www.compare-online.co.uk
Search for the best insurance, mortgage, bank account, and other services with this handy comparison site. For more finance busting check:
www.confused.com
www.moneysupermarket.com

Debt Advice
www.debtadvicecentre.co.uk
Get yourself out from the hole.

Earnings Whispers
www.earningswhispers.com
When a stock price falls upon the release of higher-than-expected earnings, chances are that the expectations being "whispered" amongst traders prior to opening were higher than those circulated publicly. Here's where to find out what's being said.

Financial Planning Horizons
www.financial-planning.uk.com
Good, unbiased information on the full range of financial products available in the UK.

Financial Times
www.ft.com
Business news, commentary, delayed quotes and closing prices from London. It's free until you hit the archives.

Find
www.find.co.uk
The Financial Information Net Directory houses six thousand links to UK financial sites, organized into categories such as investment, insurance, information services, advice and dealing, bankings and savings, mortgages and loans, business services and life and pensions.

Foreign Exchange Rates
www.xe.net/ucc
Round-the-clock rates, conversion calculators and intraday charts on pretty close to the full set of currencies. To chart further back, see:
pacific.commerce.ubc.ca/xr/plot.html

Frugal Corner
www.frugalcorner.com
Learn how to be thrifty from the experts. See also:
www.moneysavingexpert.com

FTSE
www.ftse.com
All the data and indices you could ever want.

HedgeWorld
www.hedgeworld.com
Allowing the average Joe a peek inside the secretive world of hedge funds.

Hoovers
www.hoovers.com
Research US, UK and European companies.

iCreditReport
www.icreditreport.com
Dig up any US citizen's credit ratings.

Investment FAQ
www.invest-faq.com
Learn the ropes from old hands.

InvestorWords
www.investorwords.com
Can't tell your hedge rate from your asking price? Brush up on your finance-speak here.

Island
www.island.com
See US equity orders queued up on dealers' screens.

MAXfunds
www.maxfunds.com
Great site that allows you to track the performance of mutual funds. You have to register, but it's free. For more on managed funds and unit trusts, try:
www.funds-sp.com
www.trustnet.com

Missing Money
www.missingmoney.com
Reclaim those US dollars you're owed. More dosh up for grabs here:
www.findcash.com

MoneyChimp
www.moneychimp.com
Plain English primer in the mechanics of financial maths.

MoneyExtra
www.moneyworld.co.uk
Compare financial products and get the best deals.

Money Facts
www.moneyfacts.co.uk
Impartial financial advice from this top site, with calculators, guides and hot tips. worth a look.

Motley Fool
www.fool.co.uk
Forums, tips, quotes and sound advice. More people telling you what to do with your money at:
www.citywire.co.uk
www.thisismoney.com

Money Origami
members.cox.net/crandall11/money
It's not how much you earn – it's the way you fold it.

Tax returns

These days you can do your tax return online – it's easy. For more details and information on obtaining a logon ID, and to get tax information straight from the horse's mouth, go to:

Inland Revenue www.inlandrevenue.gov.uk

To find a qualified adviser, try:

The Chartered Institute of Taxation www.tax.org.uk

For a rough estimate of how much you'll have to pay, try:

UK Wage/Tax Calculator listen.to/taxman

For more help and advice with your tax return, as well as links to providers of tax-calculating software, visit:

Advice Guide www.adviceguide.org.uk/em/index/life/tax/tax_returns.htm
QCK www.tax-advice.qck.com
TaxBuddies www.taxbuddies.com

Music Guard
www.musicguard.co.uk
Specialist insurers for musicians.

PayPal
www.paypal.co.uk
Arrange online payments through a third party. The payment method of choice for many on eBay.

Peer Group Online
www.pgpartners.co.uk
Peer Group Online provides contacts, knowledge, experience and new opportunities for people too young to retire.

Pension Sorter
www.pensionsorter.com
Protect yourself against the scandals of the 1980s with this site's impartial advice. Also check out the Pension Advisory Service, and for the Government's angle, try Pension Guide or the DWP's site:
www.opas.org.uk
www.pensionguide.gov.uk
www.dwp.gov.uk/lifeevent/penret

www.allenbukoff.com

Pro Funding
www.fundinginformation.org.uk
News and information for those involved in raising funds for not-for-profit organisations.

Screentrade
www.screen-trade.co.uk
General insurance site, offering quotes from a range of insurers. Try also 1st Quote and InsuranceWide:
www.1stquote.co.uk
www.insurancewide.co.uk

Tax & Accounting Sites Directory
www.taxsites.com
Links to everything you need to know about doling out your annual pound of flesh.

Tax Café
www.taxcafe.co.uk
UK tax advice guides and tips for paying less.

Wall Street Journal Interactive
www.wsj.com
Not only is this online edition equal to the print one, its charts and data archives give it an edge. That's why you shouldn't complain that it's not free. After all, if it's your type of paper, you should be able to afford it, bigshot.

Where Have I Been?
www.wherehaveibeen.com
Find out where your money goes – literally!

Museums & galleries

Homepages of bricks-and-mortar museums:

British Museum www.thebritishmuseum.ac.uk
Guggenheim www.guggenheim.org
The Hermitage www.hermitagemuseum.org
Louvre www.louvre.fr
Metropolitan Museum of Art www.metmuseum.org
Museo Del Prado museoprado.mcu.es
Museum of Modern Art www.moma.org
National Gallery www.nationalgallery.org.uk
National Portrait Gallery www.npg.org.uk
Natural History Museum www.nhm.ac.uk
Tate Gallery www.tate.org.uk
Uffizi Gallery www.uffizi.firenze.it
Victoria & Albert Museum www.vam.ac.uk

And if you want to track down a specific artist:

Leonardo da Vinci sunsite.dk/cgfa/vinci
Matisse www.ocaiw.com/matisse.htm
Michelangelo www.ibiblio.org/wm/paint/auth/
michelangelo
Monet webpages.marshall.edu/~smith82/monet.html
Picasso www.tamu.edu/mocl/picasso
Rembrandt www.ibiblio.org/wm/paint/auth/rembrandt
Van Gogh www.vangogh.com

The American Package Museum
www.packagemuseum.com
Browse through product packaging from yesteryear.

Artcyclopaedia
www.artcyclopedia.com
Resource for finding art exhibits on the web.

ArtMuseum
www.artmuseum.net
Infrequent exhibitions of modern US classics.

Bitstreams
www.whitney.org/bitstreams
A fine exhibit of minimal digital art from New York's
Whitney Museum, with downloadable art.

Brandon Bird
www.brandonbird.com
Online gallery of the artist's work, which includes a

painting of Christopher Walken building a robot and one of Michael Landon cradling a dead squid.

British Lawnmower Museum
www.lawnmowerworld.co.uk
SEE: the world's fastest lawnmower. SEE: Prince Charles's lawnmower. SEE: the water-cooled egg boiler lawnmower. SEE: Vanessa Feltz's lawnmower.

Dia Center for the Arts
www.diacenter.org
Web exclusives from "extraordinary" artists, plus the lowdown on the NY Dia Center's upcoming escapades.

The Exploratorium
www.exploratorium.edu
No substitute for visiting this great San Francisco museum in the flesh, but the Exploratorium's website is filled with fun and educational sections on sports medicine, the solar system, the Hubble telescope and the Panama Pacific Exposition.

Interesting Ideas
www.interestingideas.com
A wonderful site which encompasses roadside art, prison art, outsider art, visionary environments and a whole variety of other creations. The comprehensive links page is one of the best for anyone interested in this area.

Isometric Screenshots
whitelead.com/jrh/screenshots
An online exhibition by artist Jon Haddock in which he has rendered some of the twentieth century's defining moments (the protests at Tiananmen Square, the beating of Rodney King, the assassination of Martin Luther King) in the visual style of video games.

MOMA
www.moma.org
The Museum of Modern Art's site has a compre-hensive online archive of works, with detailed background on each exhibit.

MOOM
www.coudal.com/moom.php
The Museum of Online Museums collects together the best galleries to be found on the web. Everything from an exhibition of fading billboard ads to art treasures from Kyoto.

The Museum of Bad Art
www.museumofbadart.org
A comprehensive and well organised gallery of amateur paintings marred by its slightly derogatory tone.

Museum of Menstruation and Women's Health
www.mum.org
Its curator may be a man, but this is a rather weird and wonderful site that takes its subject pretty seriously.

Plan 59
www.plan59.com
Museum of mid-20th-century illustration. Beautiful renditions of happy families sitting in grotesque cars and psychotic children grinning at hideous cakes.

The PSB Gallery Of Thriftstore Art

www.thriftstoreart.com

Hosts an inspiring online collection of discarded amateur paintings collected from thrift stores around the USA. Everything from a giant Jesus blessing an articulated truck to a series of studies of crumpled toothpaste tubes.

see also www.hugemagazine.com/thrift/index.html

The San Francisico Museum of Modern Art

www.sfmoma.org

Some good interactive programs on various aspects of modern art can be found here, alongside information about current and past exhibits.

The Smithsonian Institution

www.si.edu

The Smithsonian pages host an online magazine, exhibitions, features and educational materials covering a broad range of subjects including the arts, science, history and nature.

Sulabh International Museum of Toilets

www.sulabhtoiletmuseum.org

There goes the neighbourhood.

24 Hour Museum

www.24hourmuseum.org.uk

Portal for British museums, with an excellent search feature which allows you to look for museums with food, baby changing facilities or that tie-in with national curriculum requirements. Also try MuseumNetwork or Museums Around the World:

www.museumnetwork.com
www.icom.org/vlmp/world.html

For galleries as well as museums see the Art Guide and The Gallery Channel:

www.artguide.org
www.thegallerychannel.com

The United States Holocaust Memorial Museum

www.ushmm.org

Hosts a wealth of holocaust-related information, with video archives, personal histories and online exhibits.

Unusual Museums of the Internet

www.unusualmuseums.org

Homepage of the Unusual Museums Webring, your gateway to such exotic destinations as the Toilet Paper Museum, World of Crabs, Cigar Box Art and the Toilet Seat Art Museum.

Web Gallery of Art

www.wga.hu

For fans of everything from Giotto frescoes to Rembrandt's *The Night Watch*, this fantastic site houses digital reproductions of some eight thousand works from between 1150 and 1750.

Web Museum

www.southern.net/wm

Hosts a fantasy collection of art – like having the Louvre, the Metropolitan Museum of Art, the Hermitage and the Prado all right around the corner. There is also an extensive glossary of terms, artist biographies and enlightening comment on each of the works displayed.

Music

If you're at all into music you've certainly come to the right place. Whether you want to hear it, read about it or watch it being performed you'll be swamped with options. **Artist Direct** should be your first port of call:

Artist Direct www.artistdirect.com

Then try these directories:

About.com about.com/arts
Open Directory dmoz.org/Arts/Music
Yahoo! launch.yahoo.com

As ever, if these fail to satisfy, try:

Google www.google.com

For an astoundingly complete music database spanning most popular genres, with bios, reviews, ratings and keyword crosslinks to related sounds, sites and online ordering, see:

All Music Guide www.allmusic.com

Much of the mainstream music press is already well established online. You'll find thousands of archived reviews, charts, gig guides, band bios, selected features, shopping links, news, and various sound artefacts courtesy of these familiar beacons:

Billboard www.billboard.com

Dirty Linen www.dirtylinen.com
Folk Roots www.frootsmag.com
Mojo www.mojo4music.com
NME www.nme.com
Plan B www.planbmag.com
Q www.q4music.com
Rolling Stone www.rollingstone.com
Vibe www.vibe.com
The Wire www.thewire.co.uk

And if your concentration is up to it, MTV:

Europe www.mtveurope.com
UK www.mtv.co.uk

And if you are after hardware, don't buy a stereo component until you've consulted the world's biggest audio opinion bases:

AudioReview.com www.audioreview.com
AudioWeb www.audioweb.com
What Hi-Fi www.whathifi.com

Or if you wouldn't settle for less than a single-ended triode amp:

Audiophilia www.audiophilia.com
GlassWare www.glass-ware.com
Stereophile www.stereophile.com
Triode Guild www.meta-gizmo.com

Consult these directories for shops and other audio sites:

AudioWorld www.audioworld.com
UK Hi-Fi Dealers hifi.dealers.co.uk

Here are a few more of the best music sites to be found online:

A&R Online

www.aandronline.com
Expose your unsung talents or listen to other unsigned acts. More audition opportunities at: www.getsigned.com

Adtunes.com

www.adtunes.com
A one-stop shop for unearthing information about music from commercials, TV shows, video games, etc.

 ### African Music

www.africanmusic.org
World Music buffs should make a beeline for this library, searchable by country or artist, and with an accompanying shopping area.

All About Jazz

www.allaboutjazz.com
Don't let the expensive corporate layout fool you, this American site doesn't just cover Kenny G. As its name suggests, it aims to deal with the entire spectrum of jazz from Anthony Braxton to John Scofield. That it succeeds is down to an easily navigable layout, a wealth of info and contributions from the biggest names in jazz journalism.

Art of the Mixed Tape

www.artofthemix.org
"If you have ever killed an afternoon making a mix, spent the evening making a cover, and then mailed a copy off to a friend after having made a copy for yourself, well, this is the site for you."

The Bad MIDI Museum

littleitaly.fortunecity.com/vatican/791/midi.htm
Not that even "good" MIDI doesn't suck.

Band Family Tree

www.bandfamilytree.com
Secure your place in pop music's genealogy.

Band Name

www.bandname.com
Wanna call your band The Nine Elevens or Dragonsmell? Sorry, already taken. Check here to avoid teams of lawyers turning up at your door asking you to put a 'UK' at the end of your monicker.

The Breaks

www.the-breaks.com
Ever wondered what beat The Beastie Boys ripped off for "Shadrach" or who's sampled Isaac Hayes? This whistle-blowing website tears the lid off the record crates of hip-hop's most famous producers.

Classical Net

www.classical.net
An excellent resource for the beginner, with guides to the basic repertoire and building a CD collection. More adventurous listeners may find it a bit wanting, however.

Corporate Anthems – IBM

www.digibarn.com/collections/songs/ibm-songs
What to whistle while you work. There are loads more of these little gems out there – if you find any, please let us know.

music

The Covers Project
covers.wiw.org
The musical version of Six Degrees of Kevin Bacon.

The Cylinder Preservation and Digitization Project
cylinders.library.ucsb.edu
Browse and listen to their archive of early 20th century cylinder recordings.

The Dance Music Resource
www.juno.co.uk
New and forthcoming dance releases for mail order, UK radio slots and a stacked directory.

Dancetech
www.dancetech.com
One-stop shop for techno toys and recording tips. For more on synths, try:
www.synthzone.com
www.sonicstate.com

Dave D's Hip-Hop Corner
www.daveyd.com
Hip-hop portal, more at:
www.rapstation.com

Detritus
www.detritus.net
An excellent site devoted to the fringes working on "recycled culture".

Dial-the-Truth Ministries
www.av1611.org
So why does Satan get all the good music?

Dictionaraoke
www.dictionaraoke.org
Hilarious MIDI/Talking Dictionary versions of all your favourite pop hits.

Digizine
www.digidesign.com/digizine
E-zone dedicated to Pro Tools, *the* music editing tool.

Disco-Disco.com
www.disco-disco.com/index.html
Where disco is more than just Afro wigs and flares. More strobe-lit remembrances at:
www.discomusic.com/index.html

Downhill Battle
www.downhillbattle.org
Musical activism site with articles on filesharing, MP3s, and major labels. Also has interviews and useful links. For more dirt on the music industry you can read producer Steve Albini's infamous 'The Problem With Music' over at Negativland's fascinating site:
www.negativland.com/albini.html

The Droplift Project
www.droplift.org
Join in some plunderphonic fun by smuggling some avant-garde sampladelic CDs onto the shelves of major chain retailers.

Dusted
www.dustedmagazine.com
Intelligently written music reviews, interviews and features can be found here, mostly centred around independent labels and musicians. More at:
www.pitchforkmedia.com

MP3s

Unlike every music delivery system since the development of 331/3 and 45 rpm records, the MP3 format was not forced upon consumers by the record industry. MP3 is a file format that allows compression of recorded music without a significant degradation in sound quality, and it has become the standard way of storing music on the Internet. Most modern PCs and Macs have enough power and disk space to store and play MP3s. You will also need some MP3 player software such as **Soundjam** for a Mac or **Winamp** or **RealJukebox** for PC, though you'll probably find that your computer can already handle the files using built-in tools such as **Windows Media Player** or Apple's **iTunes** on a Mac. For more on software, see **MP3.com**, which as well as music has links to all the downloadable MP3 players and lots of information for beginners:

MP3.com www.mp3.com

You shouldn't have any trouble finding MP3 music online, though not everything you'll find is legal. The legal side consists mainly of pay-to-download tracks and free previews authorized by the record label. These tend to be from acts that can't get airplay and are eager for exposure, but that's not necessarily the case. As for pay-to-download, try these sites for legal MP3s:

All of MP3 www.allofmp3.com
Artist Direct www.artistdirect.com
AudioGalaxy www.audiogalaxy.com
ClickMusic www.clickmusic.co.uk
Dmusic www.dmusic.com
eClassical www.eclassical.com
Epitonic www.epitonic.com
Launch.com www.launch.com
Peoplesound www.peoplesound.com

There are also subscription services that provide a certain number of downloads (usually combined with lots of lo-fi streams) for a monthly fee. For example:

MusicNet www.musicnet.com
Napster www.napster.co.uk

In addition, there are new net labels springing up daily. The modern-day equivalent of the tape labels of the late 20th century, most are free and run purely for the love of music. Quality varies, obviously and there's a lot to trawl through but whatever your taste, you'll find something you like. Below are a few directories to get your search started:

Archive.org www.archive.org/details/netlabels
Erik Brown's MP3 Links www.ecbrown.org/linkpage.htm
Netlabels www.netlabels.org
Oddio Overplay www.oddiooverplay.com
Sonic Squirrel www.sonicsquirrel.net

So what about the illegal side? Basically, many programs allow computer users to "rip" music – convert a track on a CD into an MP3 file. Once that's done, they can distribute their files around the world – and download other people's – without any record company mediation.

Most illegal MP3s are exchanged not via the Web but via peer-to-peer file-sharing networks. These aren't illegal in themselves, but they are mostly used to share music (plus software and film) illegally without the copyright holder's consent. To connect to a network and search for files, a user simply needs an appropriate program for that network. The biggest networks are accessible with:

Emule www.emule-project.net
Shareaza www.shareaza.com
Soulseek www.slsknet.org

Some file-sharers claim that their activities will ultimately benefit musicians by removing the corporate domination of an art form. Naturally, the record industry – led by the Record Industry Association of America – is unconvinced and has tried to put a stop to free file exchanges. And it's not just pop stars and big business that are complaining. Independent musicians, too, are worried about their royalties. Read various points of view at:

Coalition for the Future of Music www.futureofmusic.org
Free Music Philosophy www.ram.org/ramblings/philosophy/fmp.html
RIAA www.riaa.com

Finally, there's the Apple Music Store, which can be accessed only by using Apple's iTunes software. For the full story pick up a copy of *The Rough Guide to iPods, iTunes & Music Online*.

Instruments

AAA Flight Cases
www.flight-cases.net
Ever tried to charm the lady at the check-in desk to let you take your guitar on the plane as hand luggage? Unless you have magical powers of persuasion it's probably worth looking at the range of custom and standard flight cases for all kinds of equipment on offer here.

Dawsons Music Store
www.dawsons.co.uk
This impressive store sells a wide range of instruments ranging from tenor saxophones to Fender guitars. There's also a monthly competition with some very cool prizes, or if you're fed up with the life of a struggling musician, you can offload your old kit in the classifieds section.

Guitar Amp and Keyboard
www.guitarampkeyboard.com
Brighton-based musical superstore selling everything from the guitars, amps and keyboards their name suggests to drums, microphones and recording equipment. More at Merchant City Music: www.guitarstrings.co.uk

Harmonicas Direct
www.harmonicas-direct.com
Let's face it, Bob, Neil and even the Boss himself wouldn't be nearly as popular if they hadn't added the woeful harmonies of this simple piece of metal to their blue-collar worker songs.

Howarth of London
www.howarth.uk.com
Reed and woodwind specialist with exquisite new and secondhand items.

The also offer repairs, sheet music and a rental scheme.

Piano Man
www.pianoplus.co.uk
Offering new pianos at discounted prices as well as secondhand ones – especially unusual and decorative instruments. They'll also quote for restoration, repair and removal work.

Student Music Supplies
www.studentmusicsupplies.com
Affordable brass and woodwind for those learning to play. Earplugs not included.

Wembley Drum Centre
www.wembleydrumcentre.com
More drums, percussion, accessories and electronics here than you can shake a pair of sticks at. For more things to hit, visit:

Electronic Musical Instruments
www.obsolete.com/120_years
From the Ondes Martenot to the sampler, this online museum is the liveliest, least techie source of information on the rapidly expanding world of music technology.

Evil Music
www.evilmusic.com
Don't know the difference between Black Metal and Doom Metal, or what constitutes Original Death Metal as opposed to Brutal Death Metal? Let Spinoza Ray Prozac be your guide to the dark world of the Metal underground.

Fat Lace
www.fat-lace.com
The Internet presence of the hilarious "Magazine for ageing B-boys" contains mostly copy from the print version which covers hip-hop with an irreverent slant only possible in the UK. An added bonus is the Random Old School Name Generator for all the Lord Disco Loves out there.

Funk45.com
www.funk45.com
A great entrée into the murky world of deep funk collecting. The site is chock-full of MP3s and RealAudio files of hopelessly obscure funk records. The only catch is that the files are only one minute long, with the aim being to introduce people to this arcane world rather than destroying its informal economy.

Funky Groovy Lexicon
www.funk.ch/funk-lexikon.htm
Over 322 pages (in PDF format), the FGL catalogues

nearly everything that can be construed as funky, from 100 Proof Aged in Soul to Zzebra. There's also a gallery of suave cats in dashikis and killer Afros. Believe it or not, it's from Switzerland.

Garage Music
www.garagemusic.co.uk
If you don't live in the East End and want to keep up with what the pirates are playing, click here for the latest news, events and downloads.

Gramophone
www.gramophone.co.uk
There is no better site for serious classical music aficionados. The Web home of *Gramophone* magazine boasts access to its database of 25,000 CD reviews. Need more reasons to visit? How about audio clips, the option to buy from the site, links, listings, glossary, artist bios and feature articles?

Guitar Nuts
www.guitarnuts.com
A wealth of information about improving and repairing electric guitars; if you want no-nonsense guides to shielding or potting your pickups look no further.

Sheet music

Look Music
www.lookmusic.com
There's no excuse for murdering the same show tune over and over again when there are so many pieces to chose from, no matter what the instrument.

Sheet Music Now
www.sheetmusicnow.com
If you have Adobe Acrobat you can use this site to buy and download sheet music direct to your computer. Search by composer or instrument.

Music For A Song
www.musicforasong.co.uk
Save a packet by buying used sheet music and music books. It won't always have what you're after but it's worth a look. Search by composer or instrument.

Music Room
www.musicroom.com
Whether they're after the Bach Lute Suites or a book of Beatles hits rearranged for the home organist, budding musicians can surf this site for hours.

Sibelius Music
www.sibeliusmusic.com
This site boasts the largest collection of new scores on the web and lets you view full scores online. You can buy them to download for printing if you decide they're keepers.

Harmony Central
www.harmony-central.com
Directory and headspace for musicians of all persuasions. If you're looking for a specific instrument or piece of hardware you'll find the exhaustive user reviews here invaluable.

Healthy Concerts
www.healthyconcerts.com
Want to see some live music but can't stand all that noise and smoke? Check here; someone might be playing in the kitchen next door. Much more civilised.

Hyperreal

www.hyperreal.org

Perhaps the godfather of all music sites, Hyperreal has been going since 1992. It's a one-stop window shop for all things rave and ambient. Erowid's Psychoactive Vaults host the raver's version of the *Physician's Desk Reference* – a library of info on mind-altering substances.

Jazz Review

www.jazzreview.com

Bottomless drawer of beard-stroking delights. Also dig: www.allaboutjazz.com www.downbeat.com

Last FM

www.last.fm

Online music station where you create your own personalized music page and get hooked up to others with similar tastes.

Launch.com

launch.yahoo.com

Thousands of music videos, audio channels, reviews and forums.

London Musicians Collective

www.l-m-c.org.uk

The LMC has been promoting the cause of improvised music in the capital for over a quarter of a century. Their site features content from their journal, *Resonance*, streaming audio from their radio show and information on studio facilities.

Lost and Found Sound

www.lostandfoundsound.com

Interesting archive site with unusual audio artefacts, mostly home recordings from the last one hundred years.

Lyrics Search Engine

lyrics.astraweb.com

Finding song lyrics on the Web is a science constantly fraught with difficulty due to copyright laws, but for now this site reigns. See also: www.thesonglyrics.com

The Manual

www.klf.de/online/books/bytheklf/manual.htm

Fancy trying pop superstardom? Have a glance at the essential guide to superstardom, written by the ace pranksters in The KLF.

MIDI Farm

www.midifarm.com

Synthesized debasements of pop tunes, TV themes and film scores.

Mr Lucky

www.mrlucky.com

Get smooth with rhythm 'n' booze.

Myspace Music

www.myspace.com

If there's a band playing in your town and you want to know if they're worth dragging yourself away from ER repeats for, you could do a lot worse than visit www.myspace.com/thenameofthebandinquestion and chances are they'll have a page on there.

Buying records online

Shopping for music is another area where the Net outshines its terrestrial counterparts. You can find almost anything on current issue, whether or not it's available locally, and in many cases hear previews. You might save money, too, but for overseas orders keep an eye on tax and freight costs. Consider splitting your order if duty becomes an issue.

A word of warning; web operators can boast a huge catalogue simply because they order everything on the fly, putting you at the mercy of their distributors. The trouble is your entire order might be held up by one item. The better shops check their stock levels before confirming your order.

Unless your tastes are very esoteric, you can't go wrong with the blockbusters:

Amazon www.amazon.co.uk
BOL www.uk.bol.com
HMV www.hmv.com
101 CD www.101cd.com
Tower uk.towerrecords.com
Virgin www.virginmegastores.co.uk

The More Music and Simply Vinyl sites have plenty of links to smaller UK online specialist stores:

More Music www.moremusic.co.uk/links/uk_shops.htm
Simply Vinyl www.simplyvinyl.com/links.asp

You might also want to try one of these:

A-1 Record Finders
www.aonerecordfinders.com
A huge warehouse holding over a million rare albums. There's no online shop but submit a wants list to them and they'll go take a look for you. Also see:
www.recordfinders.com

CD Wow
www.cd-wow.com
Cheap chart CDs. Also worth a look:
www.play.com
www.101cd.com

Descarga
www.descarga.com
For Latin music, this is a must. ¡Sabroso!

Dusty Groove
www.dustygroove.com
This renowned Chicago store created the blueprint for Internet record mailorder. For hip-hop, funk, soul, reggae, Latin or obscure soundtracks, it's nearly impossible to leave the site emptyhanded.

Forced Exposure
www.forcedexposure.com
The colossus of underground music, with an informative, easy-to-use website. Along with an excellent search feature (which searches personnel lists as well as main artist name), the reviews are opinionated and informative. See Also:

Aquarius www.aquariusrecords.org
CDEmusic www.cdemusic.org
Dot Shop www.dotshop.se
Midheaven www.midheaven.com
Penny Black www.pennyblackmusic.com
Volcanic Tongue www.volcanictongue.com

Global Electronic Music Market
gemm.com
One-point access to over 26 million new and used records from all over the world. See also:
www.secondspin.com

Hard to find records
www.htfr.com
Record-finding agency that specializes in hip-hop, soul and disco vinyl.

Other Music
www.othermusic.com
New York City's bastion of the weird, wacky and just plain great has made a name for itself as one of America's best record emporia. Friendly, helpful and attitude-free.

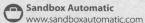

Rough Trade
www.roughtrade.com
London's underground landmark has excellent stock and the prices are reasonable. There's also an old T-shirt section, chat rooms and downloads.

Sandbox Automatic
www.sandboxautomatic.com
Without a doubt the best source for independent hip-hop on the Net. No bells and whistles, but what a choice.

Secondsounds
www.secondsounds.com
Buying used CDs online may be riskier than in an actual shop because you can't check out the merchandise, but if you're after a bargain this site is hard to beat.

Sterns African Records Centre
www.sternsmusic.com
The UK's number-one retailer of world music does a fine job online as well.

Streetwise
www.streetwisemusic.co.uk
Breakbeat, House, Drum & Bass, and other dance genres comin' atcha from, er, Cambridge. See also:
www.globalgroove.co.uk

Vinyl Exchange
www.vinylexchange.co.uk
Manchester's largest secondhand record store. For more pre-owned goodness it's always worth looking on eBay, or try:
www.reckless.co.uk

Niceup

www.niceup.com

Probably the most irie reggae site on the Net, Niceup contains discographies, articles on topics like "Studio One Riddims", a lyrics archive, histories, news and a patois dictionary.

Online Guitar Archive

www.olga.net

Awesome site for guitarists and bassists. No more scurrying through back issues of *Guitar Player* for tablature for Blue Öyster Cult's "Godzilla" – OLGA boasts some 40,000 tabs.

Opus1Classical

www.opus1classical.com

Search the world's major cities for opera and classical performances.

Original Hip Hop Lyrics Archive

www.ohhla.com

Mind-blowingly complete archive of all of your favourite rhymes.

Pancake Mountain

www.pancakemountain.com

Washington DC-based kids TV show with regular live performances from unusual indie and rock acts. Sort of like a punk rock version of Tiswas. If you like the idea of watching Deerhoof or The Go! Team playing to a room full of dancing toddlers then this is for you.

Perfect Sound Forever

www.furious.com/perfect

One of the best music sites on the Net. Mostly consisting of straight interviews, the writing on left-field heroes is passionate and informative.

Piano Tuners' Association

www.pianotuner.org.uk

Tips on piano care and what to look for when buying.

They also have a directory to help you find a qualified tuner in your area.

Rap Dictionary

www.rapdict.org

Can't understand your teenage son anymore? Log on here, dun, and you'll get the 411.

Roadie.net

www.roadie.net

No backstage pass necessary.

Rocklist

www.rocklistmusic.co.uk

Quarter of a decade's worth of best-of-the-year lists from the top mags.

Scratch Simulator

www.turntables.de

Can't afford a pair of SL 1200s? Practise your reverse orbit scratches and beat juggling here, or here: www.infinitewheel.com

Shareware Music Machine

www.hitsquad.com/smm

Tons of shareware music players, editors and composition tools, for every platform.

Shazam

www.shazam.com

When you hear a song you like but you don't know what it is, dial up Shazam on your mobile phone and point it at the sound source. Their sophisticated wave recognition system will identify the tune and send you a text message back with the details.

Sheet Music Archive

www.sheetmusicarchive.net

A great resource of copyright-free downloadable sheet music. You can download only two scores each day – but that shouldn't be a problem, unless you're a very fast learner.

Singing Fish
www.singingfish.com
Music-and-video dedicated search engine.

Smithsonian Institution
www.si.edu
Although this site is as gigantic as the famous American museum itself, if you're interested in folk music (from both America and the rest of the world) it's an absolute paradise, with info on their Folkways record label, webcasts, galleries and articles (augmented with RealAudio files).

Soul City
www.soulcitylimits.com
Listen to hundreds of 1960s and Northern Soul clips.

Soulman's World of Beats
www.worldofbeats.com/old_site
E-zine for all the crate diggers, with articles focusing on the samples from all of your favourite hip-hop records. More vinyl obsession at:
www.groundliftmag.com
www.samplehead.com

Sounds Online
www.soundsonline.com
Preview loops and samples, free in RealAudio. Pay to download studio quality. If it's effects you're after, try:
www.sounddogs.com

Taxi
www.taxi.com
Online music A&R service. And guess what? You and your plastic kazoo are just what they're looking for.

Theremin Resources
www.thereminworld.com
All the history of those "Good Vibrations", and a whole lot more. To build your own, see:
home.att.net/~theremin1

Bizarre records

American Song Poem Archives
www.songpoemmusic.com
Archive of the bizarre mid-century phenomenon where studio hacks set music to the lyrics of ordinary Joes – resulting in some of the weirdest records ever.

Frank's Vinyl Museum
www.franklarosa.com/vinyl
Exhibition of charity-shop flotsam, including such classics as Ken Demko Live at the Lamplighter Inn and an LP of Beatles covers done by dogs.

The Internet Museum of Flexi/Cardboard/Oddities
www.wfmu.org/MACrec
Records made out of metal, souvenirs from the Empire State Building and other curios.

Singing Science Records
www.acme.com/jef/singing_science
1960s educational records. Catchy, yet informative.

Songs in the Key of Z
www.keyofz.com/keyofz
Irwin Chusid's fantastic introduction to the world of outsider music.

This Day in Music
www.thisdayinmusic.com
Find out which member of The Bay City Rollers shares your birthday, and other essential music trivia.

Underground Hiphop Online
www.undergroundhiphoponline.com
The gauntlet has been thrown. Who will win the throne on the microphone?

WholeNote
www.wholenote.com
Guitar resources and chat boards. For live lessons, see:
www.riffinteractive.com

Net stuff

Anonymizer
www.anonymizer.com
Suite of software tools to prevent spyware and keep your IP address private when you surf the web. Free anonymous surfing available at the Cloak:
www.the-cloak.com

Atlas of Cybersapce
www.cybergeography.org/atlas
Mapping the geography of the web with abstract representations of electronic spaces.

Builder
builder.com.com
If you know your PHP from your ASP check out Tech Republic's web development resources page. For more coding ideas and tutorials visit:
www.wdvl.com
www.webmonkey.com
www.webreference.com

Clusty
www.clusty.com
Useful search engine that categorises your results into clusters for you.

Del.icio.us
del.icio.us
Store your bookmarks and favourites online so that you can access them from anywhere in the world or share them with friends. You can also find similar sites bookmarked by others.

Evite
www.evite.com
More than just an e-greetings site, Evite lets you manage invitation lists and utilise their exclusive party-planning content.

Grokker
www.grokker.com
Innovative search tool that presents your results in a graphical 'map' view and lets you adjust parameters such as date or source in real time.

Internet Traffic Report
www.internettrafficreport.com
Get a detailed analysis of where all the data is going.

Mess With MSN Messenger
www.mess.be
Access skins, icons, modifications and plugs for MSN messenger software.

Mozilla
www.mozilla.com
Developers of the award-winning Firefox web browser and Thunderbird email client. Both free and worth your investigation if you haven't already made the switch from Internet Explorer.

Nuthin But Net
www.nuthinbutnet.net
If you're struggling to make your first website and need a few pointers about HTML or graphics this is a helpful resource.

News, newspapers & magazines

Now that almost every magazine and newspaper on the globe from *Ringing World* (www.ringingworld.co.uk) to the *Falkland Island News* (www.sartma.com) is discharging daily content onto the Net, it's beyond this guide to do much more than list a few of the notables and then point you in the right direction for more. Find your favourite periodical by looking for its web address in a recent issue, or try entering its name into a subject guide or search engine. If you prefer to browse by subject or region, try:

Open Directory dmoz.org/News
Yahoo! dir.yahoo.com/News_and_Media

Some newspapers replicate themselves word for word online, but most provide enough for you to live without giving you the complete paper edition. Not bad considering they're generally free online before the paper even hits the stands. Apart from the portion of their print they choose to put online, they also tend to delve deeper into their less newsy areas such as travel, IT, entertainment and culture, often bolstering this with exclusive content such as breaking news, live sports coverage, online shopping, opinion polls and discussion groups. There are also a few sites that index multiple news archives, though usually at a price. Such as:

Electric Library www.elibrary.com
FindArticles.com www.findarticles.com
NewsLibrary www.newslibrary.com
Northern Light www.nlsearch.com

All of the popular news bugles have a presence online, most with an address that you shouldn't have too much trouble figuring out (www.guardian.co.uk, www.thesun.co.uk, etc). If there are any that you can't find, try **Google** or see if the address is printed somewhere on the paper version.

Like much you do online, reading news is addictive. You'll know you're hooked when you find yourself checking in throughout the day to monitor moving stories. Try these for breaking news:

Ananova www.ananova.com
Associated Press www.ap.org
BBC news.bbc.co.uk
CNN www.cnn.com
ITN www.itn.co.uk
NBC www.msnbc.msn.com
Reuters www.reuters.com
Sky www.sky.com
Wired News www.wired.com

Or perhaps best of all, use a free news aggregator,

News tickers

News tickers place a thin ticker-tape-like strip along the top or bottom of the Desktop or sometimes a floating panel, which, depending on the ticker you have, displays a continuous trickle of headlines, share prices, weather reports, etc. More often than not they are downloadable from, and updated by, one particular site, but there are also news aggregating tickers available which draw from multiple news sources. They work best with an always-on connection, but the best very thing about these little utilities is that they are free.

CoolTick (stock ticker) www.cooltick.com
Desktop News www.desktopnews.com
Weather tickers weather.about.com/cs/weathertools
WorldFlash www.worldflash.com

which taps into several sources simultaneously. These ones are good for UK content:

Google News UK news.google.co.uk
NewsNow www.newsnow.co.uk
Yahoo! News UK uk.news.yahoo.com

But there's plenty more at:

Arts & Letters Daily www.aldaily.com
Asia Observer www.asiaobserver.com
NewsHub www.newshub.com
TotalNews www.totalnews.com

If you want to search news blogs (see opposite), probably the best way is to use:

DayPop www.daypop.com

To find more specialist publications, you may want to try a directory of newspapers and news organizations on the Web, which will help you track down everything from Bulgarian National Radio to Zambian broadsheets.

NewsLink newslink.org
Editor & Publisher www.editorandpublisher.com
Metagrid www.metagrid.com
NewsDirectory www.newsdirectory.com
Online Newspapers www.onlinenewspapers.com

As for magazines, most maintain a site but they're typically more of an adjunct to the print than a substitute. Still, some are worth checking out, especially if they archive features and reviews or break news between issues. Again, check a recent issue for an address, or a directory such as:

The Magazine Boy www.themagazineboy.com

And as you might expect, there's no shortage of tech news out there on the Web:

NewsLinx www.newslinx.com
SiliconValley www.siliconvalley.com
Tech News www.news.com
TechWeb www.techweb.com
ZD Network News www.zdnet.com

And if you want e-business news:

InternetNews www.internetnews.com

AlterNet
www.alternet.org
Roundup of America's alternative weeklies.

American Newspeak
www.scn.org/news/newspeak
Celebrating the arts of doublethink, spin, media coaching and other ways to mangle meaning.

Crayon
www.crayon.net
Most of the major portals such as Excite, Yahoo! and

E-zines

"E-zines" are magazines that exist only online or are delivered by email. But because almost any regularly updated webpage or blog fits this description, the term has lost much of its currency. Although most e-zines burn out as quickly as they appear, a few of the pioneers are still kicking on. For more, try browsing a directory at:
www.ezine-dir.com
zinos.com

ABC All 'Bout Computers
personal-computer-tutor.com/abc
Loads of handy PC tips, tricks and advice.

Arts Journal
www.artsjournal.com
Dily digest of arts, culture and ideas.

Collective
www.bbc.co.uk/collective
Edgy arts and culture news from the BBC.

Drudge Report
www.drudgereport.com
The shock bulletin that set off the Lewinsky avalanche. A one-hit wonder perhaps, but still a bona-fide tourist attraction on the info goat track.

Gurl.com
www.gurl.com
Zine dedicated to hip young things pitched somewhere between the original Sassy and Jane.

IGN
www.ign.com/affiliates/index.html
The Internet Gaming Network treads similar – though generally tamer – ground to UGO, partnering mostly with high-quality gaming, sci-fi, wrestling and comic sites.

The Morning News
www.themorningnews.org
Daily news, interviews and commentary.

Pixelsurgeon
www.pixelsurgeon.com
Oddities and observations from and of the World Wide Web. As well as the regular posts, there are interviews, features and reviews, and lots of lovely pictures too.

The Register
www.theregister.com
The best source for daily tech news straight to your inbox.

Salon
www.salon.com
Smart, witty, and compelling content from this renowned ground-breaking web zine.

Spiked
www.spiked-online.com
Caustic, political e-zine from former *Living Marxism* supremo Mick Hume.

Underground Online
www.ugo.com
Big men's magazine-style network

MSN also allow you to create a custom news page that draws from several sources – though none does it quite so thoroughly as Crayon. Infobeat does similar things but delivers by email:
www.infobeat.com

DavesDaily
www.davesdaily.com
A compendium of the weirdest news and views from around the world.

 iSubscribe
www.isubscribe.co.uk
Save a mint on magazine subscriptions. More at:
www.magazinecafe.co.uk
www.uksubscribe.com

A Journalist's Guide to the Internet
reporter.umd.edu
No design whatsoever, but a useful set of links to resources for journalists. More for hacks at:
www.journaliststoolbox.com
www.cyberjournalist.net
mediapoint.press.net

MediaLens
www.medialens.org
Suspicious of our beloved "free" press? You will be once you've visited this site.

Moreover
www.moreover.com
The best free service for searching current or recent

stories across hundreds of international news sources. Also try News Index and What the Papers Say:
www.newsindex.com
www.whatthepaperssay.co.uk
Like someone to monitor the Web and assorted newswires for mention of your product or misdeeds? Try:
www.webclipping.com

MyVillage
www.myvillage.com
Online community with an emphasis on local news. Best in and around London, but slowly increasing their profile across the country.

The Onion
www.theonion.com
News the way it was meant to be.

This Is True
www.thisistrue.com
Randy Cassingham's weekly column of preposterous-but-true news stories and headlines, collated from the major wire services.

Trend Watching
www.trendwatching.com
Fascinating monthly e-zine concerned with emerging consumer trends around the globe.

WHSmith
www.whsmith.co.uk
Customers can order a single issue of a favourite magazine or subscribe to it. Plenty of specials and there's even a 'magazine of the week'.

Wired News
www.wired.com
Read and respond to archived articles from the technology and lifestyle monthly.

RSS newsfeeds

These days most news websites and blogs – and lots of other sites as well – offer "newsfeeds" based on Really Simple Syndication (RSS). Each feed consists of a series of headlines that link to a story on the site. The beauty of the system is that you can see at a glance what's new without actually having to visit the site. Browsers such as Firefox have RSS capability built in, allowing you to see the headlines at a news site directly from your bookmarks bar. Or you could use a standalone newsreader, or "aggregator", such as SharpReader (Windows) or NetNews Wire (Mac) to keep an eye on lots of sites simultaneously.

SharpReader (Windows) www.sharpreader.net
NetNews Wire (Mac) ranchero.com/netnewswire
Mozilla Thunderbird (both) www.mozilla.com/thunderbird

Wireless Flash News Service
www.flashnews.com
News service specializing in pop culture stories, featuring some of the least newsworthy headlines in history.

World Press Review
www.worldpress.org
Keeping tabs on the people who keep tabs on us. Also keep an eye on News Watch:
www.newswatch.org

Yahoo Auctions
search.auctions.yahoo.com/search/ auctions?p=magazines&alocale=1us&acc=us
Thousands of magazines are on auction here at any one time which makes it a must for collectors, whether you're after a copy of a gay magazine starring a nude Sylvester Stallone or a 1951 edition of National Geographic.

Office supplies

Big Pockets
www.bigpockets.co.uk
Excellent deals on office consumables.

CDR by Mail
www.cdr-by-mail.co.uk
Professional quality unbranded blank media from the top manufacturers (such as Taiyo Yuden) alongside items such as business-card shaped CDRs.

City Organiser
www.cityorg-pdq.co.uk
For those Luddites refusing to get on the PDA bandwagon, this is where to come for accessories and inserts for your trusty Filofax.

Data Labels Group
www.datalabel.co.uk
For retail barcodes, security labels and custom-designed labels provided to your specifications.

E Generation
www.egeneration.co.uk
Useful info on making your business ecologically sustainable with advice about how to run your office energy-efficiently and links to suppliers of environmentally friendly business services and suppliers.

Euro Office
www.euroffice.co.uk
Euro Office has a stylish site with everything from fire extinguishers and storage solutions to copier paper and rubber bands.

Furniture at Work
www.furnitureatwork.co.uk
Massive savings on desks, chairs and storage.

Home Working Solutions
www.homeworkingsolutions.co.uk
For a stylish range of home office furniture and accessories. They also offer advice on office ergonomics and have sections devoted to RSI prevention, health & safety, and setting up a home office.

Office Reality
www.officereality.co.uk
For cubicles, dividers, screens, hexagonal call-centre tables and other torture devices. They also host a classy range of bespoke reception area furniture.

OFIS Group
www.ofis-group.co.uk
A huge range of office furniture and an extensive range of supplies including stationery, legal supplies, planning and presentation and more.

Toners.Co.UK
www.toners.co.uk
Toner and copier supplies for new and not-so-new machines.

Viking Direct
www.viking-direct.co.uk
Stock up on Post-its and paper clips at this online warehouse. More at:
www.nextdayoffice.co.uk

Outdoor pursuits

Birdlinks
www.birdlinks.co.uk
Gateway to the world of birdwatching. More at:
birding.about.com
www.camacdonald.com/birding
dmoz.org/Recreation/Birding
www.birdsofbritain.co.uk

Blacks
www.theoutdoorsonline.co.uk
All the biggest (and a few smaller) brands to help you cope with the great outdoors.

The Butterfly Website
www.butterflywebsite.com
The Monarch of butterfly sites, with galleries, lists of gardens and butterfly gardens and loads of information on biology, conservation and behaviour.

Camp Sites
www.camp-sites.co.uk
Find a place to pitch in the UK. More nights under canvas here:
www.campinguk.com

Complete Outdoors
www.complete-outdoors.co.uk
A large range of big-brand trekking, rambling and camping gear, including a separate kids' section, and accessories and gizmos (pedometers, cooking equipment, tools and much more). They have regular deals on tents, sleeping bags, and other essentials.

Ellis Brigham
www.ellis-brigham.com
A great selection of outdoor clothing, footwear, rucksacks, camping, climbing and ski equipment. There are loads of clearance bargains available, and a community section with advice, competitions and a photo gallery.

Go Fishing
www.go-fishing.co.uk
Your complete angling resource. Other sites that would make Isaak Walton proud:
www.anglersnet.co.uk
www.angling-news.co.uk

Great Outdoor Recreation Pages
www.gorp.com
Ignore all the multivitamin and SUV adverts and the American bias because this is the best outdoors site on the Web. The superlative how-to pages alone make it worth navigating the pop-up ads.

Jacksons Outdoor Leisure Supplies
www.jacksons-camping.co.uk
All the comforts of home away from home are available, mostly geared to caravan enthusiasts, but plenty for campers and even just for the back garden. Also has a good line in pools and hot tubs.

Oswald Bailey
www.outdoorgear.co.uk
Everything from tents and boots to mosquito head

nets and waist wallets. Decent product descriptions and reasonable prices.

Outdoor Megastore
www.outdoormegastore.co.uk

A plethora of outdoor gear at discounted prices.

Outside
outside.away.com

Outside magazine's home page is packed with special features, gear reviews, culture and archives from previous issues.

Pennine Outdoor
www.pennineoutdoor.co.uk

Pennine Outdoor sells a staggering range of specialist outdoor fabrics – everything from fleeces and breathable waterproofs to heavy-duty neoprene-coated fabric. You can also buy patterns for outdoor gear, and accessories such as freezing-temperature zips and seam waterproofing.

Pro-Line Sports
www.proline-sports.co.uk

If the mind's willing but your flesh is weak, this is the place to come. Pro-Line Sports specialises in shoulder braces, knee supports, calf protectors, kidney belts, toe warmers, face masks…in fact, a whole range of outdoor body aids that will keep you safe from all kinds of scrapes and injuries.

Ramblers' Association
www.ramblers.org.uk

All the latest news on walking and other pedestrian pursuits. For more info, take your browser on a stroll over to Walking World or Walking Britain:
www.walkingworld.com
www.walkingbritain.co.uk

Rock & Run
www.rockrun.com

Everything you need to move up in the world, literally. There are regular bargains and reviews of products like climbing shoes, ice tools, and harnesses.

Rock Climbing in the UK
www.ukcrags.com

Great resource for British rock climbers, with news, articles, webcams, events listings, routes and crag descriptions. More great climb sites here:
www.climb-guide.com
www.bouldering.com
www.ukclimbing.com

Simply Scuba
www.simplyscuba.co.uk

Billed as the UK's biggest online dive store, this site has everything the scuba diver or snorkeller could need. They also hire equipment and have regular news & reviews.

Snow and Rock
www.snowandrock.co.uk

Big-brand skiing and climbing gear is arranged into categories (including a section for kids); you'll find the usual range of clothing, tents, backpacks, etc.

Stif Mountain Bikes
www.stif.co.uk

If you're into mountain biking, you'll find this site truly indispensable. There's a big selection of bikes on offer, plus associated "software" – bags, Oakley glasses, drinking systems (just so you know they're serious), jerseys, helmets…even replacement bike parts. The site also features plenty of biking news and views to soften the sales edge.

Parties

 Charlie Crow
www.charliecrow.com

Fun party costumes for kids. All occasions covered from Halloween to Christmas to Pirate Day, Tiger Day, Magic Day, Knights of the Round Table Day, Dinosaur Day, and any other occasion you'd care to invent. They also stock a small range of tricks, jokes and themed partyware, and offer some tips on running your party smoothly, with recipes, games, and ideas.

Jane Asher Party Cakes
www.jane-asher.co.uk

Impress the socks off your birthday boy or girl (well, their parents anyway) with a flash cake from Jane Asher's shop in Chelsea. You can choose from fruit or sponge cake, and there are a number of fancy designs including

one in the shape of a gameboy. There's also a gallery of custom-designed cakes including a toad, dead dinosaur, unfinished brick wall, and a bald man in the bath (sadly not all on the same cake).

Just For Fun
www.justforfun.co.uk

Loads of fancy dress here for kids and grown-ups alike, along with decorations, piñatas and joke items. Need the biggest afro you've ever seen or an inflatable kangaroo (and who doesn't?). Look no further.

Party Bus
www.partybus.co.uk

Available up and down the UK! It's a double-decker bus on a mission to party! Next stop: Funkytown! Oh, sorry. Blackpool.

Party Delights
www.partydelights.co.uk

A plethora of party products for all ages and occasions. All the usual stuff on offer: piñatas, confetti, balloons, toys, and themed partyware for everything from Chinese new year to St Patrick's day. Yet more at: www.partybox.co.uk

Security
www.idcband.co.uk

For those who are into party organising in a big way and are interested in dehumanising their guests, this site can supply ID wrist bands, hand-stamps and stewards' vests to guard against gatecrashers and potential terrorists. We were disappointed to find that there's no genetic fingerprinting available but watch this space.

Pets

About Veterinary Medicine
vetmedicine.about.com
About's vet pages are an excellent resource for pet owners worried about their moggie or pet lizard and are filled with advice, news, disease indices and forums.

The Aviary
www.theaviary.com/ci.shtml
Everything you'd ever want to know about companion birds – and then some.

Barbara's Canine Café
www.k9treat.com
Only In America part 346: If your mutt's got a food allergy or you just want to get your hound a "celebration gift basket" made from all-natural ingredients, look no further.

Bugs Direct
www.bugsdirectuk.com
Buy live insects online. Creepy crawlies on offer include praying mantis, tarantulas, scorpions, giant centipedes, land crabs, giant snails and more. They also sell dried & framed insects and jewellery, which seems a little bit like a regular pet shop selling badges made out of dead hamsters but that's just the crazy world we live in.

Burns Pet Nutrition
www.burns-pet-nutrition.co.uk
The Burns in the title of this site has an awful lot of letters following his name so you can be certain the health of your pet is in safe hands. Ingredients and nutritional info and guidance are on hand, and prices are good for such specialised products.

Chazhound
www.chazhound.com
Resources for dog lovers as well as screensavers, games and doggie greetings cards.

The Dogpatch
www.dogpatch.org
Advice on training your pooch, plus the best canine links on the Web.

Dogs
www.dogs.co.uk
Pages for British dog owners, including loads of links to dog-friendly accommodation.

Dogster
www.dogster.com
It was only a matter of time; this plays out like a Myspace for dogs, where dogs can enter their vital statistics, hobbies and interests, hook up with other dogs and leave bones for each other. And for cats:
www.catster.com

Equine World
www.equine-world.co.uk
Great site covering all things equestrian. See also Equiworld:
www.equiworld.net

FishDoc
www.fishdoc.co.uk
All the information you need if your goldfish is looking a bit green around the gills. For aquarium links:
www.fishlinkcentral.com

Gillrugs
www.gillrugs.com
Some people can go over the top when it comes to pet clothing but Gillrugs is about providing your dog with extra warmth, waterproof protection and even safety clothing. This family-run business offers a selection of jackets and matching extras; you just have to supply the measurements.

House Rabbit Society
www.rabbit.org
Online resource for rabbit owners. To offer a home to an orphaned rabbit, visit:
www.rabbitrehome.org.uk

Kingsnake.com
www.kingsnake.com
A mind-bogglingly enormous portal for reptile and amphibian enthusiasts.

Moggies
www.moggies.co.uk
In addition to the usual information and advice, this feline resource allows you to create a virtual cat and even offers horoscopes for Tiddles. Also, visit Frank the cat at:
www.cathospital.co.uk

Mr Winkle
www.mrwinkle.com
Ok, so how cute is Mr Winkle? But is he really real?

Museum of Non-Primate Art
www.monpa.com
Online home of the people behind the "Why cats paint" caper, with special exhibitions devoted to dancing with cats and "bird art".

New Pet.com
www.newpet.com
Friendly and informative site for new or soon-to-be owners of a cat or dog.

Pet Emporium
www.petemporium.co.uk
An obvious range of cat baskets, scratching posts and dog homes, but quite a variety of colours and materials.

Pet Mobil
www.petmobil.com
A variety of pram-like contraptions to transport your

pet anywhere you wish. They double up as shopping trolleys, but make sure you remove the cat before you dump your groceries in.

Pet Planet
www.petplanet.co.uk

As well as a huge selection of pet products and excellent prices, this site offers a handy breed selector, news, pet insurance, pet-specific forums and a whole load of other services.

The Pet Project
www.thepetproject.com

There's a whiff of New Age aromatherapy here ("the special bond between human and animal") and the focus is firmly on the US, but this is surely the most comprehensive pet resource on the Web, with all manner of advice on everything from canine nutrition to interpreting the sounds your chinchilla makes.

Pets Direct
www.petsdirect.com

Offers hundreds of items of pet paraphernalia. Luxuries range from the carousel cat bed to a mini piñata for your parrot.

Pets Park
www.petspark.com

Pets Park offers the natural way to pamper your pet with organic catnip toys and Evening Primrose vitamins, regular features on pet health and channels for a variety of different kinds of pets from dogs to reptiles. They also have a classifieds section.

RSPCA Online
www.rspca.org.uk

The RSPCA's homepage offers advice, allows the kids to adopt a cyber-pet before getting the real thing and features news and information on campaigns for animal welfare.

Save Toby
www.savetoby.com

At the time of going to press, the owner of Toby the rabbit has claimed that he will eat his fluffy friend if he doesn't receive $50,000 of online donations. By the time you read this Toby may be little more than a tasty memory, but it'll still be worth checking out the site's "hate mail" page.

Stinky Pets
www.stinkypets.com

This site is selling a recipe for making a pet odour remover out of regular household ingredients.

UK Dog Sitters
www.ukdogsitters.co.uk

Directory of people offering pet-sitting services for dogs, cats and all other kinds of animals. Sitters are rated with recommendations from previous clients which should give you a fair idea whether or not you're leaving your pussy in safe hands.

Virtual Pet Rock
www.virtualpetrock.nl

Roll Over! Play Dead! Good boy! If you'd like to take the plunge and offer a home to a real-life rock visit: adoptarock.weblodge.net

Photography

American Museum of Photography
www.photographymuseum.com
Delightful exhibitions demonstrating early attempts at making the camera lie, with sections on faux snow, ghosts & seances, and montage mischief.

Black & White World
www.photogs.com/bwworld
A celebration of black-and-white photography.

British Journal of Photography
www.bjphoto.co.uk
Homepage of the venerable magazine and a valuable resource for the professional photographer.

 ## Camera King
www.cameraking.co.uk
For serious photographers. Pro cameras, lenses, and accessories. Worth a look for the regular special offers and clearance sections.

Camerapedia
www.camerapedia.org
An online repository for camera knowledge based around specific brands and models. You can add to or edit the information wiki-style or simply find out more about your machine.

 ## Digital Camera Company
www.digital-cameras.com
Comprehensive range of digital cameras and accessories available here. More at:
www.jessops.com
www.ukdigitalcameras.co.uk

Digital Camera Resource Page
www.dcresource.com
A simple, easy-to-use site, offering reviews of loads of digital cameras and equipment as well as product news and information on issues like Mac OS X compatibility.

Digital Photography Review
www.dpreview.com
Considering a new digital camera? Rigorous testing, reviews and sample galleries here. More reviews and digital camera advice at:
www.cameras.co.uk

Digital Truth: Photo Resource
www.digitaltruth.com
Perhaps the best photographic resource for the

advanced photographer, with loads of tips, down-loadable f-stop calculation software and "the world's largest" film development chart.

Exposure
www.88.com/exposure

A beginner's guide to photography, whose neatest feature is the simulated camera which mimics the effects of adjustments in shutter speed and aperture on pictures.

Flickr
www.flickr.com

Excellent example of an online photo album site. Lets you share your pics with friends and family only or publicly. There's a handy keyword search facility and you can add comments and even tag specific areas of the picture with notes.

 **Freestyle Photographic Supplies**
www.freestylephoto.biz

For film, paper, chemicals, lighting, and all the other stuff you need if you're in the business of taking pictures.

Invisible Light
www.atsf.co.uk/ilight/photos/index.html
Your complete guide to infrared photography.

Life
www.lifemag.com

View *Life* magazine's Picture of the Day, then link through to some of the world's most arresting pho-tographs. There's even more over at *Time*'s Picture Collection and Australia's Newsphotos:
www.thepicturecollection.com
www.newsphotos.com.au

 **Lomographic Society International**
www.lomography.com

Home of the Lomo, a clunky lo-fi camera that has an idiosyncratic charm. Relive the anticipation of going to collect your pictures from the shop and wondering what they actually look like. Or visit their online shop

for some weird and wonderful products such as com-pact multi-lensed and panoramic cameras.

 London Camera Exchange Group
www.lcegroup.co.uk

New & used cameras, lenses and accessories from this specialist photographic chain.

Masters of Photography
www.masters-of-photography.com

An excellent collection of the works of some of histo-ry's greatest snappers, from Berenice Abbott to Garry Winogrand. In addition to the images, there are links to articles and other websites with biographical and technical information.

Photodisc
creative.gettyimages.com/photodisc
Plunder these photos free, or pay for hi-res versions.

Photoblogs
www.photoblogs.org

There are thousands of stunning quality photoblogs out there; photoblogs.org is a community that pulls some of them together in one location. A good place to jump around from.

Photo Friday
www.photofriday.com

Each week they post a photo assignment. You can

Online photo albums

Got some snaps you'd like to show the world – or just your friends (through selective password access)? Upload them here:

Picture Trail www.picturetrail.com
Web Shots www.webshots.com
Yahoo! Photos photos.yahoo.com
Flickr www.flickr.com
Shutter Fly www.shutterfly.com
Image Shack imageshack.us
Foto Thing www.fotothing.com

interpret the week's theme in any way you like and then post the picture you took to your website and submit your link.

Photo.net
www.photo.net
Photography portal with galleries, reviews, forums, stolen equipment lists and tips & tutorials. More at:
www.photolinks.net
www.stilljournal.com
photography.about.com

PhotoZone
www.photozone.de
This site offers comparative analysis of cameras and lenses, and loads of technical information on all sorts of equipment.

Pinhole Visions
www.pinhole.com
A great site devoted to the art of pinhole photography, a primitive form of picture-taking that creates a dreamlike effect unattainable with conventional photography.

Polaroid
www.polaroid.com
The instant camera is still alive and well.

Shutterbug
www.shutterbug.net
The home of the American *Shutterbug* magazine includes a massive archive of past articles, product reviews, news, hints, galleries, competitions and more.

Take Better Photos
betterphotos.cjb.net
No-nonsense site offering tricks and tips on correcting common photographic errors, picking the best viewpoint, compensating for parallax, computer enhancement, etc, etc. For more serious (really serious) tuition at a cost, try Photo Seminars:
www.photo-seminars.com

UK Camera
www.ukcamera.com
Take a look here for contact details and links to over one thousand specialist camera stores, browseable by category or location.

Unphotographable
www.unphotographable.com
Street photographer Michael David Murphy's compelling and poignant descriptions of the scenes he found himself unable to shoot.

Year in the Life of Photojournalism
www.digitalstoryteller.com/YITL
Tag along with pros and see what they do day to day.

Politics & government

Most governmental departments, politicians, political aspirants and causes maintain websites to spread the word and further their various interests. To find your local rep or candidate, start at their party's homepage. These typically lie dormant unless there's a campaign in progress, but can still be a good source of contacts to badger. Government departments, on the other hand, tirelessly belch out all sorts of trivia right down to transcripts of ministerial radio interviews. So if you'd like to know about impending legislation, tax rulings, budget details and so forth, skip the party pages and go straight to the department. If you can't find its address through what's listed below, try:

Yahoo! dir.yahoo.com/Government
Open Directory dmoz.org/Society/Government

For the latest election night counts, check the breaking news sites (p.173). Below is a selection of the most useful starting points.

British Politics Links www.ukpol.co.uk
Green Party www.greenparty.org.uk
Labour www.labour.org.uk
Liberal Democrats www.libdems.org.uk
National Assembly for Wales www.wales.gov.uk
Natural Law www.natural-law-party.org.uk

Northern Ireland Assembly www.niassembly.gov.uk
Plaid Cymru www.plaidcymru.org
Prime Minister www.pm.gov.uk
Scottish National Party www.snp.org
Scottish Parliament www.scottish.parliament.uk
Sinn Fein www.sinnfein.ie
Social Democratic and Labour Party www.sdlp.ie
Socialist Party www.socialistparty.org.uk
Socialist Workers Party www.swp.org.uk
Tories www.conservatives.com
Ulster Unionist Party www.uup.org

Amnesty International
www.amnesty.org
Join the battle against brutal
regimes and injustice.

Antiwar
www.antiwar.com
Challenges US intervention in foreign affairs, especially in the Balkans and Middle East.

Bilderberg Group
www.bilderberg.org
Read about the people who really rule the world.

The British Monarchy
www.royal.gov.uk
Tune into the world's best-loved soap opera.

politics & government

British Politics Pages
www.ukpolitics.org.uk
News and history for politicos, with a great links page.

Center for the Moral Defense of Capitalism
www.moraldefense.com
Is greed still good in the Y2Ks? Maybe not good but legal, says Microsoft's last bastion of sympathy. Also: www.aynrand.org

Central Intelligence Agency
www.cia.gov
Want the inside story on political assassinations, arms deals, Colombian drug trades, spy satellites, phone tapping, covert operations, government-sponsored alien sex cults and the X-files? Well, guess what? Never mind, you won't go home without a prize – see:
www.copvcia.com

Communist Internet List
www.cominternet.org
Angry intellectuals and workers unite. Also visit: www.yclusa.org

The Complete Bushisms
slate.msn.com/default.aspx?id=76886
The sublime wit and wisdom of George Dubya.

The Conspiracy Theory Research List
www.ctrl.org
Certain people are up to something and, what's worse, they're probably all in it together. Click here for the biggest cover-ups of all time.
www.mt.net/~watcher

DirectGov
www.direct.gov.uk
Not to be confused with the ISP, this UK Online aims to be the place where people interact with the Government. Like most governmental policies, it seems pretty hazy and to get anywhere you have to dig far too hard.

Disinformation
www.disinfo.com
The dark side of politics, religious fervour, new science, along with current affairs you won't find in the papers.

Doonesbury
www.doonesbury.com
Over thirty years of Gary Trudeau's legendary political cartoon.

Electronic Frontier Foundation
www.eff.org
Protecting freedom of expression on the Internet.

ePolitix
www.epolitix.com
British politics portal.

Oliver Postgate
www.oliverpostgate.co.uk
Creator of Bagpuss and The Clangers shares his world view.

Fax Your MP
www.faxyourmp.com
Pester your local member through an Internet-to-fax gateway.

FBI FOIA Reading Room
foia.fbi.gov
FBI documents released as part of the Freedom of Information Act. Includes a few files on such celebrities as John Wayne, Elvis, Marilyn and the British Royals. Check out who's most wanted now at:
www.fbi.gov

Federation of American Scientists
www.fas.org
Heavyweight analysis of science, technology and public policy including national security, nuclear

weapons, arms sales, biological hazards, secrecy and space policy.

Foreign Report
www.foreignreport.com
Compact subscription newsletter with a track record of predicting international flashpoints well before the dailies.

Free Tibet
www.freetibet.org
Favourite site of The Beastie Boys and Richard Gere.

Freedom Forum
www.freedomforum.org
Organization dedicated to free-speech issues, news-room diversity and freedom of the press.

The Gallup Organization
www.gallup.com
Keep track of opinion trends and ratings.

Gates Foundation
www.gatesfoundation.org
See where the world's second richest man is spreading it around.

Gay & Lesbian Alliance against Defamation
www.glaad.org
Stand up against media stereotyping and discrimination against those deviating from the heterosexual norm. For more news, advice and dispatches from the activist front, try:
www.stonewall.org.uk
www.actupny.org

Gendercide
www.gendercide.org
Investigates mass killings where a single gender is singled out.

German Propaganda Archives
www.calvin.edu/cas/gpa
Who did you think you were kidding, Mr Hitler?

Political blogs

As you might expect, some of the best blogs to be found online are politically charged. Browse the eTalking directory to find your political allies:

eTalkinghead directory/etalkinghead.com

Some of the most interesting political blogs are those written by MPs and councillors, honestly:

Richard Allan richardallan.org.uk (Lib Dem)
Paul Cumming www.paulcumming.blogspot.com (Conservative)
Austin Mitchell www.austinmitchell.org (Labour)
Tom Watson www.tom-watson.co.uk (Labour)

For further commentary and insight, try:

Paul Anderson libsoc.blogspot.com
Bloggerheads www.bloggerheads.com/politicians.asp
British Politics britishspin.blogspot.com

Global Ideas Bank
www.globalideasbank.org
If you think you know better than the politicians, come and post your ideas for global change – who knows, they might even read it.

Grassroots.com
www.grassroots.com
Tracks (US) political action and election policies across the board, aided by *TV Nation* champ Michael Moore, whose homepage is also worth a look. Believe it or not, some people aren't so keen on Moore's activities, see MooreWatch.com:
www.michaelmoore.com
www.moorewatch.com

Greenpeace International
www.greenpeace.org
Rebels with many a good cause.

Hindu Holocaust Museum
www.mantra.com/holocaust
Contends that the massacre of Hindus during Muslim rule in India was of a scale unparalleled in history, yet it has largely gone undocumented.

InfoWar
www.infowar.com
Warfare issues from prank hacking to industrial espionage and military propaganda.

Jane's IntelWeb
intelweb.janes.com
Brief updates on political disturbances, terrorism, intelligence agencies and subterfuge worldwide. For a full directory of covert operations, see:
www.virtualfreesites.com/covert.html

Liberty
www.liberty-human-rights.org.uk
Championing human and civil rights in England and Wales. For a more global perspective, see Human Rights Watch:
www.hrw.org

Memeorandum
www.memeorandum.com
Constantly updated news digest centred around US political developments.

Meta Mute
www.metamute.org
Mute magazine investigates politics and culture from a post-internet perspective; their site augments this with articles, updates and resources. Well worth a look.

National Charities Information Bureau
www.ncib.org
Investigate before you donate, both with NCIB and the Charity Commission. Once you're convinced, give at CharitiesDirect.com:
www.charity-commission.gov.uk
www.charitiesdirect.com

National Forum on People's Differences
www.yforum.com
Toss around touchy topics such as race, religion and sexuality with a sincerity that is normally tabooed by political politeness.

One World
www.oneworld.net
Collates news from over 350 global justice organizations.

Open Secrets
www.opensecrets.org
Track whose money is oiling the wheels of US politics. More keeping 'em honest at:
www.commoncause.org

Oxfam
www.oxfam.org
Pitch in to fight poverty and inequality. Also see:
www.roughguide-betterworld.com

Political Arena
www.planetquake.com/politicalarena/c2k.htm
Stage American elections on Quake.

The Political Graveyard
www.politicalgraveyard.com
Find out where over 81,000 politicians, diplomats and judges are buried.

Political Leanings of Selected Cartoon Characters
www.unknown.nu/cartoon
Uncover the ideologies of those seemingly innocent Saturday morning fixtures.

Political Wire
politicalwire.com
In-depth political news aggregator that is US-heavy but which does cover international politics as well.

Politics Online
www.PoliticsOnline.com
It may be subtitled "Fundraising and Internet tools for

politics", but this is actually a good general political site, with an emphasis on how connectivity is changing the face of the game.

The Progressive Review
www.prorev.com
Washington's dirt dug up from all sides of the fence. For darker soil, try the RealChange.org site:
www.realchange.org

Protest.net – A Calendar of Protest Worldwide
protest.net
Find a nearby riot you can call your own.

Public Education Network
www.penpress.org
Frightening statistics about global inequality and political madness.

Serendipity
www.serendipity.li
Read detailed theories about the World Trade Center demolition, the war on drugs, London bombings, voting machines, and other such issues. See also:
www.infowars.com

Spin On
www.spinon.co.uk
Play games such as "Stay to the Right of Jack Straw", "Egg Prescott" and the "Hague Goes Trucking Simulator".

Spunk Press
www.spunk.org
All the anarchy you'll ever need, organized neatly and with reassuring authority. More of the same can be found at:
www.infoshop.org

This Modern World
www.thismodernworld.com
Archive of Tom Tomorrow's scathing political cartoon.

Tolerance.org
www.tolerance.org
Shining the public flashlight on hate groups and political forces that threaten to undermine democracy and diversity. See also:
www.publiceye.org
www.splcenter.org

UK Census
www.statistics.gov.uk
More statistics on the UK and its citizens than you'd care to know.

Undercurrents
www.undercurrents.org
Alternative political news and opinion.

US Presidential Candidates and their Evil Genes
www.nenavadno.com/usaelections2000.html
Biocybernetic criminals from the 33rd dimension take America.

YouGov
www.yougov.com
A good attempt at using the Internet to make government more accountable. There are columns and

comment from John Humphrys, Fay Weldon and Ian Hargreaves, plus constantly updated political news. The best features, though, are the People's Parliament, which allows users to vote on the same issues as parliament, a service to create e-petitions and GovDoctor, which identifies MPs, councillors and service managers.

ZNet
www.zmag.org
Fresh stuff from dissident writers around the world, including big names such as Chomsky.

Property

The Web is a great way to look for property to rent or buy. You can see hundreds of offerings in half an hour without even leaving your front room. Try the following sites as well as those of your local estate agents:

Accommodation Directory www.accommodation.com
Assertahome www.assertahome.com
Find A Property www.findaproperty.com
Home Sale www.home-sale.co.uk
Homefile www.homefileuk.co.uk
Homepages www.homepages.co.uk
Let's Direct www.letsdirect.co.uk
LondonHomeNet www.londonhomenet.com
NAEA www.naea.co.uk
Pavilions of Splendour www.heritage.co.uk
Property Live www.propertylive.co.uk
Property World www.propertyworld.com
Right Move www.rightmove.co.uk
Vebra www.vebra.com

For commercial property, try:

Comproperty www.comproperty.com

Anti Gazumping
www.anti-gazumping.co.uk
Protect yourself from property chain nightmares with this legal agreement. This and other documents also available over at Lawpack:
www.lawpack.co.uk

Big Yellow Self Storage
www.bigyellow.co.uk
Temporarily homeless? Dump all your belongings here til you get settled.

British Association of Removers
www.removers.org.uk
Search for a mover who meets the BAR's standards of service.

Ebuild
www.ebuild.co.uk
Self-build resources, including a UK plots database, sections on building regulations, planning permission, news, and a massive trade directory. There's also a discount book and magazine subscription store.

Estate Agents
www.estate-agents.co.uk
A no-nonsense database of UK estate agents.

Help I Am Moving
www.helpiammoving.com
Tries to remove the hassle from moving, with step-by-step guides on packing up, changing address, things for the kids to do, and a nationwide database of removal firms. Also try:
www.themovechannel.com

Don't buy a home without us

Home Check
www.homecheck.co.uk
An excellent service for prospective home buyers: type in your future postcode and it will tell you if you need to worry about subsidence, pollution, air quality, flood risk or if the Triads are likely to firebomb the flat below.

Homes Go Fast
www.homesgofast.com
Sell your property privately online.

iammoving.com
www.iammoving.com
Bulk-notify UK companies of your new address.

International Real Estate Digest
www.ired.com
This site helps you locate real estate listings, guides, and property-related services worldwide.

Mouse Price
www.mouseprice.com
The mouseprice.com database contains the current valuation and historical prices paid for over six million properties in England & Wales. The catch is you have to pay them for the information.

National Security Inspectorate
www.nsi.org.uk
Keep tabs on the guys installing your alarm. To make sure your lock doesn't get picked, check out:
www.locksmiths.co.uk

UpMyStreet
www.upmystreet.com
Astounding wealth of house prices, health, crime, schools, tax and other statistics on UK neighbourhoods. Mighty useful if you're shifting base.

Buy, sell & rent

Easier
www.easier.co.uk
A huge database of private and commercial properties up for private sale and rent. If you're looking for anything from an ex-council flat near Harrods to a pied à terre in Paris, there are online brochures and plenty of tips for both sellers and buyers.

08004Homes
www.08004homes.com
Property portal with excellent choice of channels, including one for interiors and another for the experts' view of the current housing market.

House Buying Guide
www.housebuyingguide.co.uk
Everything you need to know.

House Net
www.housenet.co.uk
Dealing with both private sellers and estate agents, this site has a vast number of properties on view, from seafront flats in Hove to a traditional farmhouse with stables and barns in Warwickshire. Small classified listings are free. Links to regional estate agents are useful, as are the insurance, removals and environmental check links.

Houseweb

www.houseweb.com

The site boasts 150,000 properties and features like auto-notify to let you know when a property matching your criteria comes up.

My Des Res

www.mydesres.com

By advertising here you can save a lot of money by foregoing agent's commission fees for both sales and lettings as buyers contact vendors directly without the need for a middleman. If you have never sold a property privately you'll find their guide useful.

Property Broker

www.propertybroker.co.uk

If you live within the M25 you can avoid the middle-man and advertise your property here for a flat fee of £137.

Property Finder

www.propertyfinder.co.uk

Search engine for sorting through the thousands of properties on estate agents' books.

Really Moving
www.reallymoving.com

Practical, well-designed portal that guides you through the whole house-moving process with skill and reassurance. Includes an e-mail service to remind you of all the things you must do when moving house, from commissioning a survey to forwarding your mail. There are also online quotes on services like removals and spring-cleaning your new home.

Rent Right
www.rentright.co.uk

UK property search with the emphasis on renting.

This is London

www.thisislondon.co.uk

Stylish site which not only has property listings but a London lifestyle guide. Listings include information on new developments as well as estate agent registered homes, with some fancy extras like a quick mortgage calculator and 3D tours of some properties.

Finance

For help with getting the best mortgage see our **Money and banking** section (p.154), or see what's recommended here:

Find www.find.co.uk

MoneySupermarket www.moneysupermarket.com/mortgages

UKMortgagesOnline www.ukmortgagesonline.com

John Charcol

www.charcolonline.co.uk

The Mortgage Wizard search engine scans 45 different mortgage lenders to find the right products for you – some of which are exclusive deals done with high-street names. It can also offer you a mortgage if you're one of those people many banks won't touch

– the self-employed, those with a poor credit history, or people wanting to buy to let.

Mortgage Future
www.mortgagefuture.co.uk
Mortgage tips and links to brokers in your area. More mortgage advice, information and calculators at: www.uk-mortgage-advisors.co.uk

Council Tenants' Advice Bureau
www.counciltenantsmortgages.co.uk
Information and mortgages for council tenants. Recommended by local authorities and housing associations

Direct Line
www.directline.com
Plenty of information here about Direct Line Household Buildings and Contents Insurance (including the whole policy document to download if you're really keen on small print). The basic outline of cover, including legal protection, leads you to a tailored quotation which you can accept and purchase online.

Ecology Building Society
www.ecology.co.uk
This mortgage lender is dedicated to promoting sustainable housing, handy if you're buying an energy-efficient house, restoring a dilapidated or derelict property or are involved in some ecological enterprise, private or commercial. Not the best rates, but you may get a loan on a project other lenders would run a mile from.

Easy Quote
www.easy-quote.co.uk
No Fuss insurance quotes from the company's respected insurance partners, including Northern Rock, CGU and Norwich Union.

Grove Insurance Services
www.grove-is.co.uk
Straightforward independent site offering quotations

on policies from over sixty different insurance companies, with advice on which is likely to be best for you.

Wise Money
www.wisemoney.com
Here you'll find quotes offered on household insurance, mortgages and other financial products. If you're serious about looking for a mortgage lender or insurer, this is a good place to start.

Unusual homes

Ken Lund's Islands for Sale
www.islandsforsale.com
Always dreamed of buying your very own island? Ken Lund's your man with plenty of dreams to choose from. He specialises in the stunning islands off the coast of British Columbia, but if you're after a slice of Caribbean or Pacific heaven, he can help you there too. For more opportunities for isolation, try Tropical Islands or World of Private Islands:
www.tropical-islands.com
www.vladi-private-islands.de

Pavilions of Splendour
www.heritage.co.uk
This company specialises in unusual and historic properties, often listed and even more often in need of a great deal of TLC. Since many properties have had preservation orders slapped on them, you have to be prepared to fork out vast wads of cash and spend weekends raking through architectural supply yards just to repair a window.

Radio & webcasts

Not only do almost all radio stations have a website, most now pipe their transmissions online using RealAudio and/or Windows Media Format. Both players come with in-built station directories along with Web-based event guides that are fine for starting out, but nowhere near complete.

RealGuide realguide.real.com
Windows Media Guide windowsmedia.com

Not enough? Then buy the *Rough Guide to Internet Radio* or try one of the specialist radio directories, which list physical radio stations with websites along with full-time stations that exist only online, normally lumped together by country or genre. If they don't provide a direct link to the live feed, visit the station's site and look for a button or link that says "live" or "listen".

BRS Web Radio www.web-radio.fm
ComFM www.comfm.fr/live/radio
Live Radio www.live-radio.net
Radio Jump www.radiojump.com
Radio Locator www.radio-locator.com
RadioNow www.radio-now.co.uk
Shoutcast www.shoutcast.com
Virtual Tuner www.virtualtuner.com

Apart from the traditional single-stream broadcasters, dozens of sites host multiple feeds. These might be live, on demand, on rotation, archived or one-off events. They tend to work more like inflight entertainment than radio.

Air Bubble www.airbubble.com
Anime Hardcore animehardcore.net
Betalounge www.betalounge.com
CD Now www.cdnow.com/radio
House of Blues www.hob.com
Live 365 www.live365.com
Yahoo! Radio radio.yahoo.com

There are thousands upon thousands of webcasters sending their signals into the ether. These are some of the more familiar names and some of the oddest:

Audio Blogs
wiki.monkeyfilter.com/index.php?title=MP3_Blog_
Listing
Here you can find a massive list of audio blogs covering all genres. Not strictly web radio but worth a look.

BBC Radio
www.bbc.co.uk/radio
Auntie online, with something for everyone.

De Concertzender
www.concertzender.nl
A real boon for lovers of "highbrow" music: jazz, classical and New Music from this Dutch terrestrial station.

Mercora

www.mercora.com

Social radio networking, create your own station for others to hear, or get recommendations based on your listening habits. Similar to Last FM: www.lastfm.com

MTV

www.mtv.com

It may not be radio, but it does have hundreds of video streams available.

NPR

www.npr.org

NPR (National Public Radio) is an internationally acclaimed producer and distributor of noncommercial news, talk, and entertainment programming. Over three hundred different channels available covering most subjects.

Swank Radio

www.swankradio.com

Space-age bachelor pad muzak for cocktail enthusiasts and Tiki lovers everywhere.

Totally Radio

www.totallyradio.com

Online radio with a variety of weekly shows encompassing hiphop, indie, jazz, techno and more.

Underheard

www.underheard.org

Collects together the best independent and community radio and pocasts in one place.

Van Halen Radio Network

www.vhradio.com

Yup, all Van Halen, all the time.

WFMU

www.wfmu.org

Lucky residents of the New York metropolitan area have been able to call this treasure theirs for thirty-

---

Podcasts

Podcasts are basically MP3 files that you can download onto your MP3 player or computer and listen to as radio. The neat thing about Podcasts is you can subscribe to them using either iTunes or some dedicated RSS-aggregating software:

iTunes www.apple.com/itunes
Doppler www.dopplerradio.net
iPodder www.ipodder.org

iTunes will also give you access to a massive Podcast directory within the iTunes Music Store. Still not satisfied? The sites below pull together recommended selections of what's out there, be it music, news, or other information.

Indie Podder www.ipodder.org
Podcast Alley www.podcastalley.com
Podcast Bunker www.podcastbunker.com
Podcast.net www.podcast.net

---

odd years. Now you can listen to the best freeform radio station on earth no matter where you live.

WNUR

www.wnur.org

Another great American station (from Chicago) covering experimental and local music better than nearly anyone else. For more strange music with a UK twist try Resonance: www.resonancefm.com

Xfm

www.xfm.co.uk

Catch London's indie station live online, all the time.

If you fancy setting up your own station or listening to the online equivalent of pirate radio, try:

Icecast.org www.icecast.org
Live365 www.live365.com

Reference

There's really only one place to go these days if you want an answer fast, and that's **Wikipedia** – the encyclopedia you can be a part of. As with all "wikis", the entries of this amazing resource (quarter of a million and growing) are user-editable, so if you see a mistake or a misplaced semicolon, you can simply change it. This collaborative approach has created a surprisingly comprehensive and accurate multi-language encyclopedia, which, due to the "open-content" arrangement, will be freely available to the public until the end of time.

Wikipedia www.wikipedia.org

With the Net threatening the very foundations of the encyclopedia industry, it should come as no surprise to find most of the household names well entrenched online. While they're not all entirely free, they're certainly cheaper and more up-to-date than their bulky paper equivalents.

Britannica www.eb.com
Columbia www.bartleby.com/65
Encarta www.encarta.com
Macquarie www.macnet.mq.edu.au

Here's the best of the rest:

Acronym Finder
www.acronymfinder.com
Before you follow IBM, TNT and HMV into initializing your company's name, make sure it doesn't mean something blue. More here:
www.ucc.ie/info/net/acronyms/acro.html

All Experts
www.allexperts.com
Ask any question and let unpaid experts do the thinking. For more answers to those burning questions, try:
www.askme.com

Alternative Dictionary
www.notam.uio.no/~hcholm/altlang
Bucket your foreign chums in their mother tongue.

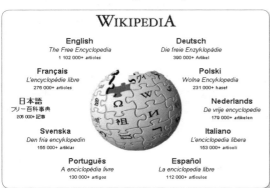

WIKIPEDIA

English
The Free Encyclopedia
1 102 000+ articles

Deutsch
Die freie Enzyklopädie
390 000+ Artikel

Français
L'encyclopédie libre
276 000+ articles

Polski
Wolna Encyklopedia
231 000+ haset

日本語
フリー百科事典
205 000+ 記事

Nederlands
De vrije encyclopedie
179 000+ artikelen

Svenska
Den fria encyklopedin
155 000+ artiklar

Italiano
L'enciclopedia libera
153 000+ articoli

Português
A enciclopédia livre
130 000+ artigos

Español
La enciclopedia libre
112 000+ artículos

American ASL Dictionary
www.handspeak.com
Learn sign language through this site of simple animations.

Anagram Genius
www.anagramgenius.com
Recycle used letters.

Answers
www.answers.com
A powerful reference tool: type in a term and you'll immediately get definitions, pronunciation, explanations and more. Unfortunately, anything more than two weeks' use will cost you.

Aphorisms Galore
www.ag.wastholm.net
Sound clever by repeating someone else's lines.

Babelfish Translator
babelfish.altavista.com/translate.dyn
Translate text, including webpages, in seconds. Though run some text back and forth a few times and you'll end up with something that wouldn't look out of place on a Japanese T-shirt.

Bartleby Reference
www.bartleby.com/reference
Free access to several contemporary and classic reference works such as the American *Heritage* dictionaries, *Columbia Encyclopedia*, Fowler's *King's English*, Emily Post's *Etiquette*, the *Cambridge History of English and American Literature* and *Gray's Anatomy*.

Biography
www.biography.com
Recounting more than 25,000 lives.

Calculators Online
www.math.com
Awesome collection of online tools.

Slang dictionaries
Aussie Slang www.aussieslang.com
Cockney Rhyming Slang www.cockneyrhymingslang.co.uk
Playground Slang www.odps.org
Modern/Web Slang www.slangsite.com
A Prisoner's Dictionary dictionary.prisonwall.org
Pseudo Dictionary www.pseudodictionary.com
Hardboiled Slang www.miskatonic.org/slang.html
Urban Dictionary www.urbandictionary.com

Cliché Finder
www.westegg.com/cliche
Submit a word or phrase to find out how not to use it.

Earthstation1
www.earthstation1.com
The twentieth century captured in sound and vision.

Encyclopedia Mythica
www.pantheon.org
Hefty album of mythology, folklore and legend.

Famous Quotations Network
www.famous-quotations.com
Perk up essays and letters with a witticism from Oscar Wilde or a Senegalese proverb. For more quotes, try: www.quotationspage.com

Find Articles
www.findarticles.com
No fuss, no muss search engine of more than three hundred magazines and journals. The results are all printable and free.

How Stuff Works
www.howstuffworks.com
Learn the secrets behind fake tans, animal camouflage and cable modems.

reference

InfoPlease
www.infoplease.com
Handy, all-purpose almanac for stats and trivia.

Itools
www.itools.com
All the search resources you need in one place. More at refdesk:
www.refdesk.com

Librarian's Index
www.lii.org
Naturally there are oodles of reference portals brimming with helpful reference tools. These are some of the best:
www.libraryspot.com
dmoz.org/Reference
www.refdesk.com
dir.yahoo.com/reference

Megaconverter 2
www.megaconverter.com/mega2
Calculate everything from your height in angstroms to the pellets of lead per ounce of buckshot needed to bring down an overcharging consultant.

Nonsensicon
www.nonsensicon.com
Non-existent words and their meanings.

Oxford Reference
www.oxfordreference.com
Mind-blowing reference library of some one hundred titles now online. Unfortunately, you have to subscribe.

Questia
www.questia.com
A contender for the title of world's biggest library, this site has the full contents of nearly half a million books and journals.

Reality Clock
www.realityclock.com
An ever-expanding source of statistics, from the bizarre and shocking to the mundane.

RhymeZone
www.rhymezone.com
Get a hoof up in putting together a classy love poem.

Roget's Thesaurus
www.thesaurus.com
New format; useless as ever.

Skeptic's Dictionary
www.skepdic.com
Punch holes in mass-media funk and pseudosciences such as homeopathy, astrology and iridology.

The Straight Dope
www.straightdope.com
Cecil Adams's answers to hard questions. Find out how to renounce your US citizenship, what "Kemosabe" means and the difference between a warm smell of colitas and colitis.

Strunk's Elements of Style
www.bartleby.com/141
The complete classic of English usage in a nutshell, though unfortunately not the latest edition. For more on grammar and style:
www.edunet.com/english/grammar
www.garbl.com

Symbols
www.symbols.com
Ever woken up with a strange sign tattooed on your buttocks? Here's where to find what it means without calling in Agent Mulder.

Technorati
www.technorati.com
Search weblogs from here.

What is?
www.whatis.com
Unravel cumbersome computer and Internet jargon without having even more thrown at you. Also visit the wonderful Webopedia:
www.webopedia.com

Whoohoo
www.whoohoo.co.uk
If you come from Berwick and find yourself in the East End unable to understand a word anyone says, this site may be of help.

The Why Files
whyfiles.org
The science behind the headlines.

World Atlas
www.worldatlas.com
Maps, flags, latitude and longitude finder, population growth and so on – though you might prefer the maps on paper. For more try:
www.nationalgeographic.com/mapmachine
dmoz.org/Reference/Maps

World Factbook
www.odci.gov/cia/publications/factbook
Information for spies from the CIA.

Xrefer
www.xrefer.com
Consult this site to query a broad selection of prominent reference works from Oxford University Press, Houghton Mifflin, Penguin, Macmillan, Bloomsbury and Market House Books.

Learn a language
Most free online language lessons serve only as an introduction, while there are many more rigorous courses available at a price from established vendors such as **Linguaphone** (www.linguaphone.co.uk). It's also worth checking **Wikibooks** (en.wikibooks.org) for comprehensive free language courses. Below are a handful of free introductory sites to get you started:

Arabic i-cias.com/babel/arabic
BBC www.bbc.co.uk/languages
French www.bonjour.com
German For Travellers www.germanfortravellers.com
The Japanese Tutor www.japanese-online.com
StudySpanish.com www.studyspanish.com
Word Reference www.wordreference.com

Yellow Pages
www.yell.com
If you're too lazy to flip through the book.

YourDictionary.com
www.yourdictionary.com
For one-point access to over a thousand dictionaries across almost every language. Try also Dictionary.com, the Free Dictionary and One Look:
www.dictionary.com
www.thefreedictionary.com
www.onelook.com

Relationships, dating & friendship

The Internet is the biggest singles bar humankind has ever created: with millions and millions of users from around the world, even the most love-lorn are bound to find someone worth cyber-flirting with. However, it's worth bearing in mind that the World Wide Web is no different from the real world and there are plenty of scam artists, hustlers, leeches and other unsavoury characters lurking in unsuspected corners. By all means enjoy dropping virtual handkerchiefs to prospective suitors, but keep your wits about you. Before engaging in any social intercourse on the Net, go to Wildx Angel (www.wildxangel.com) for advice on the safest way to go on the pull online.

To help you on your way, here are some of the Web's biggest dating agencies:

Dateline www.dateline.co.uk
Dating Direct www.datingdirect.com
Elite Dating www.elite-dating.co.uk
Friendfinder www.friendfinder.com
Lavalife www.lavalife.com
Lovefinder www.lovefinder.co.uk
Match.com www.match.com
SocialNet www.relationships.com
UDate www.udate.com
UK Singles www.uksingles.co.uk

To find a chat room, try a chat portal such as:

The Chat Room Directory www.webarrow.net/chatindex
Chat Shack Network chatshack.net
The Ultimate Chatlist www.chatlist.com

Or try the Open Directory's chat portal list:

Open Directory dmoz.org/Computers/Internet/Chat

43 Things
www.43things.com
Make a list of 43 things you've always wanted to do and meet people with similar ambitions.

Cyberspace Inmates
www.cyberspace-inmates.com
Strike up an email romance with a prison inmate – maybe even one on Death Row.

Dating Directories
www.singlesites.com
Come aboard, they're expecting you.

The Divorce Support Page
www.divorcesupport.com
Lots of friendly ears and shoulders to cry on.

Friends Reunited
www.friendsreunited.co.uk
You haven't forgotten. Now track them down one by one. More people who teased you in the common room are at:
www.classmates.com

The Hugging Site
members.tripod.com/~hugging
The history of embracing, hugging stories and tips to improve your cuddling technique.

Love Calculator
www.lovecalculator.com
Enter your respective names to see if you're compatible.

Pen Pal Directory
dir.yahoo.com/Social_Science/Communications/
Writing/Correspondence/Pen_Pals
Exchange email with strangers.

The Rejection Line
www.lazystudent.co.uk/rejectline.html
Let the professionals break it to that not-so-special someone.

Romance 101
www.rom101.com
Chat-up lines, compatibility tests and advice from men to women such as "Never buy a 'new' brand of beer because 'it was on sale.'"

Secret Admirer
www.secretadmirer.com
Find out whether your secret crush digs you back. More stalking at:
www.ecrush.com

Subster
www.snubster.com
Make lists of the people who are dead to you. And then snub them.

So There
www.sothere.com
A place to post your parting shots.

Swoon
www.swoon.com
Dating, mating and relating.

Social networks

Touted by many as the next big Internet revolution, social networks are designed to cultivate every type of relationship, from friendship and romance to business partnerships. They're based on the idea of "degrees of separation". You set up a list of your friends or colleagues and invite them to join and do the same. Soon a network is established where you can make contact with people you may not know directly, but you know are "friends of friends", "friends of friends of friends", and so on. Most also include sub-networks combining people of similar interests, occupations and the like.

Many such networks are still pretty IT- and new-media focused, but more are appearing all the time. Here are a few of the bigger networking sites worth visiting:
Ecademy www.ecademy.com
Friendster www.friendster.com
Myspace www.myspace.com
Orkut www.orkut.com
Tribe www.tribe.net

Tips for Dating Emotional Cripples
www.grrl.com/bipolar.html
The site all women must visit.

Way Too Personal
www.waytoopersonal.com
Wild and woolly adventures in Internet dating.

Weddings in the Real World
www.theknot.com
Prepare to jump the broom – or untie the knot:
www.divorcesource.com
www.absolutedivorce.com

We Want Fun
www.wewantfun.co.uk
Adult dating agency for adults. They want fun. Adult fun.

Science & nature

Science

To keep abreast of science news and developments stop by **Scitech**, which aggregates stories from the leading scientific media:

Scitech Daily Review www.scitechdaily.com

Or go straight to one of the numerous science journals, many of which let you sign up for daily, weekly or monthly news emails:

Archeology www.archaeology.org
British Medical Journal www.bmj.com
Bulletin of Atomic Scientists www.bullatomsci.org
Discover www.discover.com
Discovery Channel www.discovery.com
Edge www.edge.org
Highwire Press highwire.stanford.edu
The Lancet www.thelancet.com
National Geographic www.nationalgeographic.com
Nature www.nature.com
New Scientist www.newscientist.com
Popular Mechanics www.popularmechanics.com
Popular Science www.popsci.com
Science à GoGo www.scienceagogo.com
Science Magazine www.sciencemag.org
Science News www.sciencenews.org
Scientific American www.scientificamerican.com

The Scientist www.the-scientist.com
Skeptical Inquirer www.csicop.org/si
Technology Review www.techreview.com

Looking for something specific or a range of sites within a strand? Try searching a directory:

Hypography www.hypography.com
Open Directory dmoz.org/Science
SciSeek www.sciseek.com
Treasure Troves of Science www.treasure-troves.com
Yahoo dir.yahoo.com/science

Albert Einstein Online

www.westegg.com/einstein
An Albert Einstein portal with links to biographies, quotes, articles and essays, photos and other pages related to *Time* magazine's Man of the Century.

Amusement Park Physics

www.learner.org/exhibits/parkphysics
If your kid has absolutely no interest in potential and kinetic energy, send them to this fantastic site for the coolest science lesson on the Web, and give them the chance to design their own rollercoaster.

AnthroNet
www.anthro.net
Gateway to the world of anthropology, archeology and other subjects in the field of social science.

Battlebots
www.battlebots.com
Robots kick ass. Or for a scaled-up version visit Survival Research Laboratories.
www.srl.org

Brainwave Generator
www.bwgen.com
Tune in, turn on, zonk out.

Chemistry.org.uk
www.liv.ac.uk/Chemistry/Links/link.html
The chemistry section of the WWW Virtual Library has some 8500 links to chemistry sites. Advanced chemists should check out ChemWeb (www.chemweb.com) and its Available Chemical Directory of 278,000 compounds (you need to subscribe to gain access).

Cool Robot of the Week
ranier.hq.nasa.gov/telerobotics_page/coolrobots.html
Clever ways to get machines to do our dirty work. For a directory of simulators, combat comps, clubs and DIY bots, direct your agent to:
www.robotcafe.com

Dangerous Laboratories
www.dangerouslaboratories.org
Definitely don't try this at home.

Exploratorium
www.exploratorium.edu
An online science museum. With over 15,000 pages and interactive exhibits, webcasts and movies.

Genewatch
www.genewatch.org
Dusting crops for genetic fingerprints.

Gray's Anatomy Online
www.bartleby.com/107
The complete edition of the essential anatomical text. Or for some samples from the life's work of anatomist Frank Netter MD visit
www.graphicwitness.com/netter/

Half Bakery
www.halfbakery.com
Where lighter than air sausages rub shoulders with evil laugh-activated hand dryers.

science & nature

History of Mathematics
www-groups.dcs.st-andrews.ac.uk/~history
The life and times of various numerical bright sparks.

HotAir – Annals of Improbable Research
www.improbable.com
Science gone too far, or around the bend. Includes the Ig Nobel awards for achievements that cannot, or should not, be reproduced.

How Does a Thing Like That Work?
www.pitt.edu/~dwilley/Show/menu.html
Entertaining physics demonstration experiments.

How Stuff Works
www.howstuffworks.com
Unravel the mysterious machinations behind all sorts of stuff from Christmas to cruise missiles.

Interactive Frog Dissection
teach.virginia.edu/go/frog
Pin down a frog, grab a scalpel and follow the pictures.

Jet Propulsion Laboratory
www.jpl.nasa.gov
Keep up to date with NASA's space program and the progress of deep space exploration. Including the Cassini probe's visit to Saturn:
saturn.jpl.nasa.gov
solarsystem.nasa.gov

The Lab
www.abc.net.au/science
ABC science news and program info with Q&As from Aussie pop-science superstar, Dr Karl Kruszelnicki.

The Lifter Experiments Home Page
jnaudin.free.fr/lifters/main.htm
Make your own anti-gravity device out of some tin foil and sticks, oh, and a 30,000 Volt generator. You can read the science behind and watch video clips of electrostatic lifters being tested. See also:
www.americanantigravity.com

MadSciNet: 24-hour Exploding Laboratory
www.madsci.org
Collective of more than a hundred scientific smarty-pantses set up specifically to answer your dumb questions. More at:
www.ducksbreath.com
www.wsu.edu/DrUniverse
www.sciam.com/askexpert
www.sciencenet.org.uk

MIT Media Labs
www.media.mit.edu
If you've read *Being Digital* or any of Nicholas Negroponte's *Wired* columns, you'll know he has

some pretty tall ideas about our electronic future. Here's where he gets them.

National Inventors Hall of Fame
www.invent.org
Homepage of a museum based in Akron, Ohio, dedicated to the world's most important inventors. Includes short biographies and pictures of luminaries such as Thomas Edison, Enrico Fermi and Louis Pasteur. For more modern inventions, go to Inventions And Technologies:
www.inventions-tech.com/epanel.htm
And for questionable inventions see Patently Absurd!:
www.patent.freeserve.co.uk

Netsurfer Science
www.netsurf.com/nss
Subscribe to receive weekly bulletins on science and technology sites.

Nobel e-Museum
nobelprize.org
Read all about Nobel prize-winners.

Rocketry Online
www.rocketryonline.com
Take on NASA at its own game.

Skeptics Society
www.skeptic.com
Don't try to pull a swift one on this crowd.

The Soundry
library.thinkquest.org/19537
A fun introduction to the science of acoustics.

Space Sounds
spacesounds.com
Listen to the 'sounds' of Saturn's rings, black holes, the heartbeat of the Sun and more. It's unclear whether these are actual signals from space or if it's just some guy with a synthesiser as there's no details on the site about how these sounds were generated. But it's

fun to listen to. Its sister sites include Storm Sounds (plausible) and Dinosaur Sounds (less plausible).

Strange Science: The Rocky Road to Modern Paleontology and Biology
www.strangescience.net
A great site exploring the fallout of science's paradigm wars.

Time Travel
freespace.virgin.net/steve.preston
"We discuss many of the common objections to time travel and we show that these objections are without foundation."

Try Science
tryscience.org
Expand your kids' scientific explorations beyond trying to blow up the kitchen or torturing spiders.

VoltNet
www.voltnet.com
Celebrate the power of electricity by blowing things up.

WebElements
www.webelements.com
It's the periodic table. More elemental knowledge at:
www.chemsoc.org/viselements

Weird Science and Mad Scientists
www.eskimo.com/~billb/weird.html
Free energy, Tesla, anti-gravity, aura, cold fusion, parapsychology and other strange scientific projects and theories.

Why Files
whyfiles.news.wisc.edu
Reports on the science behind current news stories.

Nature

3D Insects
www.ento.vt.edu/~sharov/3d/3dinsect.html
Whizz around a selection of 3D bugs. They're not real insects but at least they don't have pins through their backs. Also see what's creeping and crawling at:
insects.org

African Wildlife Foundation
www.awf.org
Great site covering everything from the aardvark to the zebra.

Animal Diversity Web
animaldiversity.ummz.umich.edu
Database of animal history, classification, distribution and conservation. More at Natureserve:
www.natureserve.org

Aquatic Network
www.aquanet.com
A good site promoting sustainable aquaculture, with some great photography and solid information saving it from being too earnest.

ARKive
www.arkive.org
Electronic archive of the world's endangered species.

Birding
birding.about.com
Birds are such regional critters that one site couldn't hope to cover them all. Use this page to find the chirpiest one on your block. More fine feathered friends listed at:
www.camacdonald.com/birding
dmoz.org/Recreation/Birding

Birds of Britain
www.birdsofbritain.co.uk
Webzine devoted to our fine feathered friends, with an illustrated guide of around a hundred species.

Cetacea.org
www.cetacea.org
Excellent encyclopedic source of information on whales, dolphins and porpoises.

Dinosaur Interplanetary Gazette
www.dinosaur.org
It may be as slow and cumbersome as a brontosaurus stuck in the LaBrea tar pits, but patience does pay off with a wealth of information and features.

The Electronic Zoo
netvet.wustl.edu/e-zoo.htm
Up and running since 1993, this virtual menagerie is the best collection of animal-related links on the Web.

EMBL Reptile Database
www.embl-heidelberg.de/~uetz/LivingReptiles.html
Slither through for info on everything from turtles to amphisbaenae.

eNature.com
www.enature.com
Vibrant field guides to North American flora and fauna.

Field Trips
www.field-guides.com/vft/index.htm
A neat idea, if not perfectly executed: visit this site and take virtual field trips involving deserts, oceans, hurricanes, sharks, fierce creatures, salt marshes, volcanoes and other natural wonders.

Forces of Nature
library.thinkquest.org/C003603
Thinkquest's student-designed website devoted to avalanches, droughts, landslides, earthquakes and other natural disasters.

ForestWorld
www.forestworld.com
Timber tales from both sides of the 'dozer. More here forests.org

Great Cats of the World
www.greatcatsoftheworld.com
The homepage of the Bridgeport Nature Center in Texas functions as a mini-encyclopedia of lions, tigers, leopards and cougars.

Insects on the Web
www.insects.org
Definitely not one for your little girl, this excellent educational resource of creepy-crawlies features some rather too detailed photography of everyone's least favourite bugs.

The Natural History Museum
www.nhm.ac.uk
Plenty of features and detailed information here surrounding exhibits at the museum itself.

Nessie on the Net
www.lochness.co.uk
Watch the Loch Ness webcam, spot the monster and win £1000.

Predator Urines
www.predatorpee.com
Bewitch neighbouring Jack Russells with a dab of bobcat balm or true blue roo poo:
www.roopooco.com

Sea turtle migration-tracking
www.cccturtle.org/satwelc.htm
Adopt a bugged sea reptile and follow its trail.

World Wide Fund For Nature
www.wwf.org.uk
Teach your kids that the WWF isn't all about pile drivers and steroid cases in skimpy shorts. More animal lovers at the WSPA and the RSPCA:
www.rspca.org.uk
www.wspa.org.uk

ZSL
www.zsl.com
The Zoological Society of London's site is packed with features, news, and information. From here you can buy tickets to London Zoo or Whipsnade, find out about the new Biota project, adopt an animal, or book a 'keeper for a day' expereience.

Silver surfers

Age Concern
www.ageconcern.org.uk
Excellent site with a library of factsheets concerning issues for the over-50s, plus plenty of lifestyle content and forums on the living room section.

BBC Health: Health at 50
www.bbc.co.uk/health/50plus
Easily among the best of the BBC sites. The advice is honest and there are no bells or whistles.

Entitled To
www.entitledto.co.uk
Online calculators work out what benefits you should be getting. More information over at Direct Gov:
www.direct.gov.uk/Over50s

FiftyOn
www.fiftyon.co.uk
A portal for 50-pluses, with career advice and a vacancies database it maintains for older jobseekers.

Hell's Geriatrics
www.hellsgeriatrics.co.uk
Grow old disgracefully. Then fight ageism here:
www.wiseowls.co.uk

The Open University
www.open.ac.uk
You're never too old to learn new tricks. More adult education from lifelong learning and u3a:
www.lifelonglearning.co.uk
www.u3a.org.uk

Retirement Matters
www.retirement-matters.co.uk
Online magazine specializing in news, reviews and information for over-50s.

Saga
www.saga.co.uk
Services for the over-50s, including Saga magazine, with content from the current issue.

Senior Site
www.seniorsite.com
American online community with plenty of health and lifestyle advice, including an excellent section on protecting yourself against "senior scams". Specifically for older women there's Third Age:
www.thirdage.com

Seniority.co.uk
www.seniority.co.uk
Bustling online senior community portal.

Silver Surfers
www.silversurfers.net
If you can get past the jarring colour scheme you'll find useful links for everything from arts to travel.

Write a Senior Citizen
www.writeseniors.com
Penpals for seniors.

Sports

For live calls, scores, tables, draws, teams, injuries and corruption enquiries across major sports, try the newspaper sites (p.173), breaking news services (also p.173) or sporting specialists such as:

BBC Sport news.bbc.co.uk/sport
Eurosport www.eurosport.com
SkySports www.skysports.com
Sportal (INT) www.sportal.com
Sporting Life www.sporting-life.com
Sports.com (Euro) sports.com

But if your interest even slightly borders on obsession you'll find far more satisfaction on the pages of something more one-eyed. For clubs and fan sites, drill down through **Yahoo!** and the **Open Directory**. They won't carry everything, but what you'll find will lead you to the right forces:

Open Directory dmoz.org/Sports
Yahoo! Sports dir.yahoo.com/recreation/sports

If you can't get to the telly or are looking for webcasts of that crucial Rymans League derby, check **Sport On Air** for listings of streaming audio coverage on the Web.:

Sport On Air www.sportonair.com

If you're after in-depth news, reviews, listings and results for specific sports, try one of these pages:

American Football
www.nfl.com

Athletics
www.athletix.org
www.ukathletics.net

Baseball
www.mlb.com
www.baseball1.com

Basketball
www.nba.com
www.hosana.co.uk

Boxing
www.secondsout.com

Cricket
www.cricinfo.com
www.334notout.com
www.wisden.com

Cycling
www.cyclingnews.com
www.mtbbritain.co.uk

Football
www.footballgroundguide.co.uk
www.football365.com
www.rivals.net

www.soccerassociation.com
soccernet.espn.go.com
www.wsc.co.uk
www.soccerbase.com
www.teamtalk.com

Golf
www.golfweb.com
www.lpga.com
www.onlinegolf.co.uk

Motorsport
www.atlasf1.com
www.formula1.com
www.fia.com
www.indyracingleague.com
www.motograndprix.com
www.nascar.com
www.worldmotorsport.com
www.worldrally.net

Rugby
www.planet-rugby.com
www.rleague.com
www.ozleague.com
www.scrum.com

Sailing
www.smartguide.com
www.madforsailing.com

Skiing
www.skicentral.com
www.skiclub.co.uk
www.snowboarding.com

Snooker
www.worldsnooker.com
www.snookerclub.com

Surfing
www.surflink.com
www.britsurf.co.uk

www.eyeball-surfcheck.co.uk
www.coastalwatch.com

Swimming
www.swimmersworld.com
www.webswim.com

Tennis
www.tennis.com
www.wimbledon.org

General

 Fitness Peak
www.fitnesspeak.co.uk
Leeds-based company offering an extensive range of gym equipment from exercise bikes and heart monitors to treadmills.

 JD Sports
www.jdsports.co.uk
JD Sports has all the sportswear and accessories you need. Whether you want to head down the gym or just hang out on street corners scaring old folk, there's all the branded trackies, hoodies and caps you could need, with prices across the board.

Kitbag
www.kitbag.com
Visit one of the biggest and best known sports shops on the Internet and you'll find a huge range of football, rugby, Formula 1 and cricket kits, with accompanying accessories.

London 2012
www.london2012.org
The Olympics is coming! Don't worry, you've still got 5 years to move out of London.

M and M Sports
www.mmsports.co.uk
M and M Sports' highly competitive prices make it worth checking out; there were massive reductions of over half price when we visited, and it has a very good children's range.

Muaythai Online
www.muaythaionline.net
The wholesome home of kickboxing.

 Newitts
www.newitts.com
The UK's largest mail order supplier of sports equipment offers a vast range of clothes and equipment from boxing to bowls and tennis to trampolining.

Raise Your Game
www.bbc.co.uk/wales/raiseyourgame
Motivational website from the BBC aimed at helping you get the most out of sport.

 Simply Sports
www.simplysports.co.uk
This lively site offers more than most sports shops, including pretty much every net, hoop or goalpost used in mainstream sport. It also has exercise bikes, a sports bookstore and tennis ball machines. It's one of the best sites for outdoor or indoor games, with backgammon, chess, archery, croquet, table tennis and table football on offer.

Sportal
www.sportal.com
Broadband content with video and audio streams from the world of sport.

 Sportzwear
www.sportzwear.com
Bargain branded sportswear from Adidas to Umbro.

 Sweatband.com
www.sweatband.com
This is a well-designed site divided into tennis, squash, cricket, rugby and football shops.

Footwear

 Sportsshoes Unlimited
www.sportsshoes.co.uk
Sportsshoes Unlimited claims to be the largest sports shop in the world, with four thousand different styles of footwear. There's an enormous choice for men, women and kids, including top-brand trainers, specific sport shoes and even a Big Foot collection.

Specialist

 9 Dart Shop
www.9dartshop.com
Now all you need is a crate of beer. More darts here:
www.darts.co.uk
www.dartscorner.co.uk

Acme Whistles
www.acmewhistles.co.uk
Acme Whistles is the online trading name for Messrs J Hudson & Co of Birmingham, purveyors of police, hunting, bird-watching, marine and sports and orchestral whistles for over 130 years.

Avalon Guns
www.avalon-guns.com
Green wellies, cleaning equipment, protection togs, camouflage, books, videos, guns and ammo to appeal to your inner Dick Chaney. Good deals for hunting and shooting enthusiasts.

Denney Diving
www.divingdirect.co.uk
If you're going diving, you'll find all you need under one virtual roof at Denney Diving. Excellent for all diving goods, it has an exhaustive range of fins, masks, protective clothing and technical equipment.

The Kite Shop
www.kiteshop.co.uk
Whatever kind of kite you're looking for – sports kites, power kites or kites for beginners – you can't do much better than this. A quick flit round this site reveals a comprehensive selection of the best the kiting world has to offer, including visuals and full individual specifications.

Merlin Archery Centre
www.merlinarcherycentre.co.uk
If you were going to assassinate the president this is undoubtedly the coolest way to get the job done. Sadly no cyanide or explosive-tipped arrows but if your aim is true you won't need them.

Sweatshop
www.sweatshop.co.uk
Online branch of high-street aerobic and cross-training specialists. A bright and colourful interface guides you through history, jobs, sports injury advice or straight to a selection of equipment (running clothes, shoes, accessories, etc). There are also heaps of sale items.

Tennis Nuts
www.tennisnuts.com
A site for tennis enthusiasts by tennis enthusiasts. Also on offer are badminton and squash rackets and some sports shoes.

Fishing

Beekay International
www.beekay.force9.co.uk
The carp is king at Beekay International. You can buy carp books, carp videos, carp T-shirts and bait from the Kevin Maddocks Carp Bait Range. Trout and pike do occasionally get a look-in, but there's no mistaking the star fish here.

Bonefish Adventure
www.bonefishadventure.com
If you want to fly fish for bonefish, you can buy the equipment and even a bonefishing holiday in the

Bahamas here. Folding rods, reels, luggage and tropical accessories are all available.

Flymail
www.flymail.com

If Mini Nobblers and Boobys are your thing, this is the place find a huge selection of flies for every (fishing) occasion.

Harris Angling Company
www.harrisangling.co.uk

Hundreds of types of lures are on sale here, along with books, videos, hooks, lines and collectables. You'll also find a guide about what tackle to use where, and a bargains of the day section.

Sharpe's of Aberdeen
www.sharpes.net/sharpes/home.html

Founded in 1920, Sharpe's sells high-class rods, reels, nets and accessories. This site features in-depth product descriptions and background info on everything from Stealth Rods to the Millennium Bug (a high-tech fly that emits subtle light and the "correct frequency of sound").

Football

Christie's
www.christies.com

The auction house doesn't just sell Fabergé eggs, the international gavel banger also puts a hell of a lot of football memorabilia under the hammer, including the shirt in which Sir Geoff Hurst scored that hat-trick in 1966.

Football Directory
www.footballdirectory.co.uk

You cannot bypass this site if you want to know where on the Web you can find someone to sell you (in no particular order) floodlights, club ties, footballing figurines…This site even tells you where to buy a

trophy as well as pointing you to the usual stuff like replica kits.

JJB Sports
www.jjb.co.uk

General sports retailer with a range of replica kits for premiership and international teams amongst other sportswear and equipment.

Kitbag
www.kitbag.com

The usual selection of replica football and rugby kits. The range of extras is impressive.

Ray Taylor's Football Souvenirs
www.footballsouvenirs.co.uk

Whether it's a team-specific lunchbox or a bath towel bearing the colours of the club closest to your heart, Ray Taylor could fill that yawning gap in your life.

Signs of the times
members.aol.com/ianphipps

This virtual extravaganza of celebrity autographs has a very good football section. Worth perusing along with www.autograph-hunter.com.

Soccer Books
www.soccer-books.co.uk

For Books, a great collection of videos, that immortal CD of famous Scottish World Cup anthems and the little red book of Chinese football.

Steve Earl football programmes
www.footballprogs.freeserve.co.uk

You'll never find another football programme site quite like this. This is probably the nearest equivalent on the Internet to a garage stuffed full of the kind of stuff mum was always trying to get you throw away.

Toffs
www.toffs.com

Toffs stands for The Old Fashioned Football Shirts company. This is a treat for those who remember the game before clubs changed strips more often than some fans changed socks.

ARSENAL 1927 CUP FINAL
Product Code: 1001
→ Tell a Friend
→ Write A Review
+ Enlarge image

When Saturday Comes
www.wsc.co.uk

Lurking on the When Saturday Comes website, a small but perfectly formed selection of WSC T-shirts plus a handful of books very much reflecting the independent magazine's take on the beautiful game.

Golf

Easygolf.co.uk
www.easygolf.co.uk

An extensive online catalogue of golf equipment.

Golf Bidder
www.golfbidder.co.uk

Tidy site dedicated to auctioning off golf-related merchandise, including clubs, balls, holidays, tickets and collectibles.

Nevada Bob
www.nevadabob.co.uk

The range at Nevada Bob is vast and you can search by item or brand.

St Andrews Golf
www.standrewsgolf.co.uk

The 'home of golf' on the Net doesn't let the game or the club down. There is a useful golf clinic and plenty to buy, from branded apparel to books.

Snow sports

Edge 2 Edge
www.edge2edge.co.uk

You can buy or rent both summer and winter sports equipment from Edge 2 Edge with minimum fuss and at good prices.

Ellis Brigham
www.ellis-brigham.com

The ski section of this well-designed and speedy outdoor sports site has an excellent choice of boots, skis and other accessories. There's sound advice on offer, especially when it comes to buying boots, which it recommends you definitely try on before you buy as the fit varies so much from make to make.

Facewest
www.facewest.co.uk

Hi-tech equipment for back-country skiers and boarders and other winter sports.

JTL Skiwear
www.jtl-skiwear.co.uk

Skiwear site with jackets, trousers, all-in-ones and accessories for the whole family. Prices are good and there are sale items on top of that.

Ski Net
www.skinet.com

When you buy skis or boots for the first time, how do you find out which are best suited to your needs? This vast ski resource is packed with up-to-date product reviews and has a Gear Finder tool which can match your skills against a database of different skis.

Snow And Rock
www.snowandrock.co.uk
There's no shortage of equipment and accessories available online here.

World Ski & Snowboard
www.worldski.com
Discounted ski holidays, equipment hire and insurance all available here.

You can get further technical information on the skis you're considering at the following manufacturers' websites:

Elan www.elanskis.com
Dynastar www.dynastar.com
K2 www.k2skis.com
Rossignol www.skisrossignol.com
Salomon www.salomonsports.fr

 Boards Online
www.boardsonline.co.uk
Snowboards, bindings and boots can all be bought online from this smart yet vibrant site. Before you begin, the advice section offers useful tips for novice boarders, such as how to decide what length of board to choose.

 Slam City
www.slamcity.com
A simply designed skate and snowboarding store, with a well-stocked online catalogue of clothing, accessories and boards. Prices are good, with plenty of accessories for you to customise your own board.

 Snowboard Asylum
www.snowboard-asylum.com
Nice site with plenty of product details and a useful icon guide for each item. There's also a gear guide and 'Board Selecta' to help you chose the right board.

Snowboard Club
www.snowboardclub.co.uk
Snowboarding portal with news, reviews, articles, and all the usual portal stuff, including links to find the best dry and snow slopes in the country!

Watersports

 Jag Wet Suits
www.jagwetsuits.co.uk
Jag, one of the UK's biggest suppliers of all things neoprene, has all the outfits and accessories your need for messing about in the water.

 Robin Hood Watersports
www.roho.co.uk
Robin Hood starts at the bottom of the ladder with Kayak Starter Packs, and moves on to the radical wave boards with flashy designs and flashy prices.

 Simply Scuba
www.simplyscuba.co.uk
With dive equipment and courses to buy, news and reviews, Simply Scuba is as comprehensive as it gets. If you're new to the sport the review sections will tell you the difference between your Aqua-Lung and your Typhoon dry suit.

Telecoms

Directory Enquiries
www.thephonebook.bt.com
BT's directory enquiries site. Or try one of these:
www.192.com
www.infospace.com
www.yell.com

Efax
www.efax.com
Free up a phone line by receiving your faxes by email.
Also worth investigating are:
www.j2.com
www.tpc.int

Engadget Mobile
www.engadgetmobile.com
Great blog site offering news and reviews of the latest developments in phone technology.

Mobile Phone Numbers
www.mobilephoneno.com
Look up mobile phone numbers.

MobileWorld
www.mobileworld.org
Assorted info on mobile phones and cellular networks.

The Payphone Project
www.payphone-project.com
Bizarre site devoted to that near-extinct dinosaur of twentieth-century technology, the payphone. Includes payphone news, history of the payphone, photos and numbers. For more payphone numbers, try the Pay Phone Directory:
www.payphone-directory.org

Internet telephony

Most instant messaging programs allow you to make video and audio calls to other users of the same programs, in effect offering free international phone calls between any two people with computer, broadband, microphone and speakers.

But it's also possible to make calls to regular and mobile telephones via your broadband connection. This isn't free, but it's usually much better value than using the old-fashioned telephone. No-commitment services such as Skype, for example, let you buy a voucher and use it to call phones around the world. You could call a land line in Italy or a mobile in the US for around 1p per minute. Or you can talk to other Skype users on their computers for free; sound quality can be glitchy depending on internet traffic but is generally better than making a long-distance phone call.

Skype www.skype.com

Other so-called VoIP (Voice Over IP) services are subscription based, offering a set number of national or international calls per month. For example:

Vonage www.vonage.co.uk
BT Broadband Voice www.btbroadbandvoice.com
Voipfone www.voipfone.co.uk

WAP sites

If you've got a WAP phone or just like to pretend that you do (get a WAP emulator which enables your PC to read WML-encoded script at updev.phone.com), these are some of the best sites, or if you really want to get the full web experience from your blower, get a smart phone with web browser and you can surf away to your heart's content, albeit in minature.

Ananova www.ananova.com
Get breaking news sent as customized WAP pages to your phone.

Ents24 www.ents24.co.uk
What's-on listings for the entire country.

Genie www.genie.co.uk
Get up-to-the-minute sports results.

Mail2Wap www.mail2wap.com
Collect your POP3 mail on a WAP phone.

Mobile WAP www.mobilewap.com
The largest WAP search engine.

Pocket Doctor www.pocketdoctor.co.uk/wap
Never forget to take your medicine, or get symptom descriptions sent to your mobile.

Railtrack railtrack.kizoom.co.uk
Why talk to an operator at the National Rail Enquiries line when you can have the info zapped to your phone instead? To check out how long your delay on the Tube will be, go to: www.tflwap.gov.uk

Retrotopia Wireless Intellivision www.intellivisionlives.com/retrotopia/wireless.shtml
Play 1980s classics like Astrosmash and Night Stalker on your mobile phone.

WAP Translator langues.ifrance.com/langues/index.wml
Translate to and from English, French, Italian, Spanish, German and Dutch with your phone.

Reverse Phone Directory
www.reversephonedirectory.com
Key in a US phone number to find its owner. For UK locations see:
www.ukphoneinfo.com

Splash Mobile
www.SplashMobile.com
Ring tones, logos, games and other essential accessories for your mobile. The site pays fees to the MCPS, so you can rest assured that the composer of the *Knight Rider* theme will get his just royalties. Other ringtone sites:
www.jippii.co.uk
www.mobiletones.com
www.phoneringsong.com
www.mob.tv
www.yourmobile.com

Telephone Preference Service
www.tpsonline.org.uk
Register your phone number here (it's free and takes about ten seconds) to stop receiving unwanted cold calls from telemarketers.

UK STD Codes
www.brainstorm.co.uk/uk_std_code_search.htm
Keep up to date with the labyrinthine complexities of the UK's phone exchanges.

What Does Your Phone Number Spell?
www.phonespell.org
Enter your phone number to see what it spells. The reverse lookup might help you choose a number.

World Time & Dialling Codes
www.whitepages.com.au/wp/search/time.html
International dialling info from anywhere to anywhere, including current times and area codes.

Television

Most TV stations maintain excellent sites with all kinds of extras such as live sports coverage and documentary follow-ups. We won't need to give you their addresses because they'll be flashing them at you at every opportunity.

For personalized listings, perhaps delivered by email, try your local **Yahoo!** or:

Ananova www.ananova.com/tv
OnTheBox.com www.onthebox.com

The best of these, however, is **Digiguide** (www.digiguide.co.uk) which is a customizable listings database that covers terrestrial, cable, digital and satellite. You download the site's software, tell the program which region you live in and then download the next few weeks' worth of listings for a small yearly fee.

Atom Films
www.atomfilms.com
For spoof music videos and other culture jamming.

Bigglethwaite.com
www.bigglethwaite.com
With its comprehensive links page to UK TV websites, this is a good place to start any search.

BlinkX
www.blinkx.tv
Sophisticated search engine for finding digital video content online.

DigiReels
www.digireels.co.uk
If you can't get enough of them on TV, then point your browser here immediately and search a mind-blowing database of over 100,000 adverts. Also check out UK Television Adverts:
www.uktvadverts.com

Drew's Script-O-Rama
www.script-o-rama.com/snazzy/tvscript.html
A huge set of links to an astonishing array of pre-dominantly American television scripts and episode transcripts. Also try:
www.simplyscripts.com

Epguides
epguides.com
If you're serious about TV – really, really serious – this site is your holy grail. Containing complete episode guides for over 1700 shows (mostly American), which are linked to the Internet Movie Database for cross-referencing, this is an amazing research tool for academics, journalists, enthusiasts and general freaks. For similar coverage of Britcoms, try one of these:
www.phill.co.uk
www.episodeguides.com
www.televisionwithoutpity.com

FT2
www.ft2.org.uk
Provides training for freelance assistants in the construction, production and technical areas of the film and television industry.

Independent TeleWeb
www.itw.org.uk
The history of independent commercial television in the UK.

Jump The Shark
www.jumptheshark.com
Named after that episode in *Happy Days* when Fonzie ski-jumped over a shark, starting the show's inexorable downward spiral, this brilliant site is dedicated to documenting the moment when your favourite programme goes south. Signals of impending doom include same-character-different-actor, puberty, "A very special…" and the presence of Ted McGinley (aka Jefferson on *Married With Children*).

Like Television
www.liketelevision.com
Watch episodes of classic TV like *I Dream Of Jeannie*, *The Three Stooges* and *Bugs Bunny*.

Live TV
www.comfm.fr/live/tv
Tune into live video feeds from hundreds of real-world television stations. To record US cable shows and play them back in RealVideo (court case pending) see: www.snapstream.com

Sitcoms Online
www.sitcomsonline.com
If you're looking for any information on a Yankee comedy, this is the first place to look. There are also games, discussions and polls that are fun for any comedy enthusiast regardless of nationality.

Regional TV archives
With big media companies like Carlton and Granada dominating ITV, the halcyon days of regional broadcasting are almost gone. However, since television breeds lunacy like no other medium, there are a number of enthusiasts throughout the country dedicated to preserving the memory of low production values, terrible clothes and hopeless segues.

Border Television Area www.bordertvarea.co.uk
Harlech House of Graphics www.hhg.org.uk
ITV Southern England members.tripod.co.uk/Southern_TV
Television Southwest www.televisionsouthwest.com
Tyne Tees Logo Page www.ttlp.org.uk

Soap City
www.soapcity.com
Keep up with who's doing what to whom, who they told and who shouldn't find out in the surreal world of soap fiction.

Test Card Circle
www.testcardcircle.org.uk
The homepage of Test Card Circle, an organization of enthusiasts of the music that accompanied the test card sequences that reigned over British TV in the dark days before cable.

The 30 Second Candidate
www.pbs.org/30secondcandidate
A fascinating history of the political TV spot from PBS, America's answer to the BBC.

Transdiffusion
www.transdiffusion.org
A truly fantastic resource for anyone interested in the history of British broadcasting, this site hosts the archives of the Transdiffusion Organization, which is dedicated to preserving the history of

radio and TV in the UK. Included are screen grabs from TV coverage of historical moments, jingles, theme tunes, in-depth articles and course notes for students and teachers.

TV Ark
www.tv-ark.org.uk
The television museum where you can watch episodes and excerpts from TV shows like 'Boys from the Black Stuff', 'Survivors' and 'Children of the Stones'. There's also a huge public information film section with enough 'Charlie Says' and 'Protect and Survive' to keep you going for hours. More PIFs over at the National Archive:
www.nationalarchives.gov.uk/films

TV Eyes
www.tveyes.com
Informs you when your search term is mentioned on the telly.

TV Go Home
www.tvgohome.com
Onion-style parodies of *the Radio Times*.

TV Party
www.tvparty.com
Irreverent, hilarious and more fun than a barrel of Keith Chegwins, this American site is the hall of fame

that the medium truly deserves. Included are an amazing archive of uncensored out-takes, in-depth articles about all manner of televisual ephemera and pull-no-punches features on programmes.

TV Tickets
www.tvtickets.com
Secure your chance to clap on cue.

VCR Repair Instructions
www.fixer.com
How to take a VCR apart and then get all the little bits back in so it fits more easily into the bin.

Virtue TV
www.virtuetv.com
This virtual channel features independent short films, an archive of music concerts and sports footage, and classic movies such as Roger Corman's *Little Shop of Horrors* and Buster Keaton's *Steamboat Bill Jr.*

WWITV
wwitv.com
Watch obscure TV stations from around the world.

You Tube
www.youtube.com
Watch thousands of streaming videos from this truly on-the-edge site. Whether it's archived TV appearances of obscure cult figures, urban acrobatics or remixed movie trailers (*The Shining* recut to make it look like a feelgood movie, for example) you'll find plenty to keep you entertained right here. More amazing footage and viral video over at Video Bomb and iFilm:

Time

Calendarzone
www.calendarzone.com
Calendar links and, believe it or not, calzone recipes.

DateReminder
www.datereminder.co.uk
Remind yourself by email.

The Death Clock
www.deathclock.com
Get ready to book your final taxi.

Horology – The Index
www.horology.com
Portal to all things pertaining to the science of time-keeping includes information on collecting timepieces, email addresses of "cyber-horologists" and links to horological organizations.

International Earth Rotation Service
hpiers.obspm.fr
Ever felt like your bed's spinning? The truth is even scarier.

iPing (US)
www.iping.com
Arrange free telephone reminders for one or many.

Metric Time
www.billcollins.com.au/bc/mt
Decimalized excuses for being late.

Time and Date
www.timeanddate.com
Instantly tell the time in your choice of cities. Keep your PC clock aligned with a time synchronizer:

The Time Capsule
www.thetimecapsule.org.uk
Young or old, share your memories on this communal website from Age Concern. Submit stories from any period of your life for others to read.

Time Cave
www.timecave.com
Schedule emails to be sent at a specific time in the future.

U.S. NATIONAL DEBT CLOCK

The Outstanding Public Debt as of 04 May 2006 at 01:38:02 PM GMT is:

$8,353,340,819,614.62

US National Debt Clock
brillig.com/debt_clock
Watch your children's future slip away.

USNO Master Clock Time
tycho.usno.navy.mil/what.html
Compute the local apparent sidereal time in your part of the world or listen to a live broadcast of the USNO Master Clock announcer.

Toys

Aardmarket
aardmarket.aardman.com
Specialising in 3D animation models, predominantly from the Nick Park stable: Wallace & Gromit, Chicken Run, and others.

Action Man
www.actionman.com
The Action Man site will have you reaching for the asprin after a couple of minutes of its agitated 'extreme' multimedia content screaming at you. There's also a link to a UK online store where you can buy the figures and the associated accessories.

Active Robots
www.active-robots.com
All the materials, kits and projects you need to make your own robot. From beginner's Lego sets to advanced control boards, sensors and other parts.

Airfix
www.airfix.com
Another dream site for overgrown kids. All the models you could ever imagine at cheap-as-you-like prices. Classic ships, cars, war heroes and space models. Sizes and skill levels are included in the descriptions. There's also handy modelling how-to guides, downloadable PDF instructions and a free quarterly e-zine.

Babies "R" Us
www.babiesrus.co.uk
The baby version of Toys"R"Us offers baby products such as nappies, a range of gadgets and larger items

like prams, car seats and high chairs, as well as a pretty decent selection of baby toys like activity cottages, Mr Potato Head figures and a musical pop-up piano.

Bootleg Action Figures
www.bootlegactionfigures.com
Gallery of mis-shapen bootleg Spice Girls, Teletubbies, Batman, and practically every other character you could conceivably make a cheap plastic figure of.

Dawson and Son
www.dawson-and-son.com
A delightfully old-fashioned specialist in quaint, romantic wooden toys and games. Jack-in-the-Boxes, spinning tops and old-fashioned pastry sets are usually still hits with small children, although the knitting sets and flower-press kits are perhaps a little optimistic. The toys are quite pricey but they are beautifully made and built to last.

Early Learning Centre
www.elc.co.uk
A good, reliable site where you can shop by age, category and type of toy if you're stuck for ideas. Includes some decent discounts in the sale section. The toys are organised into interesting sections such as Imagine, which includes dressing-up clothes, as well as the more self-explanatory Sport and Activity and Discover.

Flying Toys
www.flyingtoys.com
For kites, gliders and powered planes, this shop is really taking off.

Hamleys
www.hamleys.co.uk
Hamleys has generally been ranked on a par with Harrods as one of those stores only found in the capital, and is now regarded as more of a tourist stop rather than an actual business. Now Hamleys has launched itself online, open to everyone.

Holz Toys
www.holz-toys.co.uk
Quality wooden toys, including marble runs, wooden bricks and mortar construction sets, forts, farm sets, puzzles and more.

Huggables
www.huggables.com
Gold, red and blue teddy bears, chimney sweep bears, mohair lambs, terriers and even polar bears. Yep, you guessed it, Huggables is a cuddly toy site.

Kidds Toys
www.kiddstoys.co.uk
Antique and collectable toys from around the world, from a Hungarian traffic control set to an 'East European' rock'n'roll rabbit and a selection of toys connected with children's TV shows such as Fraggle Rock and Trumpton. They don't come cheap but the selection on offer is intriguing.

Letterbox collection
www.letterbox.co.uk
Presents, dressing-up clothes and a whole range of personalised items are on sale here, but steel

yourself for some spectacularly un-politically correct costumes such as the Blushing Bride and Red Indian Chief outfits. Still, there's a decent range of goods focusing on fun and imagination rather than the practical.

 Mail Order Express
www.moetoys.co.uk
Mail Order sells every toy, game, piece of clothing and collector's card associated with must-have brands such as Lego, Scalextric, Barbie and Playmobil.

 On Tracks
www.ontracks.co.uk
Boasting 35,000 model and hobby items to buy. Aside from Hornby model railways, baseboards and landscape, On Tracks also offers a substantial catalogue of slot cars, radio-controlled toys and kit cars and fantasy figures.

 Outdoor Toys Direct
www.outdoortoysdirect.co.uk
Trampolines, wendy houses, slides, swings and go-karts all available here with some decent discounts to boot.

Paper Toys
www.papertoys.com
Completely free to download and print, then cut & glue to make paper toys as simple as a party hat or as complex as Angkor Wat, the Taj Mahal, or even Bill Gates' house!

 Shop 4 Toys
www.shop4toys.co.uk
Yet another site that can sort you out with toys, activities and accessories branded with all your children's favourite cartoon characters. Furry creatures of the moment include Barney, the Mr Men and the Tweenies.

 Smart Start Toys
www.smartstart-toys.co.uk
Educational toys and games for kids, everything from wooden train sets and toys to fun science kits. More at:
www.brightminds.co.uk

 Toy Craft
catalog.com/uk/toy
The interface is a little clunky but worth persevering with to get to a nice selection of toys and games including Safari Race, which is somewhere between a board game and a set of building blocks, and magnetic building marbles.

 Toy Robots
www.toyrobots.com
Obviously not your run-of-the-mill toy selection, here you'll find a fine range of tin robots, plastic robots, and even a robot clock, as well as space toys. Some of these are close to one-offs – like the red Russian robots bought from a now-defunct factory. More at:
www.robot1968.com
www.robotisland.com

 Toys "R" Us
www.Toysrus.co.uk
Just as the shop itself is a lurid assault on the senses, this site isn't easy on the eye. But there are benefits in shopping at such an outlet, the biggest bonus being that there is a huge range of toys.

UK Toy Museums
www.toy.co.uk/museums
Links to toy and model museums around the UK.

 Westwell Character Toys
www.character-toys.co.uk
All your favourite characters under one roof, neatly divided into their own sections, including Miffy, Fireman Sam, Pingu, Wallace & Gromit, Clangers and a whole load more.

Travel

Whether you're seeking inspiration, planning an itinerary, shopping for a ticket or already mobile, there'll be a tool online worth throwing in your box. You can book flights, reserve hotel rooms, research your destination, monitor the weather, convert currencies, learn the lingo, locate an ATM, find a restaurant that suits your fussy tastes and plenty more. For detailed listings, buy a copy of the *Rough Guide to Travel Online*. If you'd like to find first-hand experiences or travelling companions, hit the **Usenet** discussion archives at **Google** (groups.google.com) and join the appropriate newsgroup under the rec.travel or soc.culture hierarchies. As with all newsgroups, before you post a question, skim through the FAQs first:

Rec.Travel Library www.travel-library.com

Then see what the major guidebook publishers have to offer:

Bradt www.bradt-travelguides.com
Dorling www.dk.com
Fodors www.fodors.com
Frommer's www.frommers.com
Insiders www.insiders.com
Let's Go www.letsgo.com
Lonely Planet www.lonelyplanet.com
Moon Travel www.moon.com

Robert Young Pelton www.comebackalive.com
Rough Guides www.roughguides.com
Rough Guides Directions www.directionsguides.com
Routard www.club-internet.fr/routard

Alternatively, check out online guides such as:

CityVox www.cityvox.com
IExplore www.iexplore.com
World Travel Guide www.wtg-online.com

While it might seem like commercial suicide for the Rough Guides to give away the full text of its guides to more than ten thousand destinations, the reality is that books are still more convenient, especially on the road when you need them most. If you'd like to order a guide or map online you'll also find plenty of opportunities either from the above publishers, the online bookshops (p.32), or from travel bookshops such as:

Adventurous Traveler atb.away.com
Stanfords www.stanfords.co.uk

Many online travel agents also provide destination guides, which might include exclusive editorial peppered with chunks licensed from guidebooks linked out to further material on the Web. For example:

Away.com away.com

The biggest problem with browsing the Web for regional information and travel tools is not in finding the sites, but wading through them. Take the following directories, for example:

About Travel travel.about.com
Budget Travel www.budgettravel.com
Excite Travel travel.excite.com
Lycos Travel travel.lycos.com
My Travel Guide www.mytravelguide.com
Open Directory dmoz.org/Recreation/Travel
Traveller Online www.travelleronline.com
Virtual Tourist www.vtourist.com
World Travel Guide www.travel-guide.com
World Travel Net www.world-travel-net.com
Yahoo! Directory www.yahoo.com/Recreation/Travel
Yahoo! Travel travel.yahoo.com

These are perfect if you want to browse through regions looking for ideas, or find a range of sites on one topic – health, for example. But if you're after something very specific, you might find it more efficient to use a search engine such as **Google**. Keep adding search terms until you restrict the number of results to something manageable. If you'd like your vacation to coincide with a festival or event, go straight to:

What's on When www.whatsonwhen.com

Or for entertainment, eating, and cultural events, a city guide:

Citysearch www.citysearch.com
Time Out www.timeout.co.uk
Wcities.com www.wcities.com

Yahoo! Local local.yahoo.com
Zagat (Dining) www.zagat.com

If you're flexible, you might find a last-minute special. These Net exclusives are normally offered directly from the airline, hotel, and travel operator sites, which you'll find through **Yahoo!** There are also a few Web operators that specialize in late-notice and special Internet deals on flights, hotels, and so forth, such as:

Bargain Holidays www.bargainholidays.com
Best Fares www.bestfares.com
Lastminute.com www.lastminute.com
Lastminutetravel.com www.lastminutetravel.com
Opodo www.opodo.co.uk
Smarter Living www.smarterliving.com
Travel Zoo www.travelzoo.co.uk

Booking a flight online isn't too hard, but bargains are few. Unless you're spending someone else's money you'll want to sidestep the full fares offered on these major services:

Expedia www.expedia.co.uk
Travelocity www.travelocity.co.uk
Travel Select www.travelselect.co.uk

Although they list hundreds of airlines and millions of fares, the general consensus is that they're usually better for research, accommodation and travel tips than cheap fares and customer service. So if you think it's worth the effort, drop in and check which carriers haul your route, offer the best deals and still have seats available. You can then use their rates as a benchmark. Compare them with the fares on the airline sites and discount specialists such as:

Bargain Holidays www.bargainholidays.com
Cheap Flights www.cheapflights.com
Deckchair www.deckchair.com
EasyJet www.easyjet.com
Ebookers.com www.ebookers.com
Flight Centre www.flightcentre.com
OneTravel.com www.onetravel.com
Ryanair www.ryanair.com

Or compare the prices across several agencies simultaneously, using these sites:

Farechase www.farechase.com
Hotwire www.hotwire.com
QIXO www.qixo.com
Sidestep www.sidestep.com

Need a hotel? Try one of these sites to book internationally; it's usually cheaper than booking direct and many have reviews from people who have actually stayed there, invaluable for cutting through the jargon. You'll also be able to get a general idea of the locality of your chosen crib.

Accomline www.accomline.com
Easy Hotel www.easyhotel.com
Hostels.com www.hostels.com
Hotel Discount www.hoteldiscount.com
Skoosh www.skoosh.com
Octopus Travel www.octopustravel.com

Finally, see if your travel agent can better the price. If the difference is only marginal, favour your agent. Then at least you'll have a human contact if something goes wrong.

A2Btravel.com
www.a2btravel.com
Resources for getting into, around, and out of the UK,

Travel health online
Don't ignore medical bulletins if you're planning to visit a potential hotspot or health risk, but seek a second opinion before postponing your adventure.

Foreign Office www.fco.gov.uk
Australian Government www.dfat.gov.au
US State Department travel.state.gov

Also take a look at these useful sites:

Rough Guide to Travel Health travel.roughguides.com/health
Masta www.masta.org
Travel Doctor www.tmvc.com.au
TravelHealth.com www.travelhealth.co.uk
World Health Organization www.who.int

Then brace yourself against the bugs eagerly awaiting your arrival. For a list of travel medicine clinics worldwide, see:

such as car-rental comparison, airport guides, train timetables and ferry booking.
www.ferrybooker.com
www.webweekends.co.uk

The Africa Guide
www.africaguide.com
Good, general guides of a region that nearly all the major guide books and travel services ignore. Try also: www.africanet.com

Art of Travel
www.artoftravel.com
How to see the world on $25 a day.

ATM Locators
www.visa.com/atms
Locate a hole in the wall willing to replenish the hole in your wallet.

travel

Attitude Travel
www.attitudetravel.com
No-nonsense independent travel advice.

Backpacker.com
www.backpacker.com
Excellent site for wilderness trekkers, including destination guides, tips on keeping your boots in shape and the real dope on DEET-free insect repellents.

The Bathroom Diaries
www.thebathroomdiaries.com
One of the most essential sites on the Web: You're in Bamako, Mali, when nature calls and you're after a good, clean Western-style toilet, click here to find out the nearest one.

Bed & Breakfast.com
www.bedandbreakfast.com
Secure a good night's sleep worldwide.
www.bedandbreakfast-directory.co.uk
www.babs.com.au
www.innsite.com

Bugbog
www.bugbog.co.uk
Nice, compact mini-guides for people wanting to go somewhere a bit out of the ordinary. Good features include the best beaches in the world by month, and a destination finder giving you options such as colourful culture, festivals and weather.

Caravan Sitefinder
caravan-sitefinder.co.uk
Where to hitch your rusting hulk of steel without looking like hippy scum. For places to pitch your tent, try Camp Sites:
www.camp-sites.co.uk

CIA World Factbook
www.cia.gov/cia/publications/factbook
Vital stats on every country. For the score on living standards:
www.undp.org

Danger Finder
www.comebackalive.com/df
Adventure holidays that could last a lifetime.

Electronic Embassy
www.embassy.org
Directory of foreign embassies in DC plus Web links where available. Search Yahoo! for representation in other cities.

Family Travel Files
www.thefamilytravelfiles.com
Look here for help on what to do when the little monsters start asking, "Are we there yet?"

Flight Arrivals & Departures
www.flightarrivals.com
Stay on top of takeoffs and touchdowns across North America.

Gap Year
www.gapyear.com
Excellent site dedicated to students about to take a year out, with loads of travel tips and stories.

Global Freeloaders
www.globalfreeloaders.com
Take in a globetrotting dosser.

Grid Skipper
www.gridskipper.com
Irreverent and sassy urban travel guide.

How far is it?
www.indo.com/distance
Calculate the distance between any two cities.

IgoUgo
www.igougo.com
Packed full of travellers' photos and journals, this roughguides.com partner site offers candid first-hand information.

International Home Exchange Network
www.homexchange.com
Trade your dreary digs for a palatial beach house. Or try: www.homebase-hols.com

International Student Travel Confederation
www.istc.org
Save money with an international student card.

Journeywoman
www.journeywoman.com
Reporting in from the sister beaten track.

OAG
www.oag.com
Largest database of flight schedules on the Net, which can be downloaded to your Palm or mobile.

The Original Tipping Page
www.tipping.org
Make fast friends with the bell-hop.

Resorts Online
www.resortsonline.com
Your way through three thousand resorts throughout the world categorized by beach, golf, spa, ski, etc.

Roadside America
www.roadsideamerica.com
Strange attractions on US highways.

Sahara Overland
www.sahara-overland.com
Leave the city in a cloud of dust.

Seat Guru
www.seatguru.com
Detailed seating maps of various different kinds of plane on different airlines, with the good and bad seats clearly mapped out so you can avoid things like spending thirteen hours with a large metal container where your legroom should be.

Subway Navigator
www.subwaynavigator.com
Estimate the travelling times between city stations worldwide.

Theme Parks of England
themeparksofengland.com
Reviews and info on all the major high G-force thrills to be had without leaving the country.

TNT Live!
www.tntmagazine.com
Survive London and venture onward with aid from expat streetmags, *TNT* and *Southern Cross*.

Tourism Offices Worldwide
www.towd.com
Write to the local tourist office. They might send you a brochure. For even more propaganda, try Official Travel Info:
www.officialtravelinfo.com

Traffic and Road Conditions
www.accutraffic.com
Live traffic and weather updates. Also found here:
www.rac.co.uk/check_traffic/?view=Standard&nav

Traffic Signs of the World
www.elve.net/rcoulst.htm
Next time you're in Kyrgyzstan, you'll know when to look out for the men at work.

Travelmag
www.travelmag.co.uk
Several intimate travel reflections monthly.

Travel Paperwork
www.travelpaperwork.com
Sort out the red tape before you hit the border.

Trains & Buses

The Man in Seat 61
www.seat61.com
A superb resource – how to get from London to anywhere in the world by train (and the occasional boat).

Megabus
www.megabus.com
Travel by coach around the UK for as little as £1 per journey. More cheap fares available from National Express (check their Fun Fares section):
www.nationalexpress.com

Network Rail
www.networkrail.co.uk
Depress yourself at the state of the country's railways. To book tickets online try The Train Line or Q Jump, and for general public transport see

Traveline:
www.thetrainline.com
www.qjump.co.uk
www.traveline.org.uk

Rail Britain
www.railbritain.com
A big site aimed at both the traveller and the enthusiast. For British rail history, see:
www.trackbed.com

Trip Advisor
www.tripadvisor.co.uk
Browse over four million unbiased travel reviews covering locations, local attractions, hotels and more..

Unclaimed Baggage
www.unclaimedbaggage.com
You lose it; they sell it.

UK Passport Agency
www.ukpa.gov.uk
Speed up your passport application at this streamlined site.

Underbelly
www.underbelly.com
Short, sharp, shocked guides to the places tourists rarely ever see.

Universal Currency Converter
www.xe.com/ucc
Convert Tunisian dinars into Central African francs on the fly. More at Oanda:
www.oanda.com

Vindigo
www.vindigo.com
Is Vindigo the future of travel guides? Download its Palm Pilot or AvantGo city guides and decide for yourself.

Virtual Tourist
www.virtualtourist.com
Database of travel reviews written by ordinary people, not travel journalists on press junkets. The reviews are hooked up to maps and links to other sites.

Walkabout
www.walkabout.com.au
Get the lowdown on the land down under.

WebFlyer
www.webflyer.com
Keep tabs on frequent flyer schemes.

What's On When?
www.whatsonwhen.com
Annoyed you've missed Thaipusam or the turning of the bones yet again? Get your dates right here.

World Heritage Listing
www.unesco.org/whc
Plan your itinerary around international treasures.

World Travel Tips
www.worldtraveltips.net
A good, all-round destination site; the layout is clear, maps are good, and there are Yahoo! links for news headlines of each destination.

Weddings & bar mitzvahs

Alternative Gowns
www.alt-gowns.co.uk

An unusual venture selling alternative wedding dresses, evening gowns and bridal accessories from a variety of stores. Styles include Celtic, medieval and speciality couture from Yorkshire. Not likely to suit every taste (PVC undies?) but useful if price and making a statement are your priorities. More at:
www.uptight-clothing.co.uk
www.18thcenturycorsets.com
www.avalonweddings.co.uk

Alternative Wedding List
www.thealternativeweddinglist.co.uk

If you have all the toasters you need, consider an alternative wedding list where your guests can make donations to your selection of charities.

Celtic Bride
www.celticbride.com

Handcrafted Celtic style tiaras, crowns and jewellery items to add an extra slice of chic.

Confetti
www.confetti.co.uk

Alongside the usual guff about etiquette, there's some cracking stuff here to calm a harassed bride. Our favourite is the rotating dresses section where you can see what a selection of gowns looks like from all angles before you try them on. There's also a selection of pretty and reasonably priced tiaras for those who are not fortunate to have a diamond one in the family, and jewellery thank-you gifts for bridesmaids. Truly a one-stop shop.

Hens and Stags
www.clickandbuild.com/cnb/shop/hensandstags

Online shop for party supplies aimed at hen parties and stag nights. Fake breasts, furry handcuffs, inflatable men and women – you get the drift.

Martha Stewart
www.marthastewart.com

Martha is the uncrowned US queen of the stylish wedding. Her website has a whole section devoted to wedding ideas (think discreet luxury rather than raucous knees-up).

The Occasional Poet
www.theoccasionalpoet.com

Commission a poem which is tailored to you and your intended's lives. Or better still, get someone to write your whole wedding speech for you:
www.finespeeches.com

Web Wedding
www.webwedding.co.uk

Weddings portal with advice on all aspects of getting hitched, forums, and an ask the expert section. More resources available at:
www.weddings.co.uk
www.weddingchaos.co.uk
www.weddingguide.co.uk
www.hitched.co.uk

Photos & video

Guild of Wedding Photographers
www.gwp-uk.co.uk
Advice on what to look for in a good photographer, plus contact details and links to Guild members. More photographers to be found here: www.findaweddingphotographer.co.uk

PIC Productions
www.pic.clara.net
These wedding videographers provide plenty of stills from actual wedding videos so that you can get a real idea of the coverage and service they offer.

Studio Images
www.studioimages.co.uk
Representing photographers all over the UK who specialise in modern wedding photography. There are loads of pictures to look through to help you choose, and an online request form for more information or contact details.

Stationery

Big Leap Designs
www.bigleapdesigns.com
Bright and cheerful wedding invitation and thank-you card site. There are plenty of designs to choose from and they also do orders of service, candles, place cards, evening invitations and reply cards.

Shadi Cards
www.shadicards.com
Suppliers of invitations and cards. There are lots of different designs, and insert paper is included in the price for you to print on your own printer, or for a bit extra they can print them for you.

Wedding locations

Country House Wedding Venues
www.wedding-venues.co.uk
Enter your region and the number of guests and get a list of posh country manors to get hitched in.

Federation of Professional Toastmasters
www.federationtoastmasters.fsnet.co.uk
If you're planning a big do, consider hiring a toast-master (generally a man with a moustache, red jacket and a loud voice) to keep things running smoothly.

For Better For Worse
www.forbetterforworse.co.uk
Directory for a wide variety of sites for UK civil weddings. There are stately homes, country house hotels and unusual venues such as football grounds.

Bar & bat mitzvahs

The Cake Company
www.thecakecompany.co.uk
This cake order service can design a kosher cake for any occasion. View the very elaborate examples to get your mouth watering. E-mail with enquiries.

Jewish.co.uk
www.jewish.co.uk
General site with a useful directory of specialist firms who supply invitations, photographers and kosher catering for a Bar or Bat Mitzvah celebration.

Talit.com
www.jewishheart.com
Online mall of Jewish products directly from Israel. Many items are handmade and holy products such as Talis are certified kosher. Prices are in US dollars but they ship anywhere. For UK suppliers try: www.judaicastore.co.uk

Weird

Absurd.org
www.absurd.org
Please do not adjust your set.

Aliens In The Bible
aliensinthebible.com
Fact: spooky space dudes are stealing our souls. The Bible wouldn't lie about something that important. If you think you may be an alien (not necessarily in the Bible), see the Alien Counsel at:
www.angelfire.com/md/aliencounsel

American Association of Electronic Voice Phenomena
www.aaevp.com
Capture voices from the dead on tape. It's easy once you know what you're listening for.

American Pie and the Armageddon Prophecy
www.roytaylorministries.com
How Madonna testified against the descendants of Israel all the way to number one. But what tragedy awaits her?

Animal Mating Zone
www.matings.co.uk
Hardcore sex: the type you only get to see in wildlife documentaries.

Bayraider
www.bayraider.tv
Strange celebrity artefacts auctioned on eBay. From Elvis' number science book to Michael Jackson trial juror notebooks.

The Bicycling Guitarist
www.thebicyclingguitarist.net
Site dedicated to Chris Watson, the man who can ride a bike and play guitar at the same time, and his radioactive beagle Daiquiri.

Borgstrom.com
www.borgstrom.com
Hours of fun hitting a man with a beard around the face with your mouse pointer.

The Church of the Subgenius
www.subgenius.com
The religion of choice for artschool dropouts back in the 1980s.

Christian Guide to Small Arms
www.frii.com/~gosplow/cgsa.html
"He that hath no sword, let him sell his garment and buy one" – Luke 22:36. It's not just your right; it's your duty, darnit.

Circlemakers
www.circlemakers.org
Create crop circles to amuse New Agers and the press.

A Citizen from Hell
www.amightywind.com/hell/citizenhell.htm
If Hell sounds this bad, you don't want to go there.

Clonaid
www.clonaid.com
Thanks to the Raelians, we now know all life on earth was created in extraterrestrial laboratories. Here's where you can buy genuine cloned human livestock for the kitchen table. Ready as soon as the lab's finished.

Corpses for Sale
distefano.com
Brighten up your guestroom with a life-sized chew-toy.

Corrugated Iron Club
www.corrugated-iron-club.info
It's metal. It's wavy. It rocks.

The Darwin Awards
www.darwinawards.com
Each year the Darwin Award goes to the person who drops off the census register in the most spectacular fashion. Here's where to read about the runners-up and er…winners.

Deep Black Magic
www.mindspring.com/~txporter
Forty years of CIA research into mind control and ESP. For the perspective of a Finnish immigrant to Canada on mind control, see:
hackcanada.com/canadian/freedom/mylife.html

Derm Cinema
www.skinema.com
Know your celebrity skin conditions.

Dr MegaVolt
www.drmegavolt.com
The Doc sure sparked right up when they switched on the power, but could he cut it in the big league? www3.bc.sympatico.ca/lightningsurvivor

 ### Eerie Evenings
www.eerie-evenings.com
Spend a night in a haunted house.

English Rose Press
www.englishrosepress.com
Diana sends her love from Heaven.

Entrances To Hell
www.entrances2hell.co.uk
Damnation is to be found in the strangest of places.

Evil Clown Generator
scottsmind.com/evil_clown.php
It does exactly what it says on the tin.

Fetish Map
www.deviantdesires.com/map/map.html
Join the dots between piggy-players, fursuiters, inflators, crush freaks and where you're standing now.

 ### Food-blender and telephone
www.cycoactive.com/blender/
It's a telephone and a food-blender all in one!

Fool's World Map
zen.chakuriki.net/world/
Did you know that the China-appointed governor of Tibet is Adam Yauch of the Beastie Boys? Find out more at this daft remix of planet Earth.

Form

www.c3.hu/collection/form

This kind of defies description, we're still not actually sure what it is.

Fortean Times

www.forteantimes.com

Updates from the print monthly that takes the investigation of strange phenomena more seriously than itself. See also:

www.bizarremag.com

Frozen Feline

frozenfeline.com

Frozen Feline trawls clipart collections to bring you the best bits. Not only that but they write little poems to go with them.

Future Horizons

www.futurehorizons.net

Snap off more than your fair share through solid-state circuitry.

Ghost Study Webcams

www.ghoststudy.com/camlinks.html

Links to webcams pointed at haunted rooms and places around the UK; see anything strange?

God Channel

www.godchannel.com

Relay requests to God via His official Internet channel.

Gum Blondes

www.gumblondes.com

Portraits of your favourite blondes lovingly fashioned from chewed bubblegum.

Great Joy In Great Tribulation

www.dccsa.com/greatjoy

Biblical proof that Prince Chuck is the Antichrist and key dates leading to the end of the world. For more enlightenment, including how to debug the pyramids, see:

www.bibleprophecy.net

Half Bakery

www.halfbakery.com

The Halfbakery is a communal database of original, fictitious inventions, edited by its users. It was created by people who like to speculate, both as a form of satire and as a form of creative expression. Lighter than air sausages brush shoulders with evil laugh-activated hand dryers.

Human For Sale

www.humanforsale.com

Because you're worth it.

I Am With You Always

members.aol.com/JesusImages

Larry Van Pelt's charming renditions of Christ gently helping people go about their day jobs.

I Can Eat Glass Project

www.geocities.com/nodotus/hbglass.html

Deter excess foreign suitors and carpet dealers with the only words you know in their language.

Illuminati News
www.illuminati-news.com
Storm into secret societies and thump your fist on the table.

Info Wars
www.infowars.com
Investigative journalist Alex Jones exposes America's dark secrets, from 9/11 conspiracies to his infiltration of Bohemian Grove, where the president meets up with the rich and powerful to make sacrifices to a huge owl effigy. More Alex Jones here:
www.prisonplanet.tv

International Ghost Hunters Society
www.ghostweb.com
They never give up the ghost. Nab your own with:
www.ghostresearch.org
www.maui.net/~emf/TriFieldNat.html

International Trepanation Advocacy Group
www.trepan.com
Don't try it at home with your Black & Decker; learn how to get your third eye opened properly here.

Itz Fun Tew Be Dat Kandie Kid
www.angelfire.com/ma/talulaQ/kandie.html
Mothers – don't let your babies grow up to be ravers.

Kook Sites
www.kooksites.com
Plenty of dumb links to dumb stuff.

Lego Death

www.thefrown.com/player.php?/games/blockdeath
Unpleasant death scenes from the guillotine to Elvis dying on the crapper rendered with block toys. For Bible stories illustrated with plastic blocks, go to:
www.thereverend.com/brick_testament

Life Gem

www.lifegem.com
Have your corpse transformed into a diamond.

A Mathematical Survey of the English Language
www.geocities.com/garywaterbury
Plot your future through simple arithmetic.

Mount St Helens VolcanoCam
www.fs.fed.us/gpnf/volcanocams/msh
Don't hold your breath.

Mozart's Musikalisches Würfelspiel
sunsite.univie.ac.at/Mozart/dice
Compose a minuet as you play Monopoly.

Mudboy
www.mudboyuk.com
Some get their kicks from muddy boots.

Museum of Non-Primate Art
www.monpa.com
Become an aficionado of moggy masterpieces.

Neuticles
www.neuticles.com
Pick your pet's pocket but leave his dignity intact.

News of the Weird
www.newsoftheweird.com
www.thisistrue.com
www.weirdlist.com
Dotty clippings from the world press.

Nibiruan Council
www.nibiruancouncil.com
Stock your bar to welcome the heroic Starseeds, Walkins, and Lightworkers from the Battlestar Nibiru, who will finally usher in the fifth dimensional reality.

Noble Title

www.elitetitles.co.uk
You know that lordship you've always dreamt of? Well now it can be a reality. Man, this century rules!

Nobody Here
www.nobodyhere.com
Sometimes things with the least purpose are the most enthralling.

Non-escalating Verbal Self Defence
www.taxi1010.com
Fight insults by acting insane.

The Ozone Cow
theozonecow.cjb.net
The story of the two most unsuccessful children's book writers in history, ever.

PhobiaList
phobialist.com
So much to fear, it's scary.

Planetary Activation Orzganization
www.paoweb.com
Prevent inter-dimensional dark forces from dominating our galaxy by ganging up with the Galactic Federation of Light.

Pointless But Cool
www.pointlessbutcool.com
Because your life isn't complete till you own a robotic chimp's head, emergency cufflinks and reindeer paté.

Pushin Daisies
www.pushindaisies.com
Fancy a chocolate human heart or hearse-shaped cookie cutters? Pushin Daisies has all the mortuary-related gifts you'll need. Within reason.

Reincarnation.org
www.reincarnation-org.com
Stash your loot with this crowd, then come back to collect it in your next life.

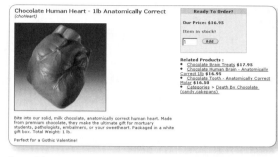

Chocolate Human Heart - 1lb Anatomically Correct *(choHeart)*

Ready To Order?
Our Price: $16.95
Item in stock!
1 Add

Related Products :
- Chocolate Brain Treats $17.95
- Chocolate Human Brain - Anatomically Correct 1lb $16.95
- Chocolate Tooth - Anatomically Correct Molar $16.50
- Categories > Death By Chocolate (candy,cakepans)

Bite into our solid, milk chocolate, anatomically correct human heart. Made from premium chocolate, they make the ultimate gift for mortuary students, pathologists, embalmers, or your sweetheart. Packaged in a white gift box. Total Weight: 1 lb.

Perfect for a Gothic Valentine!

Reptoids
www.reptoids.com
Was that an alien or merely the subterranean descendant of a dinosaur?

The Republic of Texas Provisional Government
www.republic-of-texas.net
Rednecks for liberty, fraternity and equality.

Roland Winbeckler's Cake Sculptures
www.winbeckler.com/sculptures1.asp
How often do you get to see a lifesize cake of Cher?

The Sacred Geometry Stories of Jesus Christ
www.jesus8880.com
How to decode the big J's mathematical word puzzle.

Sanguinarius
www.sanguinarius.org
Because a vampire isn't just for Christmas.

Sightings
www.rense.com
Fishy newsbreaks from talk-radio truth ferret Jeff Rense.

Steve's Ant Farm
www.stevesantfarm.com
Watch blurry black punctuation marks build tunnels.

Streakerama
www.streakerama.com
Get to the bottom of the streaker phenomenon.

Stunning Stuff
www.stunning-stuff.com
Weird news from around the globe.

Sulabh International Museum of Toilets
www.sulabhtoiletmuseum.org
Follow the evolution of the ablution at the world's leading exhibition of bathroom businessware. No need to take it sitting down:
www.restrooms.org

Tell Me Where On Earth
www.tellmewhereonearth.com
Your one-stop shop for alligator tongues, deer jaw dream catchers, kangaroo scrotum money pouches, kangaroo paw back scratchers, walrus whisker earrings, shrunken heads, deformed alligator heads, fossilised mud…You get the picture.

The Twinkies Project
www.twinkiesproject.com
Only here can you find out what happens to a Twinkie when you drop it from a great height or expose it to

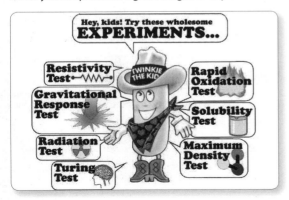

radiation, and then read the results of such experiments in haiku form.

Terry J. Hokanson Lives Under the Mafia
www.geocities.com/terry_tune
Mild-mannered inventor speaks out against the crime syndicate that controls his life through government hypnotists.

Time Travellers
time-travelers.org
Step back to a time that common sense forgot.

Toilet-train Your Cat
www.karawynn.net/mishacat
How to point pusskins at the porcelain.

Why I will never have a girlfriend
www.nothingisreal.com/girlfriend
Derived from first principles, and confirmed by his nickname.

Two Guys Fossils
www.twoguysfossils.com
Elton John need look no further for his next hair transplant. Here he can buy some two-million-year-old hair with one careless owner: a Siberian woolly mammoth. But hurry, Elton – there are only four samples left! Among the other prehistoric artefacts on this site are a sabre-toothed tiger's skull and what's left of a 36-million-year-old wolf spider.

World Database of Happiness
www.eur.nl/fsw/research/happiness
Discover where people are happiest.

Xenophobic Persecution in the UK
www.five.org.uk
If you're below British standards, MI5 will punish you by TV.

Yellow Snow
pi.pwp.blueyonder.co.uk/snow.html
It's better than pissing into the wind. Just.